MW00856818

Len Riskin is a pioneer in bringing both mediation
He is self-reflective, witty and seriously thoughtful-
work, *Managing Conflict Mindfully: Don't Believe Everyt*
better selves—a road map to understanding and ma
with grace and skill. If we all followed Len's thought.... .... managing our stress,
handling our emotions, and negotiating our conflicts, the world would be a seriously better
place.

I have taught from Len's writings for years and cannot wait to teach from this one as well.

—Claudia Bernard
Chief Circuit Mediator Ninth Circuit Court of Appeals (Retired)
Independent Mediator, Trainer and Consultant

We know that conflicts take place not only between us, but within us; that they make us feel
bad; that we become confused and lose touch with who we really are; that we end up behaving
badly toward others; that we forget what matters, and argue endlessly and aggressively about
things that don't. Now, thanks to Leonard Riskin's brilliant, insightful and immensely useful
book, there is something we can do about it. *Mindful Conflict Management* offers marvelous new
tools, important not just for mediators and negotiators, but everyone who has slipped into
conflict's dark, downward spiral. He has written an exciting, energizing, practical book that
can change your life, and I recommend it highly.

—Kenneth Cloke
Founder and past president, Mediators Beyond Borders; author or co-author of 19 books on
mediation, leadership, and management, including *The Dance of Opposites: Explorations in
Mediation, Dialogue and Conflict Resolution Systems Design;* 2013) and *Mediating Dangerously* (2001)

Managing Conflict Mindfully: Don't Believe Everything You Think is a *tour de force*. Len Riskin
juxtaposes and combines three quite different models of how humans behave in conflict and
how they can move through it. Using real-life examples, and drawing on extensive literature,
he illuminates the links between inner and outer conflict. Anyone who wants to better
understand and manage conflict, inside and out, would benefit from this book.

—Gary J. Friedman
Co-Director of the Center for Understanding in Conflict, co-founder of understanding-
based mediation. Renowned mediator, trainer, and commentator. Author, *Inside-Out: How
Conflict Professionals Can Use Self-Reflection to Help Their Clients* (2015)

Managing Conflict Mindfully: Don't Believe Everything You Think is a masterpiece written by a master
practitioner, scholar and teacher of dispute resolution and mindfulness. Everyone should read
this wonderful book. In our time of polarized politics, racial tensions, and endless conflicts,
this book helps all of us learn to bridge our differences in sustainable ways. Riskin infuses his
delightful book with helpful examples, insightful exercises, welcome humor, pearls of wisdom,
and thought-provoking appendices. Based on his own research and building on that by others,
this book pioneers a novel framework (and memorable Venn diagram) combining elements
of three domains: negotiation theories, mindfulness practice, and Internal Family Systems.
This is a one-of-a-kind book or treatise which offers interpersonal, intrapersonal, and
professional life lessons. This book is a pure joy to read! There are roadmaps, reviews,
summary boxes, and worksheets to help readers apply the frames, ideas, mindsets,
perspectives, and techniques of this book. Don't miss Len's funny, priceless, and serious light
verse poem about *Managing Conflict Mindfully*!

—Peter H. Huang
Ph.D., J.D., Author of *Disrupting Racism: Essays by An Asian American Prodigy Professor*, and
retired chaired professor, University of Colorado, Boulder Law School

With *Managing Conflict Mindfully: Don't Believe Everything You Think*, Leonard Riskin enriches our understanding of ourselves and our capacity to live a more fulfilled life. His many years of experience, wisdom and humor come together to formulate a method for managing conflict that is unique, accessible and deep, a rare combination. By brilliantly integrating insights and approaches to negotiation, mindfulness, and internal family systems, he helps us better understand why we do what we do and develop the tools to meaningfully relate to, manage, and resolve conflict. *Don't Believe Everything You Think* emerges just when we need it most, offering us the opportunity not only to transform the quality of our lives, but to help the world become a better place.

—Scott L. Rogers

J.D., M.A. Founder and director, Institute for Mindfulness Studies and the Mindfulness in Law Program at the University of Miami School of Law. Co-founder and co-director, University of Miami's Mindfulness Research & Practice Initiative. Author, *The Mindful Law Student: A Mindfulness in Law Practice Guide* (2022)

This book is a bit of a dream come true for me. To have an award-winning law school professor, who is also an influential expert in mediation and negotiation, bring my IFS model to those realms fulfills a vision. Len Riskin not only skillfully applies IFS to working with conflicts of all kinds, he combines it with mindfulness and negotiation skills to create an approach that invites each party to explore their full range of motives and emotions and then to lead their contentious interactions from a place of calm, curiosity, and even compassion for their opponent. His writing is clear and full of the kind of engaging self-disclosure that one doesn't expect from a prominent lawyer, but which not only illustrates his points well but also serves as a model for readers' self-exploration and disclosure. This is a paradigm-changing book that can revolutionize this important field.

—Richard C. Schwartz

Ph.D., founder of Internal Family Systems and the IFS Institute. Author, *No Bad Parts: Healing Trauma & Restoring Wholeness with the Internal Family Systems Model*

This book is a masterpiece—sophisticated, witty, and eminently practical! Professor Len Riskin—a revered figure in the field of conflict resolution—explains how the biggest saboteur to negotiation success often lies not in an obstinate counterpart but in the failure to manage our own psyche. He illuminates a powerful, humanistic path forward that draws on his wide-ranging experience as a lawyer, law professor, mediator, and Second-City improv student. I have had the privilege to teach with him for more than a decade and have observed firsthand the impact of his work: Countless individuals of all backgrounds have applied his ideas and completely transformed the way they deal with conflict. Read this book and the same might just happen to you.

—Daniel L. Shapiro

Ph.D., Founder and Director of the Harvard International Negotiation Project. Co-author (with Roger Fisher) of *Beyond Reason: Using Emotions as You Negotiate*

Renowned negotiation expert Len Riskin masterfully integrates negotiation and internal family systems theory with the latest thinking and practices on mindfulness. Riskin powerfully argues that knowing the right negotiation theory, while essential, is not enough; one must also know oneself. His years of experience teaching, researching, and practicing mindfulness combine to make Riskin an invaluable guide.

Anyone interested in improving their negotiation skills should read this book.

—Douglas Stone and **Sheila Heen**

Co-authors (with Bruce Patton), *Difficult Conversations: How to Discuss What Matters Most*; co-authors, *Thanks for the Feedback: The Science and Art of Receiving Feedback*

Leonard Riskin is a lawyer, a law school professor, a seasoned mediator and trainer, and a long-time meditator. He is also a committed student of conflict—the conflicts large and small that arise in our work and personal lives, day to day. How can we learn to be more skillful participants in conflict? How can we achieve better outcomes and better relationships at the same time?

In this book, Professor Riskin takes us on a tour of conflict from multiple perspectives, including the habitual patterns of negotiation that we take that can lead to poor outcomes, as well as the psychological traps that prevent us from participating more skillfully. The exciting aspect of this book is Riskin's in-depth description of the multiple and often conflicting perspectives on conflict we hold unconsciously, and the role habits of thought and emotion can play in blocking success. He doesn't leave us there but provides a well-reasoned explanation of how traditional "win-win" negotiation strategies, combined with mindfulness practices used with the Internal Family System psychological model of our minds can lead to deeper and wiser insights into ourselves and others in conflict. The book, supplemented by a website, provides a broad array of readily grasped materials designed to take us deeper into the practice of conflict resolution.

This book is for anyone who deals with conflict, anyone. Scholarly yet accessible. A fine accomplishment from a master of the field.

—Michael Zimmerman
Retired Utah Supreme Court Justice, attorney, mediator, and Zen teacher

MANAGING CONFLICT MINDFULLY

DON'T BELIEVE EVERYTHING YOU THINK

Leonard L. Riskin

Visiting Professor of Law
Distinguished Senior Fellow, Center on Negotiation, Mediation, and Restorative Justice
Northwestern University Pritzker School of Law

Chesterfield Smith Professor of Law Emeritus
University of Florida Levin College of Law

WEST
ACADEMIC
PUBLISHING

To Casey, Andrew, Tricia, Margot, and Janet,
with love and appreciation.

NOTE TO THE READER (AKA PREFACE)

———————

"Don't put anything important into the introduction," a friend advised. "No one reads introductions." I disregarded my friend's advice. So please read the Introduction and Roadmap and Guide, to get your bearings.

ACKNOWLEDGMENTS AND GRATITUDE

I might have finished this book, or something resembling it, a long time ago, except for events in 2010. I had been teaching in law schools since 1974 and, since about 1982, had focused on conflict resolution through studying, teaching, writing, and practicing. In 2002, I published the first of a series of articles on mindfulness in law and conflict resolution. By 2010, I been struggling with drafts of a book on that topic; it never seemed good enough. In 2010, my long-time friend and colleague, David Hoffman, introduced me to Internal Family Systems (IFS) and to its founder, Richard C. Schwartz, who has become a new friend and colleague. I realized quickly that adding IFS to the book-in-process could make it much more valuable, and I hope I was correct. Since then, I have included IFS in most of my law school courses and executive education programs, and have collaborated with Dick and David and others to introduce IFS to the law and conflict resolution communities.

Many people, organizations, and resources—more than I can remember or name—helped me write this book and enabled the book get into your hands, or onto your device. I am deeply grateful to the following people and organizations.

Friends and colleagues who reviewed all or most of the book and gave me very wise and helpful comments and suggestions: Dan Shapiro, Dick Schwartz, Catherine Damme, Charles Wiggins, Doug Stone, Sheila Heen, David Hoffman, Rachel Wohl, Bob Cohen, and Bachte Cohen.

Friends and colleagues who gave me wise and helpful comments or support concerning issues in or about the book: Ava Abramowitz, Danielle Anderson, M.D., James Austin, M.D., Lisle Baker, Howard Bellman, G. Daniel Bowling, Bob Burns, Baruch Bush, Alyson Carrel, Miriam Millhauser Castle, Ken Cloke, Jonathan Cohen, Lynn Cohn, Tom Durkin, John Elson, Richard Erhard, Jerry Faich, Brenda Fingold, Joan Goldsmith, Charles Halpern, Ruth Hoberman, Joe Holtgreive, Peter Huang, Daniel Kim, M.D., Andy Koppelman, Russell Korobkin, George Langford, Stewart Levine, Steve Lubet, Eddie Mordujovich, Diane Reibel, Richard Reuben, Scott Rogers, Donna Silverberg, Leo Smyth, Flint Sparks, Richard Sylvia, Lynn Taussig, and K.M. Zouhary.

Participants in courses, workshops, and other events who have provided suggestions and questions. These include:

Law students in courses I have taught using portions of the manuscript for this book at Northwestern University Pritzker School of Law; the University of Florida Levin College of Law; and the University of Missouri School of Law.

Participants in training programs I led or co-led, sponsored primarily by Northwestern University School of Professional Studies or Pepperdine University Caruso School of Law Institute for Dispute Resolution.

Participants in conferences or other events at which I have made presentations, sponsored by various organizations, including the Program on Negotiation at Harvard Law School; the Southern California Mediation Association; the Oregon Mediators Association, and the IFS Institute.

University of Missouri School of Law Center for the Study of Dispute Resolution. My years as a professor and the first director of the Center for the Study of Dispute Resolution laid the foundation for this book. I am grateful to Dean Dale Whitman for conceiving and supporting the Center and to the exceptionally creative and collaborative faculty. Special thanks to the following members of the Center: Bob Bailey, Chris Guthrie, Art Hinshaw, John Lande, Ilhyung Lee, Jim Levin, Bobbie MacAdoo, Jean Sternlight, Jennifer Robbennolt, and Josh Stulberg.

Northwestern University Pritzker School of Law, where I have been a visiting professor since 2010. My appointment at Northwestern Law commenced at about the same time as I became aware of Internal Family Systems. And shortly thereafter I decided to include internal family systems in what was then a book-in-progress on mindfulness in law and conflict resolution. In this effort, I received terrific support from my wonderful colleagues in the Center on Negotiation, Mediation, and Restorative Justice: Lynn Cohn, Alyson Carrel, Annie Buth, and Daniel Gandert, who tested and helped refine some of the ideas in the book, and Sara Buffett and Nancy Flowers, who provided extraordinary administrative help. Special thanks to the late Tim Jacobs and to Annamarie Jedziniak, faculty assistants, who help in countless ways. To Jamie Sommer, my library liaison, who never failed to find what I needed. To Kent Lawrence and the M.R. Bauer Foundation for funding the Harris H. Agnew Visiting Professorship of Dispute Resolution. And to the law school's incredible IT department, especially Stephan Martone, Nasser Doleh, and Patrick Montag, whose technical skills and reliability were exceeded only by their patience. Many other Northwestern Law colleagues also have supported this work, including Cliff Zimmerman and Rob Durr and others whom I have acknowledged above.

Northwestern University School of Professional Studies, which has sponsored a Negotiation Institute that Dan Shapiro and I have co-led, sometimes with K.M. Zouhary, annually (except for two years) since 2005. It has welcomed and accommodated the kind of innovations that we introduced, including mindfulness, Internal Family System, and improvisation. Special thanks to Dean Tom Gibbons, Erica Wilke Bove, Jake Hume, Suzanne Rovani, and Tom Durkin.

Harvard Law School Program on Negotiation. In the absence of the (PON) this book certainly would not have come into existence; I could not have written or even conceived of it. The PON has enabled and promoted a good deal of work that led to or appears in this book. I am especially grateful to PON faculty and staff for their enthusiasm and their willingness to present, consider, and use potentially transformative ideas, including mindfulness and Internal Family Systems: Bob Bordone, Erica Ariel Fox, Susan Hackley, Sheila Heen, Bob Mnookin, Bruce Patton, the late Frank Sander, Dan Shapiro, Doug Stone, Larry Susskind, and Mike Wheeler.

Pepperdine University Caruso School of Law Straus Institute for Dispute Resolution. For the last decade or so, the Straus Institute has hosted workshops that Rachel Wohl and I led on mindfulness, conflict resolution, and IFS, drawing participants from far and wide. Many thanks to Randy Lowry, Peter Robinson, Tom Stipanowich, Suksimranjit Singh, and Lori Rushford for their support and receptiveness.

People who helped me with mindfulness. This list could go on almost indefinitely. In 1974, Charles Wiggins introduced me to writings on Eastern philosophy, psychology, and religious thought, as well as Transcendental Meditation. (He and I are still talking about these and related matters.) I first learned about mindfulness more than a decade later. Since about 1987, my mindfulness/insight/Vipassana meditation has benefitted from many great teachers, including Joseph Goldstein, Jon Kabat-Zinn, Shinzen Young, Matt Flickstein, Ginny Morgan, the late Ferris Urbanowski, Melissa Blacker, and Sharon Salzberg. I have had the joy and privilege of co-teaching with some of these teachers, primarily Ferris and Melissa, in offering some of the earliest mindfulness programs for lawyers and mediators. In recent years I have been strongly influenced and enriched by the writings and online teachings of Tara Brach and Judson Brewer.

Melody Daily and Mary Trevor. Melody, my long-time friend and colleague, and Mary, who became a new friend and colleague, separately and together, gave splendid editorial advice, laced with patience, encouragement, and support. My gratitude to them is enormous.

West Academic Publishing. I am grateful for West Academic's willingness to depart from some of it its usual practices in formatting and marketing. Special thanks to Jon Harkness, Senior Acquisitions Editor, for his enthusiasm, constancy, understanding, wisdom, and patience; to Moriah Hamstad, Senior Publication Specialist, for extending herself beyond the call of duty and producing, with good cheer, excellent proofs that responded to my many requests; to Production Manager Greg Olson, who gave Moriah support and space to do her exceptional work before his recent retirement; and to Michele Bassett, who assumed the Production Manager position only a short time ago and made sure that everything came together in the final product.

My family: Casey, Andrew, Tricia, Margot, and Janet, for their love, support, and tolerance (especially for the many moments, hours, weeks, and years I devoted to this book). You have taught me more than I can say.

SUMMARY OF CONTENTS

TABLE OF CONTENTS

SECTION B. MINDFULNESS,
THE SECOND DOMAIN

SECTION C. BACK TO THE FIRST DOMAIN, NEGOTIATION: THE THREE CONVERSATIONS

SECTION D. INTERNAL FAMILY SYSTEMS (IFS), THE THIRD DOMAIN

MANAGING CONFLICT MINDFULLY

DON'T BELIEVE EVERYTHING YOU THINK

INTRODUCTION

Had I not participated—quite poorly—in two negotiations, several decades ago, I never would have written this book. At the time, I considered myself a mature professional negotiation expert, but I performed like an utter amateur. The episodes left me embarrassed, ashamed, and bewildered. Partly as a result, in the ensuing years, I have gradually developed a method for better understanding and addressing conflict, which I call Mindful Conflict Management. This book invites you to sample, consider, test, and—if you like—learn to use it.

The first of my failed negotiations arose in Luxor, Egypt, in the midst of a luxurious vacation with my wife and twelve-year-old son. I bargained hard with a carriage driver, who told me he struggled to support his wife and six children. A menacing presence, I thought, he subtly threatened me, then blatantly cheated me out of almost five dollars. As a result, I dropped into a funk, infused with anger and craving for revenge, that ruined our last evening in Egypt.

A year later, I found myself in Manila, after co-conducting a mediation-training program for the Philippine Bar Association, for which I received ample compensation, luxurious accommodations, and business-class air travel. Once again, I haggled—this time over the price of a woven blanket and a table runner—with a lovely woman who worked in a theme park. I saved about two dollars. Later, I learned that she had been on the verge of losing her store, having made no sales for two weeks; and more: she believed that God had sent my colleagues and me to save her and her children.

I wrote an essay about these two negotiations, in which I concluded that my need for self-esteem had undercut wise negotiation behavior, and then solicited comments on the manuscript. "I don't think you should publish this," a close friend said. "It makes you look like *such a jerk*!" I published it nonetheless.[1] And for many years, I suffered intermittent pangs of guilt—and the suspicion that I really *was* a jerk, a hypothesis for which I have accumulated, and revealed, other anecdotal evidence.[2]

These incidents reeked with irony. When they occurred, I had been studying, teaching, and writing about negotiation, mediation, and other conflict-resolution processes for well over a decade. I had fully explored, and *thought* I had internalized, the two most important ideas in the realm of conflict resolution: the difference between positions and interests, and the potential benefits, in a negotiation, of emphasizing or at least including

1

underlying interests. Our *positions* are what we say we want. Our *interests* are the reasons we assert such positions—the goals, motives, wishes, or impulses that we seek to serve (consciously or subconsciously) through our positions.

Several years earlier, I had resolved a family conflict using these principles. Picture the scene: my wife Casey, our son Andrew (then about seven years old), and I are about to leave for dinner at a semi-nice restaurant, when Andrew says, "I am taking ten Teenage Mutant Turtles"—bizarre but popular action figures, then and now. "No, you're not," I reply. "Yes, I am," says Andrew. As we continue to exchange these "positions," our voices rise and our tempers flare. Casey intervenes to coach me: "Ask him *why* he wants to take them." I do, and he says, "So they can play basketball." I ask, "Could they play with two on each team?" He says, "Yes," and we have a deal (four Turtles rather than ten) that serves all of our principal interests: Andrew's interests in avoiding boredom and enjoying himself, his parents' interest in relaxing at the dinner table.

In other words, understanding interests can create opportunities for mutual gain.

As Mick Jagger and Keith Richards put it,

> You can't always get what you want
>
> . . .
>
> But if you try, you just might find
> You get what you need[3]

For these reasons and others, I have deliberately stressed interests in my professional life—writing, teaching, training, negotiating, and mediating. I have tried to do so in my personal life as well. Yet on that balmy evening along the Nile, I succumbed to my anger, which drove me to rely almost totally on my positions—my demands about the fee. And I ignored and eventually damaged the interests of all concerned: my wife and son's interests (and my own) in having a nice evening, and certainly some of the driver's interests, such as supporting his family. In Manila, my conduct was even less discerning and more embarrassing: there, I felt empathy toward the woman with whom I bargained, and I saw several opportunities to satisfy her interests as well as mine. But I did not seize them.

These are not my worst negotiation performances when I knew better, or should have, though they are the worst that I am willing to tell you about right here. *All* of us—including leaders and so-called experts in conflict management and in virtually every other field—sometimes make (retrospectively) unwise decisions related to conflict with others. These decisions can produce undesirable outcomes—from missed opportunities, suboptimal agreements, and damaged relationships, to interpersonal violence, terrorism, state-sponsored war, and the accompanying suffering.

Here is a condensed version of the book's central thesis:

1. When we are in conflict with others—or think we are—we frequently make significant errors, which can lead to unwise processes or outcomes and avoidable suffering.

2. Such errors result from many factors; for simplicity and convenience, however, I organize them into inadequate management of external aspects of conflict (conflict between people); awareness and attention; and internal aspects of conflict (conflict within a person).

3. We can improve our ability to manage conflict and other problematic situations in any sphere by learning, practicing, and drawing upon methods for understanding and responding to conflict that are associated with three domains:

   Negotiation, primarily for managing external aspects of conflict, usually through discussion between the parties or their representatives.

   Mindfulness, primarily for managing awareness. Mindfulness means paying attention to our present-moment experience, primarily with kindly curiosity instead of judgment or assessment.

   Internal Family Systems (IFS), primarily for managing internal aspects of conflict. IFS is, at once, a theory, a model of the mind, and a method of psychotherapy; and its influence is growing rapidly in North America, Europe, and other parts of the world. For a quick and entertaining sense of *some* features of IFS, see *Inside Out* (Disney-Pixar 2015) or even a trailer.[4]

This book offers the first framework for managing conflict and other problematic situations using elements of negotiation, mindfulness, and Internal Family Systems. Each of these domains, alone, can help individuals manage conflict and enhance their abilities—and tendencies—to behave with wisdom, compassion, and kindness toward themselves and others. Each domain offers unique ways of understanding and responding to conflict. Each has vulnerabilities. And each can also support and reinforce the others.

Box I-1 presents a macro view of the three domains and their relationships.

Box I-1. The Venn of Conflict Management: Negotiation, Mindfulness, and Internal Family Systems

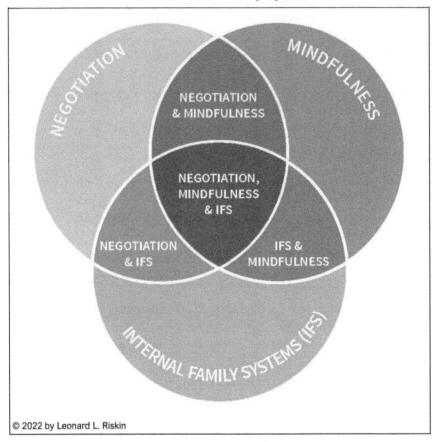

© 2022 by Leonard L. Riskin

The large circles in Box I-1 represent the three domains—negotiation, mindfulness, and IFS. The zones of overlap (smaller and darker) show that we are able to draw on more than one domain. When we do, the domains involved can reinforce or support one another, increasing our chances of skillfully managing the situation at hand. The central zone (the darkest shade), where all domains overlap, depicts the sweet spot; when our minds are in that zone, we are capable of using tools from all three domains. This will become clearer as we proceed through the book.

* * *

This book grew out of my background in studying, practicing, writing about, and teaching law (since 1974), negotiation and mediation (since 1980), mindfulness (since 1990), and IFS (since 2010). I have used drafts of this book in my courses at Northwestern University Pritzker School of Law and the University of Florida Levin College of Law and portions of it at the University of Missouri School of Law and in many other courses, programs, and workshops. Feedback from students and participants has helped improve it in many ways.

When I began to teach negotiation, mindfulness, and IFS together, most of my students had had little or no exposure to any of these areas. Yet they typically began using aspects of these domains almost immediately. Many reported that negotiation, mindfulness, and IFS helped them, not only in dealing with conflict, but also in performing and feeling better in a wide range of circumstances, such as participating in a class or a meeting, studying, taking exams, interviewing for jobs, or carrying out nearly any kind of task in their professional or personal lives, especially under stressful conditions—which might include spending a holiday weekend with their families. Combining the three domains has helped me and some of my colleagues and in similar ways—though not always, of course.

Not long ago, I heard from a former student in my course called *Conflict Management in Legal Practice* at Northwestern Law, which was based on a draft of this book. He told me he was an associate in a large commercial law firm and explained how much he had benefitted from this course:

> [T]he office. . . is full of type A folks on steroids trying to outdo one another in an effort to "be the best". . . . The course content, especially with respect to being more mindful of the reactions of others to one's behavior was pivotal in surviving this job. [In] . . . several instances . . . we were given an assignment and three hours to complete it. The task begins by seeming impossible, one tends to feel lost then panicked at the same time unable to produce coherent work product—until one gets a chance to do some meditation in the privacy of their office and suddenly everything makes a lot more sense with a lower heart rate.
>
> One thing that really helped was . . . internal family systems . . . . Separating emotions . . . has been a game changer when it comes to having to switch from family and personal concerns to work related activities. It's helped me better understand my wife and her range of emotions, which are far broader and more complex than mine. Being better prepared for personal life and able to deal with its stresses made it easier to focus on work.

Of course, I cannot guarantee that you will manage as well as this young lawyer appears to have done, and specific work, community, and family situations will differ. But if you take this book seriously and learn its lessons, you should be better able to manage your focus and awareness, as well as external and internal aspects of conflict. That, in turn, should help increase your skillful behavior, decrease your unskillful behavior, and reduce your chances of acting like a jerk. Along the way, these lessons should also guide you toward a fuller understanding and acceptance of yourself and others.

If that sounds good, or at least intrigues you, keep reading.

ROADMAP AND GUIDE

I hope to persuade you, or at least encourage you to consider, that you could improve your ability to wisely manage conflict by learning to use and integrate, as appropriate, three domains—negotiation, mindfulness, and internal family systems (IFS)—each of which contains its own theories, knowledge, and practices. To coax you in that direction, the book explains and illustrates these domains, using cases based on real events, and offers exercises and other opportunities to help you use all three domains, separately and together.

No one else has written a book of this nature, and you may wonder why I did. I have been obsessed with conflict and how to understand and deal with it since my youth. I grew up in the long shadow of the Holocaust, in which many of my relatives died, and I directly experienced the fear of nuclear war that pervaded the U.S. during the decades that followed. When my immediate family drove from Milwaukee to Miami Beach for a vacation (in the summer, to save money), I was confused and disgusted by the "Whites Only" signs on water fountains and restrooms. Perhaps that background led me to study psychology and then to attend law school.

Sections A and C offer current, but simplified, pictures of the negotiation domain, by presenting four different but related perspectives on conflict and negotiation. The first perspective focuses on positions, the second on interests, the third on core concerns, and the last on the "three conversations."

Much of legal education and law practice rests on—and wrestles with—positional, adversarial perspectives, but I did not consider this a problem until I started teaching in law school; then I quickly noticed widespread mental and emotional suffering and stress among law students and lawyers. A good deal of this harm derived from adversarial mindsets and practices, which I realized only gradually. In about 1980, I learned new perspectives and practices in negotiation and mediation that rested on a different approach; it attended to interests more than positions; and it sought solutions that were mutually beneficial to the extent feasible (colloquially called "win-win"). In the ensuing years, negotiation theory, knowledge, and practice have expanded exponentially, and interest-oriented perspectives have increasingly exerted influence.

As I studied, practiced, wrote about, and taught negotiation and mediation, I began to perform better—usually. Sometimes, however, I failed;

7

in these situations, my clarity vanished—because I had succumbed to my emotions, thought about myself too much, acted out of habit, or failed to manage my attention and awareness. By the time I encountered the Luxor carriage driver, I had been practicing mindfulness meditation for five years, though not intensively. After Luxor, I realized, slowly, that mindfulness could help me, and others, overcome or mitigate such conflict-management problems.

Section B presents mindfulness—the second domain—as a method for managing awareness and attention, and more. It explains the nature of mindfulness, describes how to cultivate it and apply it in situations of conflict, and demonstrates how it can help someone negotiate more wisely.

Mindfulness seemed to enable me—as well as many of my students and colleagues—to deal better with conflict and a range of problematic or difficult situations. But mindfulness is difficult to establish and maintain, especially in or near the heat of conflict. Luckily, in 2010 I discovered another approach to managing primarily internal aspects of conflict, an approach that also can support and reinforce mindfulness (as well as draw support and reinforcement from mindfulness). Known as IFS (for Internal Family Systems), it rests on the idea that the mind is composed of two wholly different kinds of entities—Parts and a Self—that interact as a system in ways that resemble relationships within human families or groups.

Internal Family Systems is the third domain. Section D leads us into IFS and shows how it interacts synergistically with negotiation and with mindfulness. Finally, Section E combines the three domains—negotiation, meditation, and IFS—into mindful conflict management.

Each section presents foundational information about how to understand and work with negotiation, mindfulness, or internal family systems, alone or combined, as well as exercises to enhance your skills. And each section concludes with two reviews, one of which offers a few stanzas of light verse from a poem that appears in its entirety at the end of Section E. I feel compelled to disclose that it rhymes, and I mean it to be both funny and serious.

This book can help prepare you to immediately bring some of its ideas and skills into your life—especially if you use the exercises—and then to continue developing your ability to manage conflict mindfully.

Here are a few clarifications:

The principal cases or stories used to illustrate the ideas in the book are relatively simple. They involve conflicts primarily between two individuals, which they managed, or might have managed, through negotiation. But the book's principal claims and suggestions also apply in other situations. They are equally relevant and helpful in formal negotiations that are more complex and involve many people as well as governments or various kinds of enterprises. Thus, these ideas can help us navigate conflicts and problematic situations that are connected with major national and global issues, such as climate change, inclusion and equity, health care, polarization, and even war. And these ideas apply to problematic or difficult situations that may not involve conflict or negotiation with others or between others, but in which someone is stuck, that is, they don't know what to do. For instance: should we stay or leave—a job, a relationship, a living situation, a program of study? We can look at these as internal conflicts, and manage them using the book's lessons.

Models and categories provide the scaffolding for this book, even though I am aware of their potential drawbacks. I agree with Professor George E. P. Box, who said, "All models are wrong. Some are useful."[1]

I am inviting you to learn enough about negotiation, mindfulness, and internal family systems that you can use them, at a basic level, with humility. Models enable me to help you do that. Simplification characterizes models used in science, as well.[2]

It is easy to confuse "mediation" (with one *t*) and "meditation" (with two *t*'s). The book uses both terms, as you may already have noticed, so be careful. Mediation (one *t*) is a conflict-management process; meditation (two *t*'s), as I use the word in this book, is a practice that helps us strengthen our ability to manage our awareness and attention.

I wrote this book for several audiences: professionals, academics, and students in a range of fields—most notably law, conflict resolution (especially negotiation and mediation), psychotherapy and counseling, business, and management—and for members of the public who might be interested.

You can use this book in many ways, depending on your interests, experience, and goals. I have included suggestions in the text and in endnotes.

More suggestions appear at https://tinyurl.com/ManagingConflict Mindfully, a website for the book maintained by the Center on Negotiation, Mediation, and Restorative Justice at Northwestern University Pritzker School of Law. This website contains a variety of resources, including video and audio instructions, for conflict management, mindfulness, and internal family systems exercises, and links to other materials. Instructors using this book for teaching at a law school, or in another higher-education setting, can gain access to a Teacher's Manual and additional instructional resources after registering as a faculty member at https://faculty.westacademic.com/.

SECTION A

NEGOTIATION, THE FIRST DOMAIN

In case you haven't noticed, conflict pervades human life and society. This has always been the case. But today, we can draw upon a vast array of information and advice about how to understand and deal with conflict (and other problematic situations) in virtually any sphere of human activity. This information and advice appear as theories, models, strategies, and tactics; they might be grounded in systematic research findings, experience, hunches, or characters in movies. A few of these ideas have gained widespread recognition and are easily accessible through books, videos, courses at every level of education, training programs, and, of course, the Internet. Many people take advantage of these opportunities for education. Still, we all make errors in understanding or addressing conflict.

Some such blunders occur because a person neither understands the situation nor has any notion of how to deal with it. Ted, for example, who earns his living by remodeling and reselling upscale homes, signed up for a workshop on negotiation. I asked Ted why he came to this program, and he said, "When somebody shows interest in buying one of my houses and asks the price, I give them the price that appears on the listing. Once, for instance, I said, '$746,000.' The shopper replied, 'That's too much.' At that point, I had no idea what to do next. So I said, 'Okay,' and they walked out."

But all of us—including those who have studied, practiced and mastered the most important negotiation concepts, strategies, and tactics—sometimes make unwise decisions in personal and professional life. These errors can spring from countless causes, ranging from the obvious, such as too little sleep or too much alcohol, to the more obscure, such as bacteria in the gut[1] or hormones, or because—as Yogi Berra or Nils Bohr *might* have said—"It's difficult to make predictions, especially about the future."[2] And research has confirmed that we rarely succeed at foretelling what will make us happy.[3] This book, however, focuses on five specific obstacles to skillful negotiation or skillful management of problematic situations. In subsequent sections, it presents methods for overcoming these obstacles.

CHAPTER 1

CONFLICT AND CONFLICT-MANAGEMENT PROCESSES

If you would like to improve your capacity to manage problematic situations involving two or more people, the first step is to learn about certain basic processes that are widely used for that purpose. This section uses a dispute between co-owners of a shoe business to introduce the major categories of conflict-management processes. I call it *The Shoe-Dog Split* because people who work in the shoe business often refer to themselves as shoe-dogs.[1]

Next, we shift to just one of these processes—negotiation—and set out several negotiation approaches and obstacles to using them wisely. (Don't worry. Section B will show you how to overcome these obstacles.)

The Shoe-Dog Split [2]

Twenty-five years ago, Billy and Pedro started their own firm, Billy & Pedro Shoes (BPS). The firm has enjoyed modest prosperity, making and selling just one product—a low-cut men's boot, handmade of the finest materials. BPS sells only wholesale and to a limited number of individual shoe stores or chains of stores.

Pedro was good at management and finance, while Billy excelled in sales. To facilitate management decisions, but (according to Billy) not to apportion control, they agreed to split the closely held stock unevenly, with Pedro getting 51 percent and Billy 49 percent. Pedro has worked primarily in the office, and Billy has handled marketing and sales, spending much of his time on the road. Pedro has remained physically fit. Billy's health, vigor, and mental acuity have declined, the result (Pedro thinks) of too much alcohol-related customer entertainment.

In recent years, their once-close relationship has deteriorated to the point that they avoid one another and communicate only in writing. Two issues have produced much of the stress. First, Pedro wants to modernize and expand the business, and Billy does not. Recently, Pedro announced that he has hired his daughter, Paulina, a recent MBA graduate, and assigned her to update Billy's area—marketing and sales—in which Billy is not technologically skillful. Billy relies almost entirely on personal contact. Second, Pedro would like to get rid of Billy. When Pedro told Billy—via email—about his plans for Paulina, Billy immediately hired a lawyer and brought suit against Pedro, seeking to win back some influence in the company's management. Thirty days ago, the court issued a preliminary injunction requiring Pedro to include Billy in all major decisions.

Recently, Billy returned to court, arguing that Pedro has violated the order, and asking the judge to find that, in having done so, Pedro is in contempt of court. The judge forcefully urged them to resolve this case outside of court.

* * *

What should Pedro and Billy do? First, they need to realize that they *are* in conflict. Like many other people, they trudged into this situation gradually, without knowing where it could lead. But what do we mean by conflict?

"We can understand conflict in many ways," writes Professor Bernard Mayer. "As a feeling, a disagreement, a real or perceived incompatibility of interests, inconsistent world views, or a set of behaviors."[3]

We also can distinguish between subjective and overt conflict, as does Dean Pruitt.[4] If Pedro thinks Billy's needs to drink and to golf with customers are incompatible with Pedro's goal of modernizing the firm, Pedro is in subjective conflict with Billy, even if Billy is unaware of it. If Pedro never acts to address this problem, the conflict remains subjective. The conflict becomes overt, however, when Pedro does something that brings it to Billy's attention—or vice versa.

But conflict can manifest in many other ways. Pedro might become depressed, for instance, because of his negative business and personal relationships with Billy. Rather than talk with Billy about their relationship, Pedro might gossip about him or use passive-aggressive tactics, such as scheduling a meeting when Billy will be out of town. Billy might respond in kind or in other ways, such as working less hard or undermining Pedro.

Bernard Mayer has proposed that we should understand conflict along three dimensions—behavioral, cognitive, and emotional.[5] To resolve conflict fully, he adds, we need to resolve it along all three of these related dimensions.[6] With such a resolution, Billy and Pedro would stop disputing, feel comfortable with their cognitive understanding of the outcome, and be at peace emotionally. Of course, not all conflicts or disputes get fully or even partly resolved. Just as physicians manage illnesses that they cannot cure, all human beings manage a great deal of conflict that they cannot fully resolve. Think of disputes between nations, ethnic groups, relatives, neighbors, or co-workers.

Now that you have some background on what "conflict" can mean, let's return to what Pedro and Billy might do about their situation. They have many possibilities. Consider three categories of widely used conflict-management processes—adjudicative, consensual, and mixed—as presented in Box A-1. Billy and Pedro might decide to proceed with one or more of these processes.

Box A-1. Conflict-Management Process Categories with Principal Characteristics and Examples

Process Categories	Principal Characteristics	Examples
Adjudicative	A (hopefully impartial) third party makes a binding decision after presentations by the parties or their representatives.	**Court**, in which decisions are based on applicable law. **Arbitration**, in which parties can typically decide what rules or considerations govern the decision.
Consensual	The goal is to reach an agreement through mutual consent.	**Negotiation**, in which the parties—directly or through representatives—seek a mutually agreeable outcome, usually through discussion. **Mediation**, in which a third party, the mediator, facilitates a negotiation.
Mixed	These processes include elements of both adjudicative and consensual processes.	**Mediation-arbitration (Med-Arb)**, in which, if the mediation does not produce an agreement, a binding arbitration will follow. **Early neutral evaluation (ENE)**, in which a neutral third-party makes a non-binding prediction of how a court would deal with the case. This should help the parties negotiate a settlement.

© 2022 Leonard L. Riskin

Adjudicative processes (especially in courts) typically base decisions on the law and the legally relevant facts, after considering the parties' arguments. The Pedro-Billy situation is already in court. The judge has urged them to resolve this out of court. To do so, they could use arbitration, another form of adjudication that ordinarily is faster and less formal than court proceedings.

They might also employ any of the consensual processes—such as mediation and negotiation—which can be more flexible than adjudication and can more easily consider a broad range of factors, or any of the mixed processes. Each of these processes offers several models, which have two principal functions: understanding a conflict and responding to it.

CHAPTER 2

NEGOTIATION BASICS: POSITIONS AND INTERESTS

From here on, this book centers on negotiation, the most pervasively used method of managing conflict between or among people. Negotiation typically is essential in all the other conflict-management processes and in daily life. The word *negotiation* has accumulated countless definitions, and I don't want to argue about them, but I need to tell you how I use the term in this book. Here is one definition, which appears in a book that I co-authored: "Negotiation is an interpersonal process through which we make arrangements with others to resolve disputes or plan transactions, often by reconciling conflicting—or apparently conflicting—interests. It involves communication—through the use of words or actions—of demands, wishes, and perspectives."[1]

That's a pretty good definition of negotiation that is formal, in the sense that the parties realize that they are negotiating. But that definition also fits less formal interactions about countless issues in daily life: what we will have for dinner tonight, which movie we will watch, who will take out the trash or change the air-conditioner filter, who sits where at the table or on a flight from Los Angeles to Hong Kong. Dictionary.com provides several meanings for negotiate, including "to manage; transact; conduct" or "to move through, around, or over in a satisfactory manner."[2]

Negotiation Focuses and Models

The book presents four different but complementary ways to manage conflict through negotiation, each of which has a primary focus. This section covers negotiation approaches that focus on positions, interests, or core concerns. Later, Section C presents the fourth focus: the Three Conversations.[3] For each focus, commentators have offered one or more models that provide specific guidance for working with it. I have included one model for each of the focuses.

The difference between a focus and a model, as I use the terms, is this: A focus is general; a model is specific. A focus tells you what to consider—for instance, positions, interests, or core concerns. A model is more detailed; it includes strategies and tactics for working with the relevant positions, interests, or core concerns. We've all experienced this distinction in many situations. When we are young, for instance, and going someplace alone, a parent might tell us to "pay attention to traffic," which would be a focus. Instead, or in addition, the parent might have said, "Cross the streets only at a corner; obey the traffic lights; and look both ways." That would be a model.[4]

I selected these particular focuses and models for several reasons: They are widely recognized around the world, are easy to use, and fit together readily, both in theory and in practice. The first focus—positions—may be the most familiar. The other three focuses—interests, core-concerns and three-conversations—and the models I present for them were created and popularized in books emanating from the Program on Negotiation (PON) at Harvard Law School, which has, for several decades, produced the most influential and widely known writing on negotiation; each of these models proposes ways to improve upon the positional approach. In addition, I have used these focuses and their models (but not slavishly or narrowly) for many years, in writing, research, teaching, training, negotiating, mediating, and living most aspects of my life.[5]

So let's imagine that Billy and Pedro agree to negotiate, one-on-one, at the urging of their lawyers, family, and friends. How might they do that? What choices do they have? To begin to answer that question, this chapter introduces the two most basic negotiation focuses and one model for implementing each.

The Difference Between Positions and Interests

Here comes the most fundamental and useful key to understanding negotiation—recognizing the difference between positions and interests.

A *position* in a negotiation, as generally understood in the literature and in training programs, is what you say you want or are entitled to.[6] An *interest*, in the simplest formulation, is what motivates you—consciously or subconsciously—to assert that position. Motivations could include goals, wishes, concerns, or fears (rational or irrational, conscious or subconscious), any of which might connect to identity issues or deeper human needs. Ideally, if you get what your position asserts, the interest that motivated your position would be satisfied.[7] But people sometimes do not think this through. A wonderful illustration appears in a cartoon that shows a king and a queen sitting on either side of the king's counselor. The counselor, looking at the king, says, "You say, 'Off with her head,' but what I am hearing is, 'I feel neglected.' "[8] The king's position is that the queen should lose her head. But even if he gets what he says he wants (his position), he will not get what he hoped for (his interest)—at least not from this queen.

One more important term: *issue*. An issue, as I am using the term, is a problem or question that might be included in the negotiation.

Back to Billy and Pedro. Box A-2 deals with whether Billy leaves BPS or stays, and it shows Billy and Pedro's positions on this issue, as well as their relevant interests.[9]

Box A-2. Shoe-Dog Split: Will Billy Leave BPS or Stay? Billy and Pedro's Likely *Positions* and *Interests*

Issue	Billy's positions	Billy's interests	Pedro's positions	Pedro's interests
Does Billy leave BPS or stay?	Billy stays.	Billy's dignity, sense of self-worth. Success of BPS. Avoiding tense interpersonal situation. Health care/health insurance.	Billy leaves.	Pedro's dignity, sense of self-worth. Success of BPS. Avoiding tense interpersonal situation.
If Billy stays:				
What would be his role in management?	Billy gets equal role in management with Pedro.	Billy's dignity, sense of self-worth.	Billy gets no role in management.	Pedro's dignity, sense of self-worth.
What would be his role in marketing and sales?	Billy keeps responsibility for marketing and sales.	Success of BPS. Social interaction.	Billy gets no role in marketing or sales.	Success of BPS.
If Billy leaves:		Success of BPS.		Success of BPS.
What would be his compensation?	At the rate of $2Y per share.	Dignity Economic security	At the rate of $.5Y per share.	Helping Paulina in her career.
May he continue to work in the shoe industry?	Yes.	Income. Health care/health insurance.	No.	Avoiding loss of customers to Billy.

© 2022 Leonard L. Riskin

Positions and Interests in a Conflict of Your Own

To ground your understanding of positions and interests, try this: Call to mind a conflict that was or is significant to you in any aspect of your life. It could have happened in the past or it might be ongoing. It should have an emotional element, and if it occurred in the past, it should still bother you. The exercise works best if the conflict concerns mainly you and just one other person.

Once you have such a situation in mind, close your eyes, and recall a particular event, moment, or time period associated with it.

Out of all that, try to identify positions and interests, yours and the other person's.

Then complete the form in Appendix Exercise A-1, Positions and Interests in a Conflict of Your Own.

Finally, consider whether, if you had achieved your position(s), you would have satisfied your interests.

* * *

Before we contemplate whether and how Pedro and Billy might have used either of these focuses or their models (or elements of their models), I need to tell you more about them.

A Position-Focused Negotiation Model (Extreme Version)

Positional strategies and tactics are typically most suitable when the negotiators assume that the problem to be addressed is narrow and that the purpose of the negotiation, for each party, is to get or keep as much as possible of a fixed resource—such as bitcoins or air time or lima beans— which means that whatever one negotiator gains, the other loses.[10] When those assumptions are correct, an explicit focus on positions often makes sense, especially as a starting point.

Here is an extreme, adversarial model for working with a focus on positions.

Strategies and Tactics for Understanding the Conflict or Situation

- Focus on positions, rather than interests.
- Define the problem to be addressed narrowly.
- Assume that any gain for one party means a loss for the other.

■   Learn the other side's bottom line and situation.

Strategies and Tactics for Responding to the Conflict or Situation

■   Mislead the other side about your bottom line and situation.

■   Make extreme demands or offers.

■   Make few and small concessions.

■   Persuade the other side to compromise or to agree with your position.

■   Undermine the other side's positions.

■   Walk away or threaten to do so.

Please be aware that this picture of position-oriented negotiation is extreme and skewed. There is no reason why a negotiator cannot take positions based on complex and broad issues, nor do negotiators always try to mislead one another. So, as I have described this model, it conflates the negotiator's focus with their style—as do many negotiation authorities and practitioners.

How Billy and Pedro Could Use Such Strategies and Tactics

To Understand the Conflict or Situation

Both might focus on their own and the other's positions—what they say they want from the negotiation. Here, they might express and negotiate over specific positions on a number of issues, such as whether Billy will stay or leave and what each of them would get in the event of either outcome, as illustrated in Box A-2.

They would also assume that this is a win-lose situation; whatever Pedro gains, Billy loses, and vice versa. In assessing one another's positions, they would consider what is likely to happen if a court were to decide the case, assuming their lawyers had advised them about this.

To Respond to the Conflict or Situation

In responding to the problem as they understand it, Billy and Pedro would continue focusing on positions and try to mislead one another in various ways.

For instance, each would argue that his own positions were strong, using claims grounded in power, law, morality, or fairness. Each might express absolute commitments to positions. Billy, for example, might say, "I will not leave BPS no matter what you do." He might be telling the truth, or he might be trying to mislead or threaten Pedro. And each would try to diminish the other's confidence in his own positions.

They might do this in various ways. They could make extreme demands and offers. If Billy wants $400,000 to leave, for instance, he might demand $1,500,000. If Pedro were willing to pay $300,000, he might offer $90,000. These moves exemplify a positional tactic known as "anchoring," which is based on the idea that the first offer and counteroffer frequently have strong impacts on the final agreement.[11]

Concessions would be small and infrequent. As his first concession, Billy might reduce his demand from $1.5 million to $1.25 million. Pedro might respond by increasing his offer from $90,000 to $93,000.

Generally, they would not reveal information about their own situations or interests. For instance, Billy would not tell Pedro that he would like to slow down, but wants to stay in touch with clients and needs health insurance.

An Interest-Focused Model (from *Getting to Yes,* More or Less)

The highest aspiration behind focusing on interests is to make both parties better off, usually by "expanding the pie" (a metaphor for creating value) and then "dividing the pie" (a metaphor for distributing value) efficiently. Partly for that reason, this chapter relies on (and elaborates and reorganizes, just a bit) the most influential articulation of an interest-focused model, which appears in Fisher, Ury, and Patton's *Getting to Yes. Getting to Yes* implies (or people have inferred) that the surest path to that goal depends on the negotiators revealing their interests or at least their situations. But there is no consensus about which strategies and tactics belong in an interest-focused approach.[12] Below, I divide its strategies and tactics into those directed primarily at understanding the problem or situation and those directed primarily at responding to it.

Strategies and Tactics for Understanding the Conflict or Situation

- Focus on interests, rather than positions.
- Understand the problem broadly.
- Be soft on the people.

Strategies and Tactics for Responding to the Conflict or Situation

- Be hard on the problem and soft on the people.
- Invent options before deciding.
- Insist on objective criteria.
- Develop your BATNA (Best Alternative to a Negotiated Agreement) and measure options against it.

How Pedro and Billy Could Use Such Strategies and Tactics

To Understand the Conflict or Situation

Billy and Pedro's interests (and positions) appear in Box A-2 above. Take a quick look at it. You can see that they have several overlapping or similar interests, such as the success of the firm and their own senses of dignity and self-worth. They also have individual interests, such as Pedro's wish to help Paulina in her career and Billy's needs to have health insurance and to stay connected with his customers or otherwise remain active. In following this model, Pedro and Billy are likely to reveal some of their own interests and situations and inquire about each other's.

To Respond to the Conflict or Situation

Pedro and Billy could be kind and considerate toward one another, even while each insists on a solution that works well for himself.

They could come up with options before deciding what to do. One purpose of this strategy is to help the negotiators avoid settling prematurely, that is, before they have considered other possibilities and opportunities. Brainstorming and list making are premier methods for generating options. In brainstorming, all participants suggest options that *might* respond to interests previously identified, even those that seem silly. Suggesting an option does not signify support for it. To foster creativity, no criticism is allowed during brainstorming. List making is a similar process, but each person (or each side) makes a separate list; participants can reveal individual items as and when they wish.

Based on the interests set forth in Box A-2, brainstorming or list making could produce a number of options, such as those set forth below in Box A-3.

Box A-3. Shoe-Dog Split: Options That Might Be Generated Through Brainstorming or List Making

- Billy leaves BPS.
- Pedro leaves BPS.
- Pedro buys Billy's shares, based—for instance—on an appraisal by a third party, or other methods, or vice versa.
- Pedro or Billy pays soon or periodically on a specified schedule.
- Billy retires, and BPS hires him as a consultant or in some other capacity that would enable him to continue coverage under BPS's health insurance.
- Billy trains or coaches Paulina.
- Billy introduces Paulina to customers and facilitates resolution of difficult issues.
- Billy keeps an area to manage himself.
- Billy gets a new title, such as Vice President for Client Relations.
- Billy and Pedro get separate offices.
- BPS adds a third member to the board.
- Billy and Pedro go to counseling or therapy—alone or together.
- Billy and Pedro, and perhaps others in BPS, go into mediation.
- BPS hires a management consultant to study the firm and make recommendations.
- Pedro becomes chair of the board and CEO.
- Paulina gets a nice title and office and responsibility for modernizing sales and marketing.
- Pedro or Billy or both take negotiation training.
- Pedro and Billy continue in court or submit the dispute to arbitration or mediation.
- Pedro and Billy go into psychotherapy or counseling, separately or together.

© 2022 Leonard L. Riskin

Market value and customary practices exemplify objective criteria. In this case, potentially useful objective criteria could include rules and standards a court would likely apply if it were to dissolve this closely held corporation at the request of Billy or Pedro. Objective criteria might also include customary practices about shareholders competing with one another after dissolution of a corporation or after a substantial shareholder leaves the enterprise or sells all of their stock.[13]

It is useful to distinguish "options" and "alternatives." An option is something that you can do only if your counterpart agrees. An alternative is something that you can do without your counterpart's agreement. As I've heard Dan Shapiro explain, "*o*ptions are *o*n the table; *a*lternatives are *a*way from the table." Your BATNA is the best course of action that you can take on your own, that is, without the other party's agreement. You always have a "best" alternative, even if it is not particularly attractive.

What alternatives do Billy and Pedro have? That is, what could each of them do on their own if they fail to reach an agreement with one another? One is to ask a court to dissolve the corporation. This would involve selling the assets and dividing the proceeds between Billy and Pedro—an alternative that would serve the interests of neither. Another alternative might be to continue with the current situation. Or either partner could simply work less (or less diligently) and spend time watching sports or playing video games. None of these is very good. Their BATNAs are what they actually would do, on their own, in the absence of an agreement.

And they can measure any potential agreements against their BATNAs. Working from a set of options and alternatives such as those mentioned above, Billy and Pedro (probably with help from their lawyers or colleagues) could come up with a variety of agreements that would be better for both than their BATNAs and would satisfy at least some of their interests. Perhaps, for instance, they could agree that Billy would leave his current position with BPS but remain connected through a consulting or special employment arrangement under which he would retain some of his old clients, as well as his health insurance. Perhaps he could also coach Paulina on marketing and sales. Billy and Pedro might even re-establish cordial relations.

Billy or Pedro also might enhance his own bargaining power by improving his BATNA. Billy might, for instance, secure a job offer from another company, and Pedro might identify people who could carry out portions of Billy's current responsibilities.

Another Way to Look at It: What's "The Problem"?

Billy and Pedro's abilities to recognize "the problem" and then understand it would depend, in part, upon the information they considered relevant. For instance, if they focused on positions, they might believe the problem is the disparity between their positions.

We can describe or identify Billy and Pedro's problem along a continuum ranging from narrow to broad. A narrow problem definition might emphasize law and legally relevant facts (or other claims of "right" or power). A broader understanding would include Pedro and Billy's underlying interests, and perhaps the interests of others, such as Paulina, employees, or customers.[14] In order to reach the most appropriate problem definition, it is useful to "map" the problem, that is, to understand its aspects and impacts broadly and deeply. That understanding would prepare the parties to "set" the problem, that is, to decide which aspects of the problem to address.[15] If Billy had mapped the problem, for example, they could have considered or decided which of their positions and interests to attempt to address.

A positional or adversarial focus tends to produce, or arise from, a narrower view of the problem (the problem definition) and a narrower outcome than does an interest-based focus. A narrow problem definition is congruent with "The Lawyer's Standard Philosophical Map," a mindset that I described several decades ago: "What appears on the map is determined largely by the power of two assumptions about matters that lawyers handle: (1) that disputants are adversaries—i.e., if one wins, the other must lose— and (2) that disputes may be resolved through application, by a third party, of some general rule of law . . . ."[16] This perspective has traditionally governed much of law school education and law practice, but you don't have to be a lawyer to use it. Pedro and Billy are likely to default into it, especially if they are not considering interests. Speaking generally, the easiest way to broaden perspectives on a problem is to focus on the parties' interests.

The same principles apply in trying to settle high-stakes litigation between large corporations. In the early 1980s, a division of ITT (then a prominent, global conglomerate known as the International Telephone & Telegraph Corporation) had a contract to deliver control devices to a West Coast division of another corporation, which planned to incorporate the controls into appliances that it manufactured. The West Coast firm sued ITT, claiming that the devices were defective and that, as a result, the firm had suffered extensive monetary damages. ITT denied both claims, and the two companies were unable to find a compromise between their positions, although they devoted several years and lots of legal fees to the process. Ultimately, they negotiated a settlement in which ITT agreed to pay the entire amount that the West Coast firm demanded, but to do so through discounts on future deliveries of other ITT products.[17]

As you can see, this agreement was possible because the negotiators turned their attention to their clients' underlying interests—ITT's interest in selling more of its products and the other firm's interests in saving money and getting a reliable supply of the components it needed. More broadly, this agreement addressed a fundamental interest of both firms—making a profit.

* * *

Box A-4 summarizes the chapter so far. It presents position- and interest-based negotiation focuses, a model for each, and each model's elements for understanding and responding to conflict. Note that this graphic incorporates the metaphor of levels. Positions operate on the most superficial level within a person, by which I mean they are usually easiest to access. Interests lie deeper, by which I mean they are commonly more difficult to access. In later chapters, we will explore still deeper ways to understand and address conflict.

Box A-4. Positions and Interests in Negotiation

Level & Focus	A Specific Model	Model's Components for Understanding Conflict	Model's Components for Addressing Conflict
Level 1 Positions	Model: Position-based (Extreme)	Focus on positions, more than interests. Define the problem to be addressed narrowly. Assume that any gain for one party means a loss for the other.	Mislead other side as to your bottom line and situation; learn other side's bottom line and situation. *Examples:* • Use anchoring through extreme demands. • Assert positions; undermine the other's positions. • Make few and small concessions. • Persuade other side to compromise or to agree with your position. • Walk away or threaten to do so.
Level 2 Interests	Model: *Getting to Yes*	Focus on interests rather than positions. Be soft on the people but hard on the problem. Understand "the problem" broadly.	Seek to accommodate both parties' interests. • Be soft on people and hard on problem. • Generate options before deciding.

Level & Focus	A Specific Model	Model's Components for Understanding Conflict	Model's Components for Addressing Conflict
			• Expand the pie.
			• Use objective standards.
			• Develop your BATNA
			• and measure proposed
			• agreements against it.

© 2022 Leonard L. Riskin

The Importance of Flexibility

Throughout this book, I aim to suggest ways to handle conflict most wisely and skillfully—and I recognize the ambiguity of those terms. In some situations, using one particular model would work just fine. But because each model is generally based on certain assumptions—some of which are not articulated—good negotiation often requires using strategies or tactics associated with more than one model. Some commentators have interpreted *Getting to Yes*, understandably, as suggesting that a negotiator should avoid relying on positions. But sometimes using positional strategies or tactics *is* the most appropriate, at least as part of the negotiation.

Imagine, for instance, that you want to buy a new car, specifically a new Range Rover, a luxury SUV. You have researched prices. The lowest you can get from Dealer A is $100,000. The salesperson at Dealer B, Jordan, tells you the price is $120,000. You offer $100,000, explaining that you can get the car elsewhere for $100,000. Jordan says, "I can't do that because there is huge demand for this car, but I can give it to you for $105,000, if you sign right now." You need the car quickly, and Dealer B, but not Dealer A, can deliver it right away. You can afford that price. So you accept. Or the two of you go back and forth for a short time and reach an agreement based solely on price. If that's okay for you and Jordan, there may be no reason to *explicitly* consider interests. You can have essentially the same kind of negotiation in the open-air markets in virtually any country. And sometimes it is impossible to avoid such positional processes.[18] In addition, you can modify the strategies and tactics listed for that model. You don't have to mislead or be "hard" on each other. You can be polite, considerate, and honest—and it is not unusual to find such behavior. In the Land Rover example, both negotiators served their interests through pure positional bargaining.

But in many situations, you (and your negotiation counterpart) could be better off if you attended directly and explicitly to interests. For one example, let's change the Land Rover situation a bit. Assume you and the salesperson do not reach an agreement. You are $4,000 apart, and neither of you will budge, hoping the other will eventually give in. Is there some way to use interests to produce an agreement that will be better for both of you?

What are your important interests? Imagine that you want to buy this particular car so you can drive it to your twenty-fifth high-school reunion, which occurs in a few days. But why? What is your interest in doing that? To impress your high-school sweetheart, who said you would not "make anything of yourself" and dumped you all those years ago.

With that interest in mind, you could generate alternatives—actions you could take on your own. What about renting a fancy car, or borrowing one for a day to "test drive," or hiring a chauffeur-driven limousine?

For the sake of this example, however, let's imagine that you remain set on buying this car, and you are very short on time. Does Jordan, the salesperson, have any interests that you might help satisfy, without paying a higher price? Might you help Jordan meet an end-of-the-month sales quota that would earn them a bonus? Or achieve longer-term goals, such as making a good living selling cars? What if you offer to invite them to speak at your book club or another organization? Or to distribute information about them at the high school reunion? If you happen to teach or study negotiation, perhaps you could invite them to speak to one of your classes.

Doing something like this requires expanding your focus to include interests, which requires extending your curiosity.

And there's another potential challenge.

The Negotiator's Dilemma

To negotiate effectively in many circumstances, negotiators must employ strategies and tactics associated with both position- and interest-focused approaches.[19] Most successful negotiators do this—even if they are not aware of it. Yet they may encounter a difficult challenge, "the negotiator's dilemma," which arises from the tension between interest-based (or value-creating) and position-based (or value-claiming) strategies and tactics. Sometimes, in order for negotiators to deliberately deal with a certain interest, one negotiator must reveal that interest—or the surrounding circumstances—to the other. But doing so can present risks of exploitation if the other side takes an aggressively positional approach. On the other hand, adversarial conduct that focuses primarily on positions cuts off opportunities for learning each other's interests, and thereby for developing an agreement that is better for both.[20]

Thus, some strategies and tactics associated with the position-oriented, adversarial model can interfere with strategies and tactics associated with the interest-based model. For instance, if Billy's strongest interest is maintaining his relationships with customers, and if he lets Pedro know about that, Pedro might try to exploit that knowledge by, say, agreeing to let Billy continue visiting customers only if Billy agrees to less compensation for his economic stake in the business. On the other hand, unless Pedro realizes how much Billy values this interest, the problem definition and negotiated outcomes may not include it.

One reason we sometimes encounter the negotiator's dilemma—if we pay attention—is that we don't know whether to trust the other person. If Billy and Pedro each felt confident that the other would not exploit him, they would not face this precise dilemma. Lax and Sebenius propose that to manage this dilemma, the negotiator must be aware of the tension and decide, moment to moment, how to behave.[21] And Mnookin, Peppet, and Tulumello propose a "problem-solving" approach to managing this tension and others.[22]

Similar tensions between withholding and revealing information arise in innumerable circumstances in everyday life. Let's say that you attend a conference, a class, or a social event where you meet, for the first time, someone called "Marty." The two of you decide to go out for dinner together. You are enjoying the conversation, when Marty unexpectedly tells you about some of their personal difficulties. You might then experience tension (internal conflict) about whether and how much to reveal about yourself: your worries; your hopes to leave your job, your city, or your spouse; your aspirations to play the accordion professionally; your difficult childhood; your experience with illegal drugs; or the likelihood that you will soon inherit $4 million from your Aunt Nettie. You could decide that you cannot trust Marty with such information (or fear that Marty would feel uncomfortable and think you were oversharing), and so you would keep quiet about most or all of these items. But eventually, if the two of you are to become really close friends, you may want, or need, to reveal some information of this nature.[23]

In today's world this sort of internal conflict arises frequently in online interactions, especially dating apps.

Now you know about the basic negotiation focuses and their models, the potential benefits of using elements of both focuses and models in some situations, and a fundamental challenge to our ability to do that: the negotiator's dilemma. The next chapter explores another particularly strong impediment to skillful negotiation—strong negative emotions—and a method for managing them.

CHAPTER 3

EMOTIONS AND THE CORE CONCERNS

In a negotiation or other conflict-related situation, emotions, especially strong negative ones, present both obstacles and opportunities.[1] I will tell you about the obstacles first, and then suggest ways to understand and address emotions that can lead to opportunities.

Emotions as Obstacles

Negative emotions permeate the relationship between Pedro and Billy. Pedro dislikes, perhaps disdains, Billy and feels frustrated because he believes that Billy stands in the way of two of his goals (or interests): modernizing the firm's marketing and sales efforts and enhancing his daughter's career. He condemns Billy's lifestyle, though he may also harbor a bit of envy. On the other hand, Billy resents and dislikes Pedro for excluding him. He believes Pedro is selfishly motivated to promote Paulina, and, for that and other reasons, thinks Pedro is a bad person.

Before continuing, I need to explain more generally what I mean by positive and negative emotions. Positive emotions have a positive valence, exemplified by love or joy; negative emotions have a negative valence, exemplified by sadness, fear, anger, or hatred.

Research has documented the effects of mood on negotiation. In experiments, negotiators who are in a good mood reach better, interest-based outcomes than those in a neutral mood. Positive emotions, it appears, foster good problem solving, creativity, and empathy. Negative emotions usually have negative impacts on a negotiation or its consequences. In particular, negative emotions are associated with poor judgment and less concern for others, and they can distract negotiators from attending to even their own real interests. Of course, expressing negative emotions can be helpful in some situations. Occasionally it can "clear the air," for example, or extract concessions from the other side. Yet it also can damage relations between the negotiation participants. As Roger Fisher and Daniel Shapiro put it: "In a negotiation, a positive emotion to the other person is likely to build *rapport*, a relationship marked by goodwill, understanding, and a feeling of being 'in sync.' In contrast, anger, frustration, and other negative emotions feel personally distressing and they are less likely to build rapport." Because Billy and Pedro are experiencing a storm of negative emotions, they are more likely to define their problem narrowly, take adversarial positions, and pay relatively little attention to underlying interests, either their own or each other's. They might, for instance, concentrate mainly on whether Billy should or will have an equal voice in management and take strictly contrary positions. Both might concentrate on law and legally relevant facts. If so, Pedro would rely on legal arguments based on the corporate documents, while Billy would argue that the judge who ordered Pedro to include him in important decisions had accepted Billy's argument.

If they continue to conceptualize the problem from such a "pinched perspective"[2]—as would a court—they are likely to reach the same sort of outcome that a court would produce: Billy either has or does not have an equal right to influence significant decisions. But even if Billy and Pedro have an agreement or a court judgment recognizing such a right, they might be unable to implement it unless they can recast their relationship. Their high levels of anger and hostility might prevent them from working together at all, and that could lead to BPS's liquidation (judicial or otherwise), which would satisfy few of their interests, or to a continuation of the status quo, which both find unbearable.[3]

* * *

Many of us have trouble dealing with emotions that are associated with conflict. Our ability to manage emotions is often deeply influenced by our families and the cultures in which we have grown up. Negotiators—especially those trained in law—commonly address this problem by trying to exclude emotions from negotiation. People come to this approach through observation, mentoring, training, or education. Traditional law school courses, for instance, tend to focus principally on published court opinions. These opinions typically ignore emotions of the parties, except when emotions are legally relevant.[4]

But you don't have to go to law school to adopt this narrow vision; it is the default orientation for many, perhaps most, of us. A small percentage of people have little or no conscious awareness of emotions.[5] Others ignore emotions in order to avoid uncomfortable anxiety or because they fear that bringing in emotions will overwhelm their cognitive abilities and escalate the conflict, making it more difficult to resolve.

A negotiation that excludes direct expression or consideration of emotions often enables people to settle disputes, but it also can precipitate several problems. For instance, parties frequently will not reach the best resolution because they fail to look beneath asserted positions for their underlying interests, beliefs, or perspectives.[6] As Daniel Shapiro explains, "Emotions are a means to communicate relational identity concerns."[7] Thus, to the extent that negotiators bar emotions from a negotiation process, they—or their principals—are less likely to achieve an emotional resolution because they neither understand nor address the needs associated with such emotions.[8]

In addition, despite attempts to keep them out, emotions tend to penetrate and influence negotiations. As we have seen, if these emotions are strong and negative, they can prompt adversarial perspectives and behavior, making it less likely that even the substantive interests will get attention. Unacknowledged emotions also can impair the parties' ability to think clearly, can render the parties vulnerable to exploitation, and can harm relationships.[9] These emotions can also foster passive-aggressive behavior. Thus, negative emotions can undermine the ability to skillfully conduct adversarial negotiations or to manage the negotiator's dilemma.

Emotions as Opportunities

In 2005, Roger Fisher and Daniel Shapiro published *Beyond Reason: Using Emotions as You Negotiate*.[10] Throughout the negotiation process, they assert, so many emotions are at work that negotiators cannot identify, understand, or address them directly.[11] So the book proposes a method to manage emotions indirectly, through attention to five core concerns that stem from "human wants of personal significance, usually arising within a relationship": appreciation, affiliation, autonomy, status, and role.[12] We all want to feel appreciated—at least by someone—and affiliated with someone or something. Yet we also seek autonomy—the independence to make and implement decisions. And we yearn for a meaningful role and recognition of our status. Of course, we all have these concerns in different degrees, and they vary with circumstances; culture can make a difference.

Left unsatisfied (or insufficiently satisfied), these core concerns tend to foster negative emotions, which can lead to perspectives and behaviors that do not take account of important interests. But if the relevant core concerns are satisfied, positive emotions typically result, and these should foster better, more interest-inclusive decision-making or negotiation, which can lead to a better outcome. (The core-concerns construct is equally useful in promoting skillful use of position-based or adversarial elements of negotiation.)

The core-concerns approach could have helped Billy and Pedro deal more effectively with their relationship problems, in both the negotiation and the outcome. Let's say that, before his negotiation with Billy, Pedro had read *Beyond Reason* and had taken a negotiation-training program based on it. (This would mean that he also has learned the fundamentals of interest-based negotiation.)

The Core Concerns Negotiation Model from *Beyond Reason*

To *understand* the situation, *Beyond Reason* recommends, in short, that you observe your counterpart's negative emotions and try to trace them to the unsatisfied core concerns that might have produced them, and that you do the same with your own emotions. To *respond to* the situation, *Beyond Reason* proposes that you address your counterpart's unsatisfied core concerns, and your own, and thereby build positive emotions, and then negotiate using interests.

Here is my own version of the strategies and tactics of this model:

Strategies and Tactics for Understanding the Conflict or Situation

- Observe both parties' behaviors and emotions.
- Identify any of these behaviors or emotions that might negatively impact the negotiation.
- Consider which of the other person's core concerns might have prompted such behaviors or emotions.
- Consider which of your core concerns might have prompted such behaviors or emotions.

Strategies and Tactics for Responding to the Conflict or Situation

- Stimulate positive emotions in the other person
- Stimulate positive emotions in yourself.
- Negotiate, with the benefit of positive emotions, emphasizing core concerns and interests.

How Pedro Could Use Such Strategies and Tactics

To Understand the Conflict or Situation

Pedro might use the core-concerns model to understand and respond to the situation. Before or during the negotiation, Pedro could review events in his relationship with Billy to seek core concerns that might have triggered Billy's emotions and behaviors. In so doing, Pedro might realize, for instance, that Billy believes that Pedro does not *appreciate* Billy's many contributions to BPS; that Billy worries about his *affiliation* with Pedro, with PBS, and with his customers; that Billy yearns for *autonomy* in decision making about PBS and his relationship to it; that Billy worries about his *status* in relation to Pedro,

Paulina, and BPS; and that Billy feels that his *role* in BPS is not fulfilling or appropriate.

With such awareness, Pedro could see which of Billy's unsatisfied core concerns contributed most to the development of the conflict and might remain important to Billy during the negotiation and its aftermath. Before Pedro began to use the core-concerns model, for instance, he had thought Billy was holding back the business: Billy stayed on the road too long, drank too much, grasped for power, and opposed hiring Pauline and modernizing the business. Pedro also had believed that these behaviors manifested Billy's character flaws—laziness, selfishness, rigidity, and small-mindedness.

But with his new insights, Pedro could realize that these behaviors might have grown out of Billy's unsatisfied core concerns, rather than his character. Thus, Pedro could conclude that Billy's unsatisfied concern for *appreciation* might have produced some of his surliness; that his hunger for *affiliation* could have propelled him into social and drinking relationships with his customers; that his need for *autonomy* could have kept him on the road; or that his concerns for *status* and for a meaningful *role* might have provoked anger and disappointment that fostered a range of other behaviors that bothered Pedro.

Insights such as these might diminish Pedro's negative emotions toward Billy. As Longfellow put it, "If we could read the secret history of our enemies, we should find in each man's life sorrow and suffering enough to disarm all hostility."[13] Pedro might even develop empathy, compassion, or other positive emotions toward Billy.

Pedro's review of his and Billy's interactions could also lead him to recognize some of his own beliefs and behaviors and see how they might have arisen from his core concerns, which might have precipitated or enhanced his own anger, disdain, and resentment toward Billy. Perhaps Pedro would see that he believes Billy does not *appreciate* him and his contributions to BPS; that he wants (or does not want) a stronger *affiliation* with Billy or other people in the industry; or that the current situation threatens his own concerns for *autonomy*, *status*, or *role* in managing the firm.

To Respond to the Conflict or Situation

Pedro could also use a core-concerns focus to improve the negotiation process or outcome. The new insights described above could enable him to build positive emotions in Billy and in himself by addressing their unsatisfied core concerns.[14] The resulting positive emotions could foster better negotiation processes and outcomes, as discussed in Chapter 2.

Fisher and Shapiro present overarching recommendations for developing positive emotions in your negotiation counterpart:

- Express appreciation.
- Build affiliation.
- Foster autonomy.
- Recognize status.
- Develop meaningful roles.[15]

If Pedro chooses to follow some of these recommendations, he could express *appreciation* for Billy's commitment to BPS, his strong relationships with customers, and his willingness to travel. Maybe Pedro would try to rebuild *affiliation* with Billy by recounting their long history of work and friendship; by communicating in person; or by talking about the real issues in their relationship.[16] Pedro could respect Billy's *autonomy* in the negotiation by consulting him before making any decisions about negotiation procedure. He also could propose brainstorming or ask Billy to suggest options for addressing their key issues. Pedro could acknowledge Billy's *status* as a founder of the firm, as a great shoe salesman, as a golfer, or as a *bon vivant*.[17] He could invite Billy into a *fulfilling role* as a fellow problem solver in the negotiation (i.e., a role that has "a clear purpose," is "personally meaningful," and "is not a pretense")[18] with lots of opportunities to speak freely and to influence the focus, procedure, and outcome. And, finally, Pedro could listen carefully to whatever Billy says, which itself might help satisfy any of Billy's concerns.

Using the insights about his own core concerns, Pedro might try to help Billy *appreciate him* by, say, asking Billy to paraphrase Pedro's explanations on his own states of mind.[19] Anything Pedro did to *build affiliation* could also stimulate positive emotions in himself. And Pedro could expand his own *autonomy* by making recommendations and by brainstorming.[20] Finally, Pedro might take time to privately enjoy his own *status* as the manager of a substantial business[21] and make sure that he, too, has an appropriate, fulfilling *role* in the negotiation.[22]

I do not mean to imply that Pedro should use any or all of these strategies and tactics without considering whether they are suitable, given the length and complexity of his relationship with Billy.[23]

The five core concerns overlap, as you probably have inferred; appreciation is the most important and frequently makes up a portion of the other concerns. Anything that helps satisfy one core concern is likely to have a similar impact on others.

In this case, the core concerns that are significant in the negotiation process derive from and resemble the core concerns that gave rise to the situation. Billy's core concern for a meaningful role in managing the business, for instance, might foster his concern for a meaningful role in the negotiation.

Note that core concerns sometimes are also interests, that is, motives for taking particular positions. So Pedro and Billy might use strategies and tactics of the interest-based negotiation model (discussed in the previous chapter). Thus, when generating or assessing options, they could consider the potential impact on important core concerns. They might, for instance, try to satisfy Billy's affiliation core concern through various arrangements that could enable him to maintain contact with customers, with Pedro, or with BPS employees.

* * *

Box A-5 summarizes what I have said about Pedro and Billy's positions, interests, and core concerns that are associated with whether Billy will stay or leave.

Box A-5. Shoe-Dog Split: Will Billy Leave BPS or Stay? Billy and Pedro's Likely Positions, Interests, and Core Concerns

Issue	Billy's positions	Billy's interests	Billy's core concerns	Pedro's position	Pedro's interests	Pedro's core concerns
Does Billy leave or stay?	Billy stays.	Billy's dignity & sense of self-worth.	Appreciation Affiliation Autonomy Status	Billy leaves.	Pedro's dignity & sense of self-worth.	Appreciation Affiliation Autonomy Status
		Success of BPS.	Role		Success of BPS.	Role
		Health care/health insurance.			Avoiding tense interpersonal situation.	
		Income.			Keeping customers.	

Issue	Billy's positions	Billy's interests	Billy's core concerns	Pedro's position	Pedro's interests	Pedro's core concerns
If Billy stays:						
What would be his role in management?	Billy gets equal role in management with Pedro.	Billy's dignity & sense of self-worth. Success of BPS.	Appreciation Affiliation Autonomy Status Role	Billy gets no role in management.	As above	Appreciation Affiliation Autonomy Status Role
What would be his role in marketing and sales?		Billy keeps responsibility for marketing and sales.	Appreciation Affiliation Autonomy Status Role	Billy gets no role in marketing and sales.	As above	
If Billy leaves:						
What would be his compensation?	$2Y per share.	Billy's dignity & sense of self-worth. Success of BPS. Health care/health insurance. Income.	Affiliation Autonomy Status Role	$.5Y per share.	Success of BPS. Keeping customers.	Appreciation Affiliation Autonomy Status Role
May he continue to work in the industry?	Yes.			No.		

© 2022 Leonard L. Riskin

To get a better sense of the core concerns, bring to mind a conflict in which you are or were involved, primarily with one other person, that has or had a significant emotional component. This conflict could be the one you used in Appendix Exercise A-1.

Once you have selected a conflict, recall a particular moment, event, or time period during the conflict. Put yourself into it mentally. Notice who is present and what they are doing or saying. Observe any of your emotions, body sensations, or thoughts, as best you can.

Next try to trace them to core concerns that were significant for you and for the other person.

Then complete the form in Appendix Exercise A-2, Core Concerns in a Conflict of Your Own.

Back to the Big Picture: The Interrelationships Among the Three Negotiation Focuses and Their Models

Positions, interests, and core concerns are related in many ways, and Box A-6 gives us a good start toward grasping these connections.

Box A-6. Positions, Interests, and Core Concerns in Negotiation

Level & Focus	A Specific Model	Model's Components for Understanding Conflict	Model's Components for Addressing Conflict
Level 1 Positions	Model: Position-based (Extreme)	Focus on positions, rather than interests. Define the problem to be addressed narrowly. Assume that any gain for one party means a loss for the other.	Mislead other side as to your bottom line and situation; learn other side's bottom line and situation. *Examples:* • Use anchoring through extreme demands. • Assert positions; undermine the other's positions. • Make few and small concessions. • Persuade other side to compromise or to agree with your position. • Walk away or threaten to do so.
Level 2 Interests	Model: *Getting to Yes*	Focus on interests rather than positions. Be soft on the people but hard on the problem. Understand "the problem" broadly .	Seek to accommodate both parties' interests. • Be soft on people and hard on problem. • Generate options before deciding. • Expand the pie. • Use objective standards. • Develop your BATNA and measure proposed agreements against it.

Level & Focus	A Specific Model	Model's Components for Understanding Conflict	Model's Components for Addressing Conflict
Level 3 Core Concerns	Model: *Beyond Reason*	Observe both parties' behaviors and emotions. Trace your emotions to the core concerns—appreciation, affiliation, autonomy, status, and role—that may have produced those emotions. Trace your counterpart's emotions to the core concerns—appreciation, affiliation, autonomy, status, and role—that may have produced those emotions.	Address unsatisfied core concerns in order to stimulate positive emotions in the other party; for example: • Express appreciation, • Build affiliation, • Foster autonomy, • Acknowledge status, and • Create fulfilling roles. Address your own unsatisfied core concerns. For instance: • Help your counterpart understand them. • Reframe them. • Negotiate, with the benefit of positive emotions, using core concerns and interests.

© 2022 Leonard L. Riskin

Notice that, once again, the focuses and their models appear in levels of accessibility, though the metaphor of depth is not perfect in this context. I put positions on Level 1 because, in a negotiation, positions usually are explicit or at least easy to discern. Interests appear on Level 2 because it's generally more difficult to identify them. The core concerns rest, a bit uncomfortably, on Level 3. Sometimes they serve as interests, in the sense that they are the reason a person asserts (or might assert) a particular position. And an unsatisfied core concern can produce strong emotions that impede someone's ability to assert a position that could satisfy that core concern.

Why should you care about the interrelationships among these three focuses and their models? *Getting to Yes* presents its model of interest-based negotiation as a great improvement over, and replacement for, positional negotiation. *Beyond Reason*'s authors consider their book an advanced version of *Getting to Yes* that can help people use the *Getting to Yes* model, and it surely can do that. But it can just as readily help people use positional strategies and tactics.

Given that you will sometimes benefit from using elements of both position- and interest-focused models, knowledge of the core concerns offers special benefits. It can help you consider whether your negotiation plan is internally consistent, that is, whether your positions, interests, and core concerns are aligned; and if they are not, whether and how to do something about it. For instance, Billy's position that he is legally entitled to participate in important decisions about the business might not serve his interest in relaxing more (though it might serve his core concerns for appreciation or affiliation). If Billy becomes aware of this misalignment, he may want to change, reconsider, or abandon that position; this could happen, for example, if he realizes that he cares more about having additional free time than about affiliation. (Pedro could help Billy recognize this non-alignment.)

In other situations, if you become aware that your concern for appreciation manifests as a need to win or to defeat your negotiation counterpart, and you realize that this need is running roughshod over others, you could decide whether to allow that situation to continue. If not, you could deliberately let go of the appreciation concern or the need to win—or consider other ways to satisfy them.

* * *

Understanding the core-concerns system is not difficult, and I hope that you now have a sense of how to work with it, in combination with positions and interests. But actually using the core concerns is not always easy, as the next chapter shows.

FIVE OBSTACLES TO SKILLFULLY USING THE CORE CONCERNS (AND POSITIONS AND INTERESTS)

The previous chapter gave you a sense of the multiple connections between positions, interests, and core concerns. And I hope it is clear that a negotiator can frequently benefit from using elements of more than one focus and model. If the core-concerns construct can enable us to manage strong negative emotions, it should help us, not only in formal negotiations, but also in daily interactions with other people (and with some of our pets, such as our late family border collie, Barney). The method is clear and easily grasped from reading *Beyond Reason*. In courses and training programs that include *Beyond Reason*—through lectures, demonstrations, and role-play exercises—participants quickly learn to identify unsatisfied core concerns in themselves and others and to develop ways to address them.

And yet, it's not so easy. I have observed—in myself, students, former students, and colleagues—certain common obstacles to skillfully using the core concerns, alone or combined with positions or interests. Even negotiators who are familiar with these focuses and models, and who intend to use them, sometimes fail to do so, or fail to do so skillfully. Looking back, they regret this failure; they believe that using the core concerns—or using them more skillfully—would have produced a better process and outcome.

If something like this happens to Pedro after he has taken the core-concerns negotiation training, what could have caused it?

Of course, countless ingredients might be at play, but five related factors are most obvious:

Automatic, habitual ways of thinking, feeling, or behaving;

Excessively self-centered perspectives;

Inadequate management of emotions;

Insufficient social skills;

Inadequate management of awareness and focus.

Here is some detail about the five obstacles and how they might play out in the Billy-Pedro situation.

Automatic or Habitual Ways of Thinking, Feeling, or Behaving

Automatic or habitual ways of thinking, feeling, or behaving can save us a great deal of time and energy. But sometimes, they cause problems.

Psychologist Daniel Kahneman elucidates two kinds of thinking that people use in making decisions under conditions of uncertainty. He calls them fast and slow.[1] Fast thinking is automatic and intuitive. It "includes both variants of intuitive thought—the expert (when you know something so well, you do not need to think) and the heuristic (using short-cut rubrics or rules of thumb)—as well as entirely automatic mental activities of perception and memory, the operations that allow you to know there is a lamp on your desk or retrieve the name of the capital of Russia."[2] Slow thinking is deliberate, so it takes much more effort. It's the "control that keeps you polite when you are angry and alert when you are driving at night. It is mobilized to increased effort when it detects an error about to be made."[3]

Although slow thinking has ultimate control over decision-making, at least in theory, it usually defers to the recommendations or proposals from fast thinking—out of "laziness, a reluctance to invest more effort than is strictly necessary."[4] Thus, fast thinking essentially makes most of our decisions, the bulk of which are adequate or better.

But fast thinking frequently interferes with wise negotiation. For instance, many negotiators routinely use a particular negotiation focus and model out of habit. The best example is the position-focused approach, which is very commonly—maybe pervasively—employed by many who negotiate for a living.

Other negotiators more deliberately employ elements of the *Getting to Yes* model of interest-based negotiation. This model engenders a good deal of passion, and some of its strategies—such as considering options and trying to satisfy interests of all concerned—have so infused the wider culture that they routinely appear in television programs and in movies. Many negotiators, especially students, embrace this focus and model, sometimes with too much fervor and too little discernment or skill. In some law school negotiation competitions, for instance, students try to outdo one another in collaboration, occasionally to the detriment of their hypothetical client and to the scores they receive from the competition judges.

Even if Pedro had studied interests and core concerns, his ability to use them might be impaired by "top-down,"[5] automatic (fast) ways of thinking, feeling, and behaving that might not consider interests and core concerns. Some of these are cognitive biases.

Sometimes we are aware of such biases, or could become aware of them through brief introspection: these biases are called "conscious" or "explicit." When my wife and I started dating, for instance, she told me that she had never tasted french fries; I was just as surprised to hear this as you are to read it. Her reason? As she explained while we sat in a McDonald's in Washington, D.C., she expected to dislike french fries because she assumed they would taste like her mother's mashed potatoes. I persuaded her to sample one, and she loved it, of course. (I *still* cannot get her to try watermelon.)

But we lack awareness of some of our own biases. Psychologists call these "unconscious" or "implicit" biases.[6] Studies suggest, for instance, that many people act upon biases based on group membership,[7] race,[8] or age.[9] Some errors caused by bias involve incorrect attributions of intention. The "fundamental attribution error"—the tendency to attribute another person's behavior to their character rather than to circumstances[10]—is a common example. Thus, as I suggested above, Pedro might assume that Billy's excessive socializing springs from a weak character, rather than from circumstances (perhaps including his unsatisfied core concerns). Similarly, the phenomenon known as "reactive devaluation"—devaluing a proposal that comes from a source that seems untrustworthy[11]—might lead Pedro to underappreciate an offer from Billy, just because it comes from Billy, and vice versa. Each probably would suffer, too, from "optimistic overconfidence" and think their "case" or argument or position is very strong. And either or both might be influenced by the "anchoring bias" and pay too much attention to the first offer or demand.[12]

Often these biases and habits develop through life experience, which can include studying, practicing, and observing negotiation strategies and tactics. Imagine, for instance, that Pedro wants to focus heavily on core concerns and interests in his negotiation with Billy, but most of his extensive negotiation experience has emphasized positions almost exclusively. As a result, his automatic thoughts, perspectives, and behaviors could override his ability to use interests and core concerns.

On the other hand, Pedro could become overly attached (as have many of my students) to the core-concerns model and see it as a set of rules that he must or should follow. In that event, he might try to use strategies and tactics of that model in circumstances in which they are unlikely to help or might even backfire. For example, *Beyond Reason* suggests straightforward methods to satisfy your counterpart's core concerns—express appreciation, foster autonomy, and the like—in order to create positive emotions. But Pedro and Billy's negative thoughts and emotions toward each other have developed through many encounters over years and are deeply engrained.

In short, rigid attachment—conscious or subconscious—to a particular focus or model can interfere with skillful negotiation. The creators of the models based on interests and core concerns made certain assumptions about the circumstances of the actual conflicts in which the models would be used. They also expected the end users to exercise common sense, and those expectations are not always met; less experienced negotiators might deploy strategies or tactics of these models in circumstances in which they would not be suitable.

Excessively Self-Centered Perspectives

The humorist Ambrose Bierce defines an egotist as "a person of low taste, more interested in himself than in me."[13] A strong orientation toward oneself is deeply ingrained in many Western societies—and may be a basic aspect of human nature. But if the orientation is too strong, it impairs our ability to care about others. The preoccupation with self-centered concerns both supports and draws reinforcement from strong emotions. Pedro's strong negative emotions, for instance, could undermine his ability to feel genuinely curious, to listen to him, or to care about him.

More broadly, Pedro could focus so strongly on himself that he could simply forget about core concerns and interests, and his intention to use them.[14]

Inadequate Management of Emotions

The core-concerns model is vulnerable to the very emotions that it was created to manage. Thus, before or during the negotiation, strong negative emotions—frequently the result of fast thinking or other automatic processes—might simply overpower Pedro's capacity or will to use the core concerns. If Billy arrives 45 minutes late for their negotiation and announces that he has to leave in 15 minutes for a haircut appointment, Pedro may feel hurt and angry. And unless Pedro is aware of these negative emotions, he will not be able to manage them.

Even if Pedro is not awash in negative emotions, he might wish—consciously or subconsciously—to avoid awareness of Billy's feelings. Pedro might fear that such knowledge would produce painful emotions in him that could overwhelm his ability to think clearly, or might change his behavior or his perception of himself. If Pedro were to recognize Billy's sadness and connect it with Billy's unsatisfied core concerns, for example, he might struggle with his own self-image as a good person.

We all encounter similar dilemmas in a variety of circumstances. While you are enjoying a Thanksgiving dinner, for instance, what might happen if you began to "see it from the turkey's point of view"?[15]

Insufficient Social Skills

Another possibility: Pedro might figure out which core concerns motivate certain of Billy's behaviors, decide what he needs to do in order to foster them, and then bungle the execution. Pedro might, for instance, determine that he needs to "express appreciation" or "acknowledge status." Yet his interpersonal skills might be inadequate to the task. Even if he figures out what to say, he might not know when or how to say it so that Billy would think it is appropriate and genuine.

A friend told me about her blind date for lunch with a man who had been highly recommended. She was stunned, offended, and angry, when, with the best of intentions, he asked her to marry him—before dessert.

Inadequate Management of Focus or Awareness

Pedro might be too distracted and unfocused to appropriately use the core concerns or make other decisions wisely. Distractions could come from emotions, thoughts, or body sensations, which, as we shall see in Section B, incessantly intrude into most of our mental lives. So even if Pedro remembers to use the core concerns to understand the situation and to plan for the negotiation, he might mindlessly abandon—or simply forget—this plan while preparing, negotiating, or reflecting back on it. Equally important, Pedro might be unable to quickly shift focus (from, say, the core concerns to positions), which may require improvising in response to changed circumstances.

I have described the five obstacles individually, in the interests of clarity. In reality, however, they sometimes overlap and can prompt, reinforce, and support one another. Self-centered perspectives are, or are entangled with, cognitive biases. In addition, the potential for negative cycles results from interactions between inadequate management of emotions, insufficient social skill, and inadequate management of focus and awareness.

* * *

To get a better sense of these obstacles, recall a conflict of your own, and put yourself, mentally, into that particular event or time period. Consider whether any of these obstacles were present in you and whether or how they might have affected your understanding or behavior. Then complete the form in Appendix Exercise A-3. Five Obstacles in a Conflict of Your Own.

* * *

REVIEW OF SECTION A

This section presents three negotiation focuses—positions, interests, and core concerns. Each focus is general and is accompanied by one model, which provides more specific strategies and tactics for understanding and for responding to a conflict or problematic situation. For the positional focus, I set forth an extreme model that draws upon common experience and stereotypical explanations. The interest-based model is based on "Principled Negotiation," presented in *Getting to Yes*, by Fisher, Ury, and Patton. Although they call their model "Principled Negotiation," it is best known for its central orientation toward interests. And for the core-concerns focus, I used the model from *Beyond Reason* by Fisher and Shapiro, which first presented the idea. In order to fit these models into the structure of this book, I rearranged them a bit.

Even negotiators who are well versed and experienced in these focuses and models sometimes fail to negotiate wisely. This frequently results from one or more of five obstacles: automatic, habitual ways of thinking, feeling, or behaving; excessively self-centered perspectives; inadequate management of emotions; insufficient social skills; or inadequate management of awareness and focus.

A word of caution:

Be careful about how you use the terminology about conflict management and negotiation that appears in Section A. Some of it is not widely known or widely used. And many people use the same ideas without the terminology. The term *interests* is a good example. As Condoleezza Rice, former U.S. secretary of state, wrote of her predecessor, George P. Shultz: 'Diplomats knew him as a good listener and a practical man. His favorite tactic was to say to his counterpart, 'You write down what worries you and I will do the same, and then we will work our way down the list.' "[1]

REVIEW OF SECTION A IN LIGHT VERSE

A. NEGOTIATION

A mountain serves as metaphor,
Which helps convey a little more.
This mountain has levels without and within,
And at the top we will begin.

Positions

Near the peak's where we seek our positions,
Which we find there in any conditions.
As for mine, I am quick to proclaim them.
And for yours, I will claim to disdain them.

Sometimes, when our outlook's positional,
Our counterpart seems oppositional.
Discussions, therefore, might get stuck
And then, of course, we're out of luck,

Interests

Unless we look beneath positions,
There to find our deeper missions.
Practicing prospecting underground
Can yield discoveries quite profound.

As the pathway for getting to yes,
Roger Fisher *et al.* clearly stress
Attending to interests, more than positions,
So to foster ripe conditions

In which you can generate options
And evaluate them for adoptions,
Which could lead to agreement success—
Pareto-ly optimal, which they say is the best.

And although "You can't
Always get what you want,"
Should wisdom succeed in exceeding greed,
Perhaps you will want no more than you need.

Core Concerns

Sources of interests and positions
May include our dispositions.

When core concerns are unfulfilled
Our spirits get distinctly chilled.

You see, we need appreciation,
Recognition of our station,
Freedom, belonging, a meaningful role—
These will soothe a tender soul.

And so, each person's heart does burn
To satisfy a core concern.
Else they may feel emotions negative,
And may require a calming sedative.

So if you're soaked with negativity—
Though that's not your main proclivity—
It could come from some core concern,
Or several, for which you yearn.

Unmet concerns, if they're galore,
Can leave you looking like a boor.
You may appear, well, too competitive,
And use language too loud and too repetitive.

Besides, your judgment goes kerplunk,
So others wonder what you thunk,
And you can't get your interests met.
You may not try, but just forget.

MINDFULNESS, THE SECOND DOMAIN

Section A, on negotiation, introduced three general negotiation focuses, along with one specific model for using each. But it ended on a pessimistic note, highlighting potential impediments to using these focuses and models wisely.

Now, Section B comes to the rescue. Its central missions are to present mindfulness and to show how, among other benefits, it can help you improve your negotiation performance and satisfaction by overcoming the five obstacles presented in Chapter 4 or by reducing their influence.

MINDFULNESS: THE SECOND DOMAIN

CHAPTER 5

MINDFULNESS: ITS NATURE AND POTENTIAL BENEFITS

In this book, "mindfulness" has a distinct meaning, the gist of which is paying attention to your present-moment experience, deliberately and without judgment.[1] (If you don't understand that sentence, you are in good company—and you will understand it soon.)

People cultivate mindfulness, most commonly, in silent meditation, and deploy it in everyday life. Mindfulness meditation originated some 2,500 years ago in what is now India and spread widely, with variations, across Asia.

In recent decades its popularity has swelled in nearly every sector of society in the U.S. and other Western countries. I begin with professional basketball, in a shameless effort to impress a certain segment of potential readers. When Phil Jackson coached the Chicago Bulls and Los Angeles Lakers teams, he hired a professional mindfulness-meditation instructor to lead the players in meditation before each game.[2] Later, as president of the New York Knicks, Jackson led these meditations himself.

Other examples include corporations (such as Google,[3] Monsanto, and Reebok); government agencies (such as the U.S. Marines and other branches of the military[4]); legislative bodies (such as the U.S. Congress[5]); law firms, legal offices in organizations, and courts;[6] non-profit, religious, and health-care provider organizations; educational institutions, at all levels;[7] psychotherapy;[8] and leadership[9] programs. Mindfulness meditation also has made inroads into legal and dispute resolution education, appearing in law school offerings that carry academic credit as well as in extracurricular courses; continuing education workshops for lawyers, judges, mediators, and negotiators;[10] and wellness and lawyer-assistance programs.

What accounts for all of that?

In short, mindfulness or mindfulness meditation offers many potential benefits. To explain that, I draw upon two related sources: Buddhist philosophy, psychology, and practice; and recent research and developments.

Buddhist Philosophy, Psychology, and Practices

Mindfulness rests on philosophical, psychological, ethical, and practice elements that developed—directly or indirectly—from teachings of the

Buddha. To practice mindfulness, you need not believe in or even be aware of this Buddhist foundation, but understanding that background should enable you to benefit more from mindfulness practice and from this book.

The Buddha understood the practice of meditation as part of a path to relieve suffering and foster happiness.[11] In this view, life involves a great deal of suffering; the cause of suffering is craving and aversion; the way to eliminate suffering is to eliminate craving and aversion or to detach from them by adopting a series of attitudes and practices involving morality and meditation.[12]

The Buddha's method was to lead a person to overcome the causes of suffering—craving and aversion—which incline us to want things to be different than they are. He believed that we can reduce our suffering by recognizing and accepting "reality": that everything is impersonal; everything is changing; and our perceptions arise from our own often-subconscious interpretations of events and our emotional and other reactions. Recognizing and accepting these concepts can produce "healthy" mindstates—such as compassion and kindness—which reduce suffering. In contrast, "unhealthy" mindstates—such as anger and hatred—often increase suffering.[13]

Craving and aversion (or wanting things to be other than they are) spring from the assumption that we can be happy (or satisfied) if we get what we want and avoid what we do not want. "I would be happy," we may think, "if I got that job at Goldman Sachs (or the local dog-rescue program, or Starbucks); if I had a relationship with so-and-so; if I lived in *that* house; or if I had a below-par golf score or a new refrigerator that produces ice cubes made of filtered water." We want pleasure—including pleasant sights, sounds, sensations, thoughts, events, relationships, and possessions. And we want to avoid unpleasant experiences—such as feeling hunger, eating broccoli, spending time with people who support X, Y, or Z, or listening to elevator music.

But this approach does not work, except perhaps in the very short term. No matter how hard we try, everything changes; unpleasant experience is inevitable. We all age, get sick, lose what we love. As Oscar Wilde said, "In this world there are only two tragedies: one is not getting what one wants and the second is getting it."[14]

Take my late Uncle Euch (short for Eugene, rhymes with Butch), for instance. He and Aunt Minnie owned Hauser's Department Store in Kansas City; despite its name, the store was small and sold only clothing. For years, he yearned for a Cadillac, partly for comfort, partly for prestige. Finally, he bought one, a shiny new 1967 Fleetwood—with more tasteful, less gigantic

fins than earlier models—and parked it in front of his store. He felt great—
happy and proud—mainly because, for a few hours, he did not want anything.
Then, while tailoring a suit, he heard a loud crash and rushed outside, to
discover that a rusty 1955 Plymouth had plowed into his Cadillac. He felt
awful—angry, disappointed, and dismayed—and began to blame himself for
parking on the street and to wonder, "Why did this happen to me?" Even if
the accident had not occurred, however, as time went by, Uncle Euch's
craving for a new fancy car might have returned: when his Cadillac broke
down or developed a squeak, or when his business rival across the street got
a newer or better model Cadillac—or even a Lincoln with a Continental tire
kit built into the trunk lid. That, too, is suffering.

The Buddha taught mindfulness meditation as part of the "Noble
Eightfold Path" to ending suffering, or at least reducing it—a path with
strong ethical components.[15] But an individual practitioner's actual goals can
range from achieving spiritual enlightenment to just lightening up; they also
might include dealing better with stress, increasing happiness, lowering blood
pressure, or improving performance at work or in school or on the dance
floor or the stage. In mindfulness practice, as in other areas of life, however,
what we want and what we get may differ. Someone could enter mindfulness
training in order to find enlightenment, but only improve their tennis game,
or vice versa.

Buddhism has many aspects and many uses. "Depending on which part
of Buddhism you grasp," Stephen Batchelor tells us, "you might identify it as
a system of ethics, a philosophy, a contemplative psychotherapy, a religion."[16]
For many people Buddhism is a religion, but others focus primarily or
exclusively on Buddhist philosophy or psychology or on mindfulness
practice. Today, people who practice any number of religions (including
Christianity[17] and Judaism[18])—or none at all—also practice mindfulness
meditation.[19] And many people in the U.S. learn or teach mindfulness
meditation with little or no awareness that it derives from Buddhist practices
and little or no knowledge of Buddhist thought. In this book, when I mention
Buddhism, I am generally referring to Buddhist psychology or philosophy.[20]

Mindfulness, as most commonly introduced in the West, *emphasizes*
nonjudgmental awareness, in contrast to—or at least ahead of—thinking or
evaluating. Modern commentators who highlight the awareness aspect of
mindfulness have conceptualized it in a variety of ways. Jon Kabat-Zinn, the
creator of mindfulness-based stress reduction (MBSR), for instance, tells us
that mindfulness "can be generally thought of as an openhearted, moment-
to-moment, non-judgmental awareness."[21]

Recent Research and Developments

Describing recent empirical research on mindfulness, ironically, is nerve-racking for me, especially because I have spent decades in academics, where we learn to rely intensely on primary sources. Thousands of published research studies address the impacts of mindfulness-based interventions. But many have limited reliability or applicability—sometimes because they have not been replicated or they contain flaws in design (which often result from limited funding). Some studies, for instance, lack sufficient numbers of subjects or controls; nearly every study contains a distinctive hypothesis and unique variables, some of which are confounding. For all these reasons, when I have described potential benefits of mindfulness, I usually have said something like this: Research has demonstrated *or suggested* a wide range of benefits from mindfulness-based interventions, including enhanced emotional intelligence (self-awareness, self-regulation, motivation, empathy, and social skills);[22] improved attention acuity;[23] increased activity in the brain regions associated with happiness;[24] improved immune response, resilience, and compassion;[25] enhanced ability to deal with some illnesses, e.g., fibromyalgia;[26] enhanced ability to deal with stress;[27] improved cognition (and Graduate Record Examination performance[28]); reduced mind-wandering;[29] increased density of gray matter (brain cells), which is associated with improved performance of many activities;[30] and reduced adverse effects of childhood stress and trauma.[31] It also has helped people quit smoking.[32]

When I say that studies have "concluded or suggested" that mindfulness can offer various benefits under specific conditions, I hope to avoid misleading readers. Still, the foregoing presentation partly explains why mindfulness has achieved such popularity in the West.[33]

Few studies have carefully considered one of the most important issues in contemplative science: the difference between mindfulness as a temporary state of mind and mindfulness as a longer-term trait.

Fortunately, two experts have done a good bit of that work, quite recently.[34]

Daniel Goleman and Richard Davidson examined the published studies on the impact of mindfulness meditation (and other forms of meditation, which I will not discuss here) on the brain. They wanted to determine what we know and don't know about which meditation practices can change mindstates and which can help transform temporary mindstates into longer term traits. The difference is significant. To the extent that your mindfulness is a state, it easily vanishes: Your previous mindstates reappear. But if mindfulness becomes a trait, you are usually mindful or "dispositionally" mindful. That's a big deal, as the benefits of mindfulness, to you and to others you affect, keep coming—as some would say, regardless of circumstances.

So, in order to determine what we know and do not know about how different forms of meditation impact the brain, Goleman and Davidson considered only the best studies—those that met medical standards for scientific research. In analyzing the literature, they separated the meditation subjects into three categories: beginners (who had less than 100 hours of practice), longtime practitioners (who averaged about 9,000 hours of meditation practice), and yogis (experts, "Olympians of meditation," who averaged 27,000 hours of practice).[35]

The impact of a particular meditation practice, they found, depended significantly on the level of the subjects' previous meditation experience and skill. They determined that reliable studies show that mindfulness practice has different impacts on beginners, long-term practitioners, and yogis.

Goleman and Davidson summarize their findings about beginners as follows:

> From the beginning hours, days, and weeks of meditation, several benefits emerge. For one, beginners' brains show less amygdala reactivity to stress. Improvements in attention after just two weeks of practice include better focus, less mind-wandering, and improved working memory—with a concrete payoff in boosted scores on a graduate school entrance exam. Some of the earliest benefits are with compassion meditation, including increased connectivity in the circuitry for empathy. And markers for inflammation lessen a bit with just thirty hours of practice. While these benefits emerge even with remarkably modest hours of practice, they are likely fragile and need daily sessions to be sustained.[36]

Results for long-term practitioners were stronger and were consistent with the development of altered traits.[37] And yogis experienced "clear signs of altered traits."[38]

Mindfulness can, not surprisingly, help people get rid of bad habits. Studies conducted by Judson Brewer and his colleagues showed that mindfulness-based interventions can help people quit smoking.[39] The studies compared a specific mindfulness-based intervention with conventional treatment (the Freedom From Smoking program presented by the American Lung Association) and with no treatment. Brewer reported that "participants in the mindfulness group . . . quit *at nearly twice the rate*" of those in the conventional treatment group.[40]

Many common claims about the benefits of mindfulness practices derive from sources other than scientific, empirical studies. These include a wealth of writings—some ancient—about the purposes and benefits of meditative practices as well as beliefs based on experiences of meditation teachers, students, and practitioners.

I hope this chapter has whetted your appetite for meditation practice experience. The next chapter offers tasting opportunities.

CHAPTER 6

FORMAL MINDFULNESS AND LOVING-KINDNESS MEDITATION

Mindfulness and mindfulness meditation do not always carry the same meaning. When we are mindful, we are observing our present-moment experience without judgment or preference. We are "present." We practice mindfulness meditation to cultivate mindfulness. We learn to cultivate mindfulness, in part so that we can enjoy its benefits both during formal meditation and in daily life. If you find this confusing, it may be because mindfulness is both the path and the destination.[1]

This chapter presents formal meditation practices for cultivating mindfulness and the related state of mind known as loving-kindness. "Formal meditation" usually means setting aside time to deliberately meditate in a certain way; so formal meditation is analogous to a planned dinner. Semiformal and informal mindfulness practices (which are covered in Chapter 8) typically involve less planning and less time; they are analogous, respectively, to an impromptu lunch or snack.

You may work with the meditation instructions in a variety of ways, depending upon your background, interests, and needs. When I began to learn mindfulness meditation, in about 1985, the teachers with whom I was familiar seemed to consider formal meditation primary and the less formal practices secondary. In recent years, however, some studies have shown or suggested that brief, less formal methods used repeatedly throughout the day can be more beneficial, at least for changing habits.[2] Of course the various forms of practice support one another.

The following formal meditation instructions draw on my own practice, study, and training and on my experience in teaching mindfulness. In all of these activities, I have focused most heavily on two closely related traditions. The first includes ancient practices that are known as mindfulness, insight, or *vipassana* meditation. The second is mindfulness-based stress-reduction (MBSR), a modern development that includes many of the same or similar practices and ideas.[3] MBSR was designed to serve medical patients who were dealing with intractable physical or emotional pain that their physicians could not alleviate. It now serves a much wider community.

Formal mindfulness practices typically are divided into two categories: directed awareness and open awareness. In directed awareness, we focus on particular "objects," such as the breath or the body. In open awareness, we have no preference about what we observe; instead, we seek to "be present" with whatever comes into our consciousness. As you will see, meditators frequently combine these two forms of awareness.

As you work through this chapter, and in your subsequent meditation practice, you may find it easier and more convenient to use the recorded instructions for these meditations at https://tinyurl.com/ManagingConflict Mindfully.

Before you take the plunge, I want to remind you to take care of yourself, in the same way that you ought to take care of yourself when training for other activities, such as baseball, break-dancing, or ballet.

If you are following or trying to follow a particular meditation instruction and feel overwhelmed or very uncomfortable doing so—perhaps because difficult thoughts, memories, emotions, or images arise—it is fine to stop meditating. It is also fine, perhaps even better, to continue meditating but to change the focus to something that seems safer. Let's try a brief preparatory meditation practice.

Box B-1. Preparatory Meditation on Sensations—Instructions

Sit on a chair with your feet on the floor and your back and neck erect and comfortable, so that you can be relaxed and alert. Put your hands on your thighs or knees or, one inside the other, on your lap. Close your eyes or cast your gaze downward, unfocused.

- Bring your attention to your hands. Do not look at them, but notice how they feel, physically. Observe any sensations, inside or outside, in the palms and the backs of your hands, in the fingers. Are they cold or warm?

- After about one minute, shift your attention to your feet. Observe any sensations, inside or outside, on the bottoms, on the tops. Are they cold or warm?

- After about one minute, shift your attention to your hearing. Just notice any sounds that come to your attention, without getting involved with them.

- After about one minute, shift your attention to sensations of breathing, wherever they are easiest for you to notice, which could be the nostrils, the chest, or the abdomen. Allow the breath to breathe itself; do not try to control it.

- After about one minute, consider:

Did any of these focuses seem more pleasant or more unpleasant than the others?
Do you prefer any of them over others?

All of the meditation instructions below include focusing on the breath, or more accurately, the sensations of breathing. If such a focus leads to feeling overwhelmed—perhaps because you are experiencing very difficult emotions, body sensations, memories, or images—just shift your attention to one of the safe places that you have identified in the preparatory meditation.

If that does not help you, it's fine to stop meditating.

Finally, avoid mixing these mindfulness meditation practices with those from other contemplative traditions—at least while you are learning mindfulness, or studying this book. Many new students of mindfulness bring backgrounds in other forms of meditation or contemplative practice, as well as from other practices, such as self-hypnosis. Sometimes, students combine this background practice with mindfulness, either deliberately or inadvertently. This is especially true of those with experience in transcendental meditation, visualizations, or any contemplative practices that include music.

In contrast to such practices, in mindfulness/insight/*vipassana*/MBSR, we do not typically try to clear the mind, manipulate the breath, visualize, or listen to music. There is nothing wrong with these other practices. But I suggest you avoid them while you are learning the methods in this book. Otherwise, you may not learn the mindfulness practices well, and you may not achieve the benefits associated with mindfulness—in managing conflict and other aspects of life.

Awareness of the Breath

For most mindfulness teachers and practitioners in the West, meditating on the breath is the first step. In essence, it involves placing our attention on certain sensations associated with breathing, and, as best we can, keeping it there.

Box B-2. Awareness of the Breath-Meditation Instructions

Sit comfortably on a chair with your back and neck erect, your feet flat on the floor, and your hands on your knees or thighs or one inside the other in your lap. Close your eyes, or if you are uncomfortable doing that, close them about two-thirds and aim your eyes, unfocused, downward.

- Take three deep breaths in this fashion:
  - Inhale through your nostrils to the count of four, so that your abdomen rises.
  - Pause for a few seconds.
  - Exhale slowly to the count of four.

Next, stop controlling your breath and allow the natural, automatic rhythm to resume. After a few minutes, bring your attention to the sensations of breathing at the place where you can most easily observe such sensations. This might be at the nostrils, as the air enters and leaves, or in the chest or abdomen, as they rise and fall with inhalations and exhalations. Focus on the sensations of one inhalation at a time, one exhalation at a time. Do not deliberately change or control the breath, simply observe it; you may notice, however, that the breath changes "on its own" while you focus on it.

- When you realize that your mind has wandered—which it will—this is a moment of mindfulness. Gently escort your attention back to the breath. If you have a lot of trouble concentrating on the breath, silently count each exhalation until you get to ten; when you reach ten, or inadvertently pass ten or lose count, begin again at one. Keep the counting in the background of your awareness, the sensations in the foreground.

- Once you feel accustomed to the basic meditation on the breath, perhaps in a subsequent session, you may want to add this more advanced practice: When you realize that the mind has wandered, instead of simply returning your awareness to the breath, notice where it is or what it is doing. Is it thinking? Is it in the past or future? Experiencing emotions or body sensations? Each time you notice such phenomena, make a gentle mental note, such as "sensing," "thinking," or "fear."

Then escort the attention back to the breath.

I suggest that you begin by following these instructions for five to ten minutes at a time. Most beginners are surprised to learn that they have difficulty focusing on the breath because their minds jump from one thing to another—a phenomenon called "monkey mind." As a result, many think, and say, that they "cannot meditate." But virtually everyone has monkey mind at times. When we do this breath meditation, we have two tasks: to concentrate on the breath, as best we can, and to learn about how our mind works—for instance, that it jumps around.

Meditation on the breath, as many have said, is simple, but not easy. I first realized this early in my meditation experience, when the teacher led a mindfulness-of-the-breath exercise and suggested counting the breaths if we were having trouble maintaining our focus. I was quite stunned to find that I had difficulty getting to ten, or even close to it. After the session, I learned that most people in the group had similar struggles. In particular, the man sitting next to me, who had advanced degrees in chemistry and had been meditating seriously for more than ten years, told me that he had never gotten past three. At that time, I was unfamiliar with Larry Rosenberg's simple instruction for meditating on the breath: When you realize that your mind has wandered away from the breath, escort it back, "and repeat. . .several billion times."[4]

Why meditate on the breath? For several reasons. First, it provides the most basic training and practice in deliberately concentrating the wandering mind. In order to concentrate, as you will see, you must be able to deal appropriately with distractions and interruptions. The mindful way to deal with distractions is to notice them and then let them be—don't get involved with them. Second, the breath is always available, so you can use this practice—or brief versions of it that appear below in Chapter 8—nearly any time.

You may encounter difficulty following the breath for another reason: human beings seek pleasant and avoid unpleasant experiences; if an experience is neutral—neither pleasant nor unpleasant—we tend to feel bored and have trouble paying attention to it. Take a look around your immediate environment, item by item—right now. Try to observe your mind making judgments about whether something—a colleague's new shoes, the painting on the wall, the wall clock that is thirty-minutes fast, or the ambient music coming from outside—seems pleasant or unpleasant or neutral, to you. For most of us, most of the time, the breath is neutral. So, when we focus on the breath, the mind automatically seeks something more pleasant, which could mean more interesting, which could include thoughts.

Meditation on the breath helps us develop the capacity to concentrate, even on something that seems boring, in two ways. First, the more we observe the breath, the more we notice differences and variations between individual breaths, which makes the breath seem more interesting and so more pleasant. Second, meditating on the breath tends to foster a calm state of mind and body that enables us to perceive and think more clearly. In short, breath meditation helps us train our attention, a skill that will be essential for doing more advanced meditations and for dealing with conflict and other problematic situations.[5]

Awareness of the Body

Some teachers consider awareness of body sensations the most fundamental and essential of the mindfulness meditation practices. The instructions below for the body scan ask us to begin with meditation on the breath (to stabilize our attention) and then to focus our attention at the top of our head and to notice, without judging, any sensations in the scalp or top of the skull. Then we gradually move our attention down the body until we reach the soles of our feet. At that point, we open our awareness to the entire body.

Please try it, following the instructions in Box B-3 or the recorded instructions at https://tinyurl.com/ManagingConflictMindfully.

Box B-3. Awareness of the Body (Body-Scan)—Instructions

Get into a comfortable position. If you are sitting on a chair, try to rest your weight on the front edge of the seat, so that you will not be supported by the back of the chair. Rest your feet on the floor, roughly five inches apart, and parallel. If any of that is uncomfortable, make adjustments. You want to be in a posture in which you can be relaxed and alert. (The ideal posture for the body is lying on your back on a yoga mat, blanket, or soft carpet or bed—with your feet falling loosely to the side, arms at your sides, with palms up.

- Take three deliberate, deep breaths in this fashion:
  - o Inhale through your nostrils to the count of three, so that you abdomen rises.
  - o Pause for a moment.
  - o Exhale slowly to the count of four.
  - o Pause
- Next, stop controlling your breath and allow the natural, automatic rhythm to resume. Bring your attention to the sensations of breathing at the place where you can most easily observe them. This might be at the nostrils, as the air enters and leaves, or in the chest or abdomen, as they rise and fall with inhalations and exhalations. Focus on the sensations of one inhalation at a time, one exhalation at a time. Try not to change or control the breath, but to simply observe it; you may notice, however that the breath changes "on its own" while you focus on it.
- After about one minute, on an out breath, move the awareness from the breath to the top of your head. Notice any sensations on the scalp, the muscles, or the skull. You may find, for instance, tingling, tension, or other sensations from contact with the air. If thoughts arise—say a wish that you had nicer hair, or more hair—try to "let them be," that is, do not engage with them, and return your attention to the scalp. If you observe no sensations at all, that is okay. When you notice that the mind has wandered away from that area, you have had a moment of mindfulness; simply escort the attention back.
- Gradually, in this manner, move your attention systematically throughout the body, more or less as follows, noticing, as best you can, any sensations in the skin, muscles, bones, or joints:
  - o the head—sides and back;
  - o the forehead, eye lids, eyes, nose, lips, cheeks, chin;
  - o the mouth—roof, floor, sides, tongue, teeth;
  - o the neck—front, sides and back;
  - o the right upper arm, elbow, lower arm, hand, fingers, and thumb (as best you can, focusing on one digit at a time);
  - o the left upper arm, elbow, lower arm, hand, fingers, and thumb (as best you can, focusing on one digit at a time).
- As you continue, if the attention is distracted by a very strong unpleasant sensation—such as a pain or an itch—instead of drawing the attention back to the area of focus, keep it on the unpleasant sensations. Simply focus on that sensation. As best you can, observe it without judgment. But as judgment arises, notice that, too. Observe the changes in the physical sensations and any thoughts or emotions

associated with them. Frequently, such thoughts or emotions relate to wishing the sensation would go away. Notice the difference between pain (from the physical sensation) and suffering (from the wish that things were other than the way they are).

- If, at a particular time, you feel lost or overwhelmed, use the breath for stability. In the same way that a swimmer, especially a beginner, may occasionally return for temporary support to the side of the swimming pool, when you lose track or get stuck in any sounds, body sensations, or emotions, bring the attention back to the breath until you feel comfortable returning your attention to the last place on which you were focusing:
  o   shoulders, upper back, lower back, chest, abdomen;
  o   buttocks;
  o   left thigh, knee, calf, ankle;
  o   right thigh, knee, calf, ankle;
  o   left foot—heel, arch, top of foot, toes (one at a time);
  o   right foot—heel, arch, top of foot, toes (one at a time).
- Now open your awareness to the entire body, noticing any sensations on the skin, in the tissue, in the bones and joints, as they arise in any part of the body. Relax. Treat each sensation with acceptance and curiosity.

Attending to body sensations enables you to quickly bring your awareness into the present moment, to calm yourself, and to develop an ability to observe body sensations that might otherwise not enter your conscious awareness. Some of these sensations send valuable information. If, for instance, as you speak with a particular co-worker or relative, you notice great tension in your jaws, mindful awareness could allow you to explicitly decide to "let it go" or "let it be" or to respond to it in some fashion.

Awareness of Breath, Body Sensations, Emotions, and Thoughts

This meditation prepares us to manage our awareness of several phenomena and helps prepare us for later meditations, such as open awareness, as well as the less-formal practices in Chapter 8.

Box B-4. Awareness of Breath, Body Sensations, Emotions, and Thoughts Meditation—Instructions

Sit comfortably on a chair with your back and neck erect, your feet flat on the floor, and your hands on your knees or thighs, or one inside the other in your lap. Close your eyes, or if you are uncomfortable doing so, close them about two-thirds and caste your gaze downward, unfocused.

- Take three deep breaths in this fashion:
  o   Inhale through your nostrils.

> o   Pause for a moment.
>
> o   Exhale slowly.
>
> o   Pause.
>
> Repeat two times.
>
> - Next, stop controlling your breath and allow the natural, automatic rhythm to resume.
> - After a few minutes, bring your attention to the sensations of breathing at the place where you can most easily observe such sensations. This might be at the nostrils, as the air enters and leaves, or in the chest or abdomen, as they rise and fall with inhalations and exhalations. Focus on the sensations of one inhalation at a time, one exhalation at a time. Do not deliberately change or control the breath, but simply observe it; you may notice, however, that the breath changes "on its own" while you focus on it.
> - When you realize that your mind has wandered—which it will—this is a moment of mindfulness. Gently escort your attention back to the breath.
> - When your awareness feels stable, gradually extend it to sensations of breathing elsewhere in the body, such as the thighs, knees, lower legs, and feet; then include the abdomen, chest, arms and shoulders; and then to the neck and head.
> - Now extend this awareness to include the entire body breathing.
> - Next, continuing to use the breath as a source of stability, try to notice thinking; that is, to become aware, without judgment, of thoughts as they arise, stay present, and drop out of awareness. That's all. For most people, this is difficult. So, you may find it helpful to silently "note" thoughts as they arise. For instance, you might say, "thinking." The main idea here is to be aware that you are thinking while you are thinking, and to have enough distance and freedom from the thinking that you can deliberately decide to let it go or let it be—and not get involved.
> - Next, while holding onto the breath as an anchor, open your awareness to emotions. Try to notice—again, without judgment—emotions such as fear, sadness, hate, joy, contentment, love, and revulsion. Thoughts will arise, of course, as will body sensations. Try to observe whether body sensations, thoughts, and emotions are related. For instance, a difficult experience or challenge may come to mind; you may experience fear, observe contraction in certain areas of your body, and notice a series of thoughts about your competence to deal with the situation. Try to be aware of such judgments and leave them alone, let them be, and do not judge yourself for having judgments. The appropriate attitude is curiosity, mingled with compassion.
> - Next, open your awareness more broadly so as to notice any body sensations, thoughts, or emotions that arise. Try gently noting any of these phenomena using terms such as "sensing," "thinking," or "feeling."

Why is it so difficult to be aware of our thoughts? First, thoughts can be ephemeral. Second, sometimes when we begin meditating on thoughts, we may not notice *any* thoughts; as a result, we may believe that we have *no thoughts whatever* at the moment and wonder what is wrong with us. Of course, all of that is *thinking*. To mentally step back from thoughts is a challenge, especially once we are so caught up in thinking that we are not aware that we are thinking. As the meditation teacher Joseph Goldstein puts it, "We hop on a train of association not knowing that we've hopped on and having no idea where the train is going. Somewhere down the line, we wake up from the dream of our thoughts, often in a completely different mental environment."[6] Third, most of us assume that thoughts come in the form of words or sentences. But many people do not think in language; according to the psychologist Charles Fernyhough, their inner voices are not speaking in words or sentences.[7]

This meditation gives us the opportunity to notice that we have almost no control over which thoughts arise, though we do have choices over how we respond to them.[8]

The expression, "Don't believe everything you think" is popular among mindfulness teachers. When we observe our thoughts, we may realize that we do not believe some of them. And we might wonder why or how they pop up. What should you do when such thoughts or questions arise in meditation? Treat them as "just thoughts" and leave them alone. If you notice any resistance to that, again, just notice the resistance.

Emotions, body sensations, and thoughts are intricately interrelated. Each can prompt the others—and strengthen or weaken them, as we will see in Chapters 7 and 8.

Open Awareness

Each of the previous meditation instructions tells us to "direct" our awareness to a particular object or objects during all or parts of a session—breath and other body sensations, thoughts, or emotions. In open awareness, in contrast, our attention is receptive to whatever arises in our awareness, indifferent about what will arise—whether body sensations, thoughts, emotions, or something we cannot categorize.

Box B-5. Open Awareness Meditation—Instructions

Sit comfortably on a chair with your back and neck erect, your feet flat on the floor, and your hands on your knees or thighs, or one inside the other in your lap. Close your eyes, or if you are uncomfortable doing so, close them about two-thirds and aim your eyes, unfocused, downward.

- Begin by meditating on the breath, noticing the sensations of breathing wherever it is easiest for you to do so. That could be the nostrils, the abdomen, the chest, or elsewhere. Let the breath flow naturally.

- When your awareness is reasonably stable, deliberately notice anything that distracts your attention from the breath, which could be other body sensations, emotions, thoughts, sounds, or other phenomena that you cannot easily categorize or label. When you observe such a distraction, make a gentle mental note, using whatever terms come to you most easily; they might include, for example, "emotion" or "feeling," "thought" or "thinking," "sound" or "hearing." When that "object" is no longer prominent, return your attention to the sensations of breathing.

- After a few minutes, as you become comfortable with this practice, shift to a more open awareness. Essentially this means that you no longer use the breath to anchor or stabilize your awareness. In other words, when you notice that your awareness has moved away from the breath, you observe the new object of awareness, but when it is no longer prominent, do not automatically return to the breath; instead, stay present with whatever arises, moment-to-moment, without judging or evaluating it. This is open awareness.

- Later, if you feel lost or lose track of what you are doing, either return your awareness, temporarily, to the breath or deliberately return your awareness to the present moment.

Open awareness (also known as "choice-less awareness" or "bare attention") as you may have noticed, seems more difficult than the methods presented above. That is why, as we are learning to meditate, we generally work up to open awareness, even during an individual meditation session; and it is not unusual to deliberately return to simpler concentration practice when that is more manageable. But open awareness gives us a taste of being present with our moment-to-moment experience—whatever it is.

Walking Meditation

Meditation traditionally has been practiced sitting, standing, or lying down. In addition, there are various forms of walking meditation, which are particularly useful in bringing mindfulness into daily life.

In formal "walking meditation" we set aside a specific amount of time (say, ten minutes) during which we walk and deliberately pay mindful attention to the experience of walking—generally, the body walking. As in other kinds of meditation, when you realize that your mind has wandered, just return it to the body.

Box B-6. Walking Meditation—Instructions

Find a space where you can walk for about ten feet and back without bothering anyone and without needing to observe your surroundings.

- Stand at one end of the "space," facing the other end. Allow your arms to hang loosely at your sides.

- Drop your attention into your body or specifically to your feet.

- Begin to walk slowly toward the other end of your space.

- As you do this, keep your awareness on your feet or more generally on body sensations. When you notice that your attention is elsewhere, gently return it to your feet or body sensations.

- When you reach the other end of your space, pause, turn around, make your feet parallel on the ground, and begin again.

- After a while you may wish to coordinate your breathing with your steps, or this coordination may arise on its own.

Formal walking meditation offers many of the same benefits as sitting meditation. It is especially useful for learning how to keep your awareness in your body, which is the simplest way to be in the present moment. It can help you develop the practice of keeping your attention in your body much of the day, which means frequently returning your attention there. In this way, formal walking meditation helps you bring mindfulness into your daily life and activities.

In many meditation retreats, walking meditation is scheduled between longer periods of sitting meditation. Sometimes in daily life, people who feel unable to sit still for meditation are nonetheless able to do walking meditation. I sometimes add an aerobic aspect by walking fast.

You can do a version of walking meditation in daily life as well, when you are walking to get from one place to another. In that sense, walking meditation is a step (pun intended) toward bringing mindfulness into your life when you are physically active or moving.[9]

Loving-Kindness

Mindfulness practice often fosters positive mindstates, including compassion and kindness to self and others. Such results are natural, to some extent, but not inevitable. And even if we do develop such states of mind in meditation, they can quickly vanish, especially when we need them most. Thankfully, the mindfulness traditions also include meditations to cultivate equanimity, compassion, sympathetic joy (delight in the happiness of others), and loving-kindness.[10] I present loving-kindness because it is the one most commonly taught and practiced in the Western world.

The central practice in loving-kindness meditation is to send certain kinds of good wishes to ourselves and to others.[11]

Box B-7. Loving-Kindness Meditation—Instructions

Sit comfortably on a chair with your back and neck erect, your feet flat on the floor, and your hands on your knees or thighs or one inside the other in your lap. Close your eyes, or if you are uncomfortable doing so, close them about two-thirds and aim your eyes, unfocused, downward.

- Take three deep breaths in this fashion:
  - Inhale through your nostrils.
  - Pause for a moment.
  - Exhale slowly to the count of four.
  - Pause.
- After a few minutes, bring to mind a person you love or care about very deeply, such as a mentor or benefactor, and send the following wishes (or similar wishes that feel more comfortable for you) to that person.
  - May you be healthy.
  - May you be happy.
  - May you be safe.
  - May you be peaceful and at ease.
- Send these same or similar good wishes to yourself.
  - May I be healthy.
  - May I be happy.
  - May I be safe.
  - May I be peaceful and at ease.

If you find it very difficult to send such wishes to yourself, imagine yourself at an earlier age, perhaps even as an infant, and send good wishes to that version of yourself.

- Next, bring to mind, one at a time, people such as the following, and send the same good wishes to each of them:
  - A friend.
  - An acquaintance.
  - A person you do not know, but see regularly, such as someone who works in a grocery store or coffee shop that you frequent or someone who walks their dog in your neighborhood.
  - A person you dislike.
  - Everyone in your city or town.
  - Everyone in other parts of the world, continent by continent.
  - All beings everywhere.

Sending such good wishes may not affect the intended recipient, but it often benefits the sender, creating feelings of kindness toward both self and others. Many experts believe that in order to send good wishes to another person—especially one for whom we harbor negative or mixed feelings—generally we must have good wishes toward ourselves. But in the West, many of us have lots of negative feelings and beliefs about ourselves, which we will explore below. This explains why many versions of loving-kindness meditations begin with sending these good wishes to ourselves.

During the first few times you do loving-kindness meditation, you may prefer to stop after "A person whom you do not know but see occasionally" and before "A person whom you dislike." If that is your inclination, feel free to follow it. As you practice loving-kindness meditation more, include the person you dislike strongly or even consider an enemy.

If sending good wishes to anyone feels insincere, I suggest that you continue doing so, nonetheless, and see what happens. Also, recall the poet Longfellow's observation, "If we could read the secret history of our enemies, we should find in each man's life sorrow and suffering enough to disarm all hostility."[12]

* * *

Through "formal" mindfulness meditation and loving-kindness meditation, we not only cultivate mindfulness and loving-kindness, but also develop the ability to establish and, to some extent, sustain these states of mind. The two practices support and reinforce one another. Mindfulness helps us maintain the focus needed to do loving-kindness practices; it not only fosters calm but also enables us to notice thoughts, emotions, and body sensations that arise as we are sending good wishes, so that we can return our attention to sending good wishes. The purpose of such practices, as Jon Kabat-Zinn tells us, is not to become a good meditator, but to live with more freedom from habitual ways of perceiving and acting, and thus to be more present in our lives and work, to enjoy life more, and to help others more readily and fully.[13]

HOW MINDFULNESS AND LOVING-KINDNESS CAN HELP YOU NEGOTIATE AND MANAGE PROBLEMATIC SITUATIONS MORE WISELY

When we last saw Pedro and Billy, you might have felt discouraged about their prospects for negotiating a good agreement. As Section A explained, if they had appropriately used elements of three models of negotiation—based on positions, interests, and the core concerns—they might have made a deal that suited both. But the section concluded with five potential obstacles to doing so: automatic, habitual ways of thinking, feeling, and behaving; excessively self-centered perspectives; inadequate awareness or management of emotions; insufficient social skills; and inadequate focus. This chapter reveals how mindfulness and loving-kindness could help someone such as Pedro overcome such impediments and better manage this situation.

The clearest foundation for what I want to say in this chapter is this: "Between stimulus and response, there is a space. In that space is our power to choose our response. In our response lies our growth and our freedom."[1]

Mindfulness can enable us to use that space to overcome or manage any or all of the five obstacles. Our ability to observe thoughts, sensations, and emotions with equanimity makes it easier to look for, or recognize, their sources and consequences, including positions, interests, or core concerns. This ability would allow us to deliberate—for instance, about our positions, interests, and core concerns—and decide whether and how to respond to them.[2]

Now, back to Pedro and Billy for some specifics. Assume that, in addition to learning the core-concerns and position-based and interest-based models of negotiation (which he did in Chapter 4), Pedro takes a training program in mindfulness meditation, practices rigorously for some time, and develops a reasonable ability to cultivate and sustain mindful awareness.[3] Then he readies himself to negotiate with Billy, intending to employ an appropriate balance of positions, interests, and core concerns. To do that well, Pedro may need to overcome or at least diminish some of these obstacles. Mindfulness could help him do so, as described for each obstacle below.[4]

Developing Awareness of—and Distance and Freedom from—Automatic, Habitual Ways of Thinking, Feeling, and Behaving

Fast thinking, as you will recall from Chapter 4, typically involves automatic or habitual thoughts, emotions, or behaviors. Some of these are mental short-cuts ("heuristics") or cognitive biases. And generally, fast thinking produces adequate decisions. But in some circumstances, real deliberation—slow thinking—enhances your chances of making a wise decision. On your next trip, a one-night visit to Cheyenne, Wyoming, for instance, you might sensibly rely on fast thinking to decide whether to stay at the Hampton Inn or the Red Lion Hotel and Conference Center. But if you are choosing between job offers in New York or San Francisco, slow thinking probably would serve you better. As you will see below, mindfulness can help establish the conditions for slow thinking. And slow thinking can help us transcend this obstacle.

Mindfulness and loving-kindness meditation can reduce bias associated with fast thinking. A study by Adam Lueke and Brian Gibson concludes that mindfulness meditation decreased implicit bias based on age and race, principally through "reducing the automaticity of responding."[5] In another study, this one looking at loving-kindness meditation training, Yoona Kang, Jeremy R. Gray and John F. Dovidio conclude that such training can reduce implicit intergroup bias.[6] Daniel Goleman and Richard Davidson tell us, based on a review of research, that

> [l]oving-kindness acts quickly, in as little as eight hours of practice; reductions in usually intractable unconscious bias emerge after just sixteen hours. And the longer people practice, the stronger brain and behavioral tendencies toward compassion become. The strength of these effects from the early days of meditation may signal our biological preparedness for goodness.[7]

Law professor Rhonda Magee shows how mindfulness can help overcome implicit bias based upon race and foster social justice.[8] And Tara Brach offers a reflection exercise for becoming aware of our implicit biases that lead to stereotyping others "depending on our social conditioning."[9]

The Triangle of Awareness, in Box B-8, offers a simple depiction of potential "objects" of awareness and opens the way to understanding the potential benefits of being aware of automatic, habitual ways of thinking, feeling, and behaving.

Box B-8. The Triangle of Awareness[10]

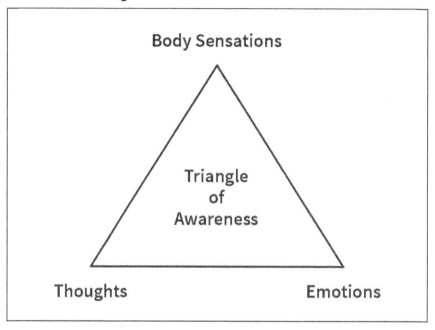

The points of the triangle are body sensations, emotions, and thoughts. These phenomena interact, and each can prompt, strengthen, or weaken the others. To explain that, I will tell you about an incident that *might* have happened when I worked at the University of Florida in Gainesville. I was walking at dusk in a nature preserve across the street from my office, and I spotted a long object on the path. As a result of fast thinking, I thought it was a Burmese Python, of which there are hundreds of thousands in the Florida Everglades, a few hours south by car. A large python can eat an entire deer. I experienced great fear and a "fight, flight, or freeze" reaction,[11] along with body sensations such as a rapid heartbeat, sweating, and tension. These responses led to more thoughts—such as, "What will happen to my wife and dog (and my students)?"—that strengthened existing emotions and body sensations. But when I calmed down enough to look carefully, I realized that the object was not a snake, but a tree branch. That new interpretation, perhaps in the form of a thought, produced dramatic changes in my emotions and body sensations, and I might even have laughed with relief.

How does this incident relate to negotiation?

Body sensations, emotions, and thoughts interact, and each can strengthen or weaken the others. If we become aware of something that we believe poses an imminent threat, if we are not mindfully aware, we are likely to rely on fast thinking and "react" automatically, out of habit. But mindfulness can interrupt the fast thinking and thus allow slow thinking, which can enable us to "respond" in a thoughtful way.

Once we become aware of thoughts, emotions, and body sensations, without judging them, we can achieve a certain "distance" from them, seeing them simply as objects of awareness rather than elements of our identity or essential self. We can understand thoughts as "just thoughts," body sensations as "just body sensations," and emotions as "just emotions." In short, we can mentally acknowledge—or notice—the presence of these phenomena, but not feel attached to or identified with them.

* * *

Back to Pedro and Billy: Imagine that, during their negotiation, Billy shrieks, "Pedro, I just can't take this anymore. You are the most *incompetent* negotiator in the world. Arrogant, inattentive, and impolite—and not overly smart." How Pedro responds could depend on whether he is mindful.

Box B-9 illustrates how the presence or absence of mindfulness could affect Pedro's internal experience and behaviors.

Box B-9. Stimulus, Internal Experiences, Awareness (Mindful or Not), and Behavior

Stimulus	Pedro's Internal Experience	Pedro's Awareness (Mindful or Not)	Pedro's Behavior
Billy calls Pedro incompetent	**Emotions:** Outrage, disgust.	**Not mindful**	**Reactive, automatic:** Returns verbal abuse, quits, walks out.
	Thoughts: Negative thoughts about Billy & himself. **Body sensations:** Rapid heartbeat, shallow breathing.	**Mindful**	**Responsive, deliberate:** Considers interests, core concerns, emotions; negotiates.
© 2022 Leonard L. Riskin & Rachel Wohl			

When Billy attacks Pedro's competence, if Pedro is not mindful, he would likely experience anger and fear, negative thoughts about Billy, insecure thoughts about himself, rapid heartbeat, and shallow breathing. He would react automatically and behave defensively. He might, for instance, denigrate Billy with harsh words or walk out.

If Pedro is mindful, he would likely experience the same thoughts, emotions, and body sensations. Yet he probably would feel calm because he is non-judgmentally aware of these phenomena. In other words, such mindfulness could act as a "wedge of awareness" that holds open the space between the stimulus (Billy's statement) and Pedro's response. This space could allow Pedro to think slowly about how he should deal with Billy's statement, which improves his odds of behaving skillfully. And in this situation, behaving skillfully might include considering interests and core concerns—Billy's and his own—and negotiating with those factors in mind.

Being mindful in this way requires a little equanimity, and produces even more of it. As psychologists Shauna Shapiro and Linda Carlson explain: "[R]eperceiving [the product of mindfulness practice] interrupts automatic maladaptive habits. People become less controlled by particular emotions and thoughts that arise, and in turn are less likely to automatically follow them with habitual reactive patterns."[12]

Diminishing Self-Centered Perspectives or Their Influence

"True humility is not thinking less of yourself, it is thinking of yourself less."[13]

Neurologist and Zen practitioner James Austin identifies two neural networks in the brain: self-centric (or ego-centric) and other-centric (or allocentric).[14] Activation of these circuits correlates with a focus on either self or others. The two networks have a "see-saw" reciprocal relationship;[15] when one is particularly active, the other is relatively inactive. Thus, when we focus primarily on ourselves, we do not pay much attention to others, and vice versa. When we do not deliberately fix our attention on either self or other, these circuits automatically trade off dominance two or three times each minute.[16] Most incoming stimuli are filtered first through the self-centric network, which gives that network a "major head start in shaping all of our priorities."[17]

When we are mindful, however, we can more easily observe and distinguish manifestations of each network, such as self-centered or other-centered thoughts, emotions, perceptions, and beliefs.[18] And we strengthen each circuit by attending to it or acting in accord with it. Meditation practice reduces activity in the self-centric network by focusing outside the self (which includes observing—but not identifying with—our thoughts, emotions, and body sensations). This, in turn, produces greater opportunities and inclinations to focus on others, or at least consider them. Thus, empathy, compassion, and kindness can arise naturally[19]—at least in theory.

Of course, most mindfulness meditation practitioners do not fully transform what Austin calls "pejorative self" or the "problematic self"[20] or even get major insights about their internal processes. But many do make progress in this direction. They get "small insights"—intuitive glimpses in the direction of "selfless insight."[21] In Austin's view, "When the hard edges of the self soften . . . or when the self recedes or is less dominant, that leaves room for our natural instincts of compassion to emerge. As self becomes less intrusive, the other networks in the brain become more active."[22]

What does all of this mean for Pedro and Billy? I suggested above that Pedro is too focused on himself to listen to Billy, or to care about him or his core concerns or interests. But if Pedro cultivates mindful awareness, it could lead to a "relative deactivation" of this self-centered network. When this happens, the other-centered network automatically becomes more active, and this could direct more of Pedro's attention to Billy and less to himself.

At a minimum, mindfulness should make it easier for Pedro to maintain non-judgmental awareness of the manifestations of *both* of the neural circuits, rather than succumb automatically to the self-centered circuit. Thus, he should be able to notice and distinguish the thoughts, impulses, and intentions that are associated with greed from those that are associated with curiosity about, and generosity toward, others. And as Pedro becomes more aware of the manifestations of what Austin calls the "problem self"—such as an intention to harm Billy or to inappropriately benefit himself—Pedro has the space to deliberately choose to ignore those self-centered impulses, or let them be.

Greater activity in the other-centered network should naturally stimulate Pedro's curiosity about Billy, as well as compassion and kindly behavior toward him. Thus, Pedro could become more inclined—and more able—to really listen to Billy, making it easier to recognize Billy's core concerns and interests and to want to accommodate them.

Enhancing Emotional Awareness and Management

Mindfulness can reduce the experience of stress, anxiety,[23] and depression;[24] enhance the ability to regulate emotions;[25] and promote the development of positive mental states.[26] For instance, mindfulness can help us notice our own thoughts and interpretations that could lead to negative emotions and resulting reactive behaviors. Then we can consider whether such thoughts and interpretations are true or important or useful, and whether to act upon them or just let them be.[27] So, if Pedro mindfully notices the thought, "I should punch that lazy bastard in the nose"—coupled with anger and an impulse to follow through—he has a chance to decide whether to actually smack Billy.

If we cultivate mindfulness through meditation, positive emotions such as happiness,[28] compassion for self[29] and others, and empathy[30] *tend* to develop naturally,[31] along with insights about the internal suffering we sometimes encounter and a recognition that others suffer in much the same ways we do.[32] And as we saw in Chapter 6, mindfulness meditation traditions also include practices, such as loving-kindness meditation, specifically intended to produce certain positive mindstates, notably loving-kindness, compassion, sympathetic joy (happiness for the good fortune of others), and equanimity.[33] Research supports the idea that practicing loving-kindness meditation can increase a person's caring and compassion for others as well as their tendency to help others.[34] That is my experience as well. In addition, we may deliberately set an intention to be kind, which should have a positive impact on our state of mind.[35]

Positive emotions could incline—or at least enable—Pedro to seek out and address Billy's interests[36] as well as his own. Recall that Pedro is infused with strong negative emotions—such as anger and disgust—toward Billy. Mindful awareness could help Pedro reduce the strength or influence of such emotions, and thereby foster non-judgmental awareness of their manifestations and causes.

If Pedro could gain such awareness, he might be able to avoid identifying with the anger or disgust, or at least with the thoughts and body sensations with which they are connected. For instance, if he could develop distance from those phenomena, he might be able to find the core concerns that prompted them. And recognizing his own core concerns might help him recognize Billy's active core concerns, and this in turn might diminish Pedro's bad feelings toward Billy.

Consequently, Pedro might be able to foster positive emotions in Billy. He could, for instance, follow *Beyond Reason*'s suggestions—express appreciation, build affiliation, foster autonomy, recognize status, and ensure meaningful roles for himself and for Billy (and Paulina). I am not suggesting Pedro should use any or all of these tools, but given his long and complex relationship with Billy, Pedro should be able to make reasonable judgments about what Billy needs, or if not, to ask Billy. Also, emotions are contagious,[37] and perhaps Billy would catch some of Pedro's positive affect.

Improving Social Skills

Pedro may know what to do—for example, express appreciation for Billy's expertise at selling shoes—but lack the social skills to do so in a way that Pedro will think is sincere.

Mindfulness tends to develop "emotional intelligence," a concept psychologist Daniel Goleman proposed and popularized.[38] Emotional intelligence entails five "basic emotional and social competencies": self-awareness, self-regulation, motivation, empathy, and social skills,[39] of which the most basic is emotional self-awareness. As Goleman tells us,

> Lacking that ability, we are vulnerable . . . to being sidetracked by emotions run amok. Such awareness is our guide in fine-tuning on-the-job performance of every kind, managing our unruly feelings, keeping ourselves motivated, tuning in with accuracy to the feelings of those around us, and developing good work-related

social skills, including those essential for leadership and teamwork.[40]

Mindfulness meditation can foster emotional self-awareness, self-regulation, motivation, and empathy;[41] these, in turn are likely to foster the fifth emotional intelligence competency—social skills.[42]

Enhancing the Ability to Manage Focus and Awareness

Mindfulness practice, as we have seen, includes and develops at least two forms of awareness: directed and open.[43] Of course, each is essential for the other. In order to focus, we often need the ability to manage interruptions and potential distractions, which may require some awareness of them, which in turn may require that we loosen up on directed awareness. William James, widely considered the father of American psychology, described the importance of these abilities:

> [T]he faculty of voluntarily bringing back a wandering attention, over and over again, is the very root of judgment, character, and will . . . . An education which should improve this faculty would be *the* education *par excellence*. But it is easier to define this ideal than to give practical directions for bringing it about.[44]

Mindfulness provides the directions that James sought, through formal practices, which appear above in Chapter 6, and semiformal and informal practices, which appear below in Chapter 8.

These practices could help a negotiator, such as Pedro, manage distractions and interruptions. As a result, Pedro should have a better chance to remember and maintain his chosen focus and strategic plans.

* * *

Box B-10 summarizes how mindful awareness could help a negotiator overcome obstacles to skillful negotiation.

Box B-10. How Mindfulness Can Help Someone Overcome Obstacles to Skillful Negotiation (a Summary)

Obstacle	Mindfulness can help	By fostering
Automatic, habitual ways of thinking, feeling, and behaving	Promote freedom from automatic, habitual ways of thinking, feeling, and behaving	Non-judgmental awareness of habitual ways of thinking, feeling, and behaving. The ability to notice and interrupt these patterns,

Obstacle	Mindfulness can help	By fostering
		which may lead to distance and freedom from them.
Excessively self-centered focus	Decrease the prominence of self-centered focus and foster the strength of other-centered focus	Understanding of and compassion for others. Recognition of interconnectedness. Insights about the nature of the self. Ability to notice and let go of self-centered perceptions and intentions. Curiosity about self and other.
Inadequate Awareness & Management of Emotions	Enhance Emotional Awareness & Management	Non-judgmental awareness of habitual ways of thinking, feeling, and behaving. The ability to notice and interrupt these patterns, which may lead to distance and freedom from them. • Equanimity.
Insufficient social skills	Improve social skills	• Emotional Intelligence: self-awareness, self-regulation, motivation, empathy.
Inadequate focus	Strengthen concentration	• The ability to notice when the mind has wandered and to bring it back to the desired focus of attention, • Equanimity.

This chapter shows how and why mindfulness can help overcome five obstacles to negotiating skillfully, both in general and in Billy and Pedro's complex long-term relationship. What about in a simpler relationship? Let's take a look in the next chapter.

CHAPTER 8

HOW TO ACTUALLY BE MINDFUL: FORMAL, SEMIFORMAL, AND INFORMAL PRACTICES

I don't know about you, but I am getting tired of Pedro and Billy. In this chapter, we meet Laura and learn how mindfulness might have helped her negotiate wisely in a less-complex relationship and conflict.

Laura's Lost Bonus [1]

Laura was an accomplished, though still junior, associate in a large law firm—until a few days ago, when she resigned precipitously.

Here is the background. Almost a year ago, Laura brought the firm a major new client, a substantial business called Zogat Industries. Shortly after that, the partner to whom Laura reported, Elaine, promised Laura an "origination fee" bonus equal to 10% of the client's fees for one year. During that first year, the client was billed and paid $500,000 in fees, so Laura anticipated an origination fee of $50,000 plus the standard bonus that members of her "class"—the group of new lawyers who started at about the same time—would receive.

At Laura's annual review meeting, however, the newly elected managing partner, Mildred, told Laura (in the presence of other partners on the compensation committee) that she had had a "good" year, and that her raise and bonus would be the same as that of the other 10 members of her class. That bonus was 5% of her $250,000 annual salary, or $12,500.

Laura was stunned and immediately replied, "What about the Zogat bonus that Elaine promised me? That's $50,000! I deserve that money, and you have to pay what you owe me. And next year, too." Mildred said, "That's ludicrous, Laura. If Elaine actually made that promise, which I doubt, she had absolutely no authority to do so, and you should have realized that. Besides, the standard 10% origination bonus in this firm is limited to equity partners. And, as I was about to tell you, the firm decided just last week that we cannot afford any more partners at this time."

After a long pause and some whispering among the most senior partners, Mildred said, "Well, under the circumstances, maybe we could give you an additional $10,000 bonus, but it would have to be strictly confidential." Mildred was poised to continue, when Laura stood up, looked around the room, and said, "You cheap, conniving bastards. You never could have gotten Zogat without me, because no one in this firm has the social or cultural background to do it. I can't stomach your greed and dishonesty. Go to hell! I quit, effective right now." Laura stormed out of the room and rushed directly to her office, where she began to write an email to everyone in the firm, announcing and explaining her resignation. Before she could do so, however, Mildred had her ejected from the firm's offices.

Subsequently, Laura has mixed feelings about the situation.

On one hand, she had been very unhappy, and very anxious, working at the firm. She thought most of the partners seemed arrogant, selfish, and crude. Their language was laced with extreme and gratuitous profanity. They were wholly insensitive to the needs of less fortunate or less powerful people, especially women, in the community and in the law firm. So, she feels very relieved that she no longer has to deal with the difficult office environment.

On the other hand, if she had delayed her resignation by five weeks, Laura would have reached the end of the fiscal year, been entitled to one or both of the bonuses, and, of course, received her salary through that time— all of which would have helped cover the down payment on a condominium that she and her fiancé wanted to buy. And she is worried about her prospects for other employment.

Laura now believes she behaved unwisely and is distressed about the situation. She is certain that she has alienated the partners to whom she spoke so rudely. But she still thinks she is right about the bonus and they are wrong.

* * *

Here is a quick picture of Laura and Mildred's positions, interests, and core concerns.

Box B-11. Laura and Mildred's Positions, Interests, and Core Concerns

Laura's Position(s)	Laura's Interests	Mildred's Position(s)	Mildred's Interests	Core Concerns of Both
	Good reputation. Good professional prospects. Financial security. Buying a condo. (This interest might rest on deeper		Keeping the other associates (as well as Laura) happy. Maintaining the firm's long-standing policy of giving the same salary increases and	

Laura's Position(s)	Laura's Interests	Mildred's Position(s)	Mildred's Interests	Core Concerns of Both
The firm owes me an origination fee of $50,000 (10% of fees Zogat paid during the first year).	Interests, such as shortening commuting time, impressing her fiancé or -Solidifying their relationship.) Paying off student loans. Demonstrating she can negotiate skillfully. Reducing or avoiding an environment she found unpleasant and stressful. (Of course, all Laura's interests are related.)	The firm owes Laura 5% of her $250,000 annual salary ($12,500).	annual bonuses to everyone in a particular "class." Maintaining the firm's policy about giving origination bonuses only to equity partners. Conserving money for the partners. Maintaining decorum. Avoiding a messy emotional conflict. Efficiency: (This could be a deeper interest underlying some of those above.)	Appreciation Affiliation Autonomy Status Role

Ironically, Laura knew better. She had recently taken a course on negotiation that emphasized interests and core concerns, and yet, in this situation, she did not deviate from her position. Mildred also stuck with her position, mainly, though she offered a compromise that, to Laura, seemed small in every way. And quite a few core concerns and interests—Laura's, Mildred's, and the other partners'—were ignored. This failing resulted from and produced negative emotions, among other things. Had Laura been mindful, she might have addressed or at least acknowledged some of Mildred's core concerns, as well as her own; both might have experienced at least some glimmers of positive emotions, which could have enabled them to actually consider interests and core concerns.

If Laura had taken account of interests and core concerns—her own, Mildred's, and the other partners'—her attitude might have shifted, which could have lessened the anger in the room. She might have suggested a break and a private conversation between her and Mildred, perhaps along with a few other partners.

Laura and the partners might have generated options,[2] such as increasing the confidential bonus above $10,000; enlarging or restructuring future origination bonuses for Zogat or other clients that Laura (and other firm lawyers who are not equity partners) might bring in; expanding Laura's client-development role; giving Laura better assignments or a better office;

giving Laura the larger bonus in exchange for her resignation; giving Laura a low-interest loan or a housing supplement to help her buy the condominium; paying off Laura's student loans. The firm's leadership might also have wondered whether other employees felt uncomfortable with profanity floating around the office and considered doing something about it. Working with such options, they might have reached an agreement that was better for all concerned.

Of course, any of the five obstacles might have impaired Laura's ability to negotiate wisely. And mindfulness might have helped Laura overcome these impediments. Still, mindfulness comes and goes; it is difficult to maintain, especially in the heat of conflict. You could be mindful when you read *this* clause, for instance, and mindless by the time you read *this* clause. In fact, mindfulness is itself vulnerable to the same five obstacles that it can help a person overcome,[3] as you will see in Chapter 10. So even if Laura had been mindful when she walked into the room, this state of mind might have disappeared as soon as Mildred called Laura's demand "ludicrous," or even before. That could have left Laura unable to deal with any of the obstacles, and consequently, unable to negotiate or behave skillfully.

What might Laura have done to enhance the likelihood that she would have been mindful during the meeting? Formal, semiformal, and informal practices might have helped her.

Formal Mindfulness and Loving-Kindness Practices (Revisited)

Formal practices include the kind of meditations presented in Chapter 6, in which (typically) a person sets aside a time for doing a particular meditation practice or practices. As we learned in Chapter 5, studies have shown that mindfulness meditation can foster mindfulness as a state of mind and that advanced practitioners can develop mindfulness as a trait.

Doing formal meditation daily is good preparation for whatever might arise almost any time. Similarly, your state of mind could be much improved if you meditate shortly before events that are likely to present challenges. These could involve negotiations or other interactions around controversial and serious current issues—such as election rules, the Covid Pandemic, rights of less-powerful individuals and groups, DIE (Discrimination, Inclusion, and Equity), and climate change. But emotional and other challenges also can arise before, during, and after negotiations or other interactions over more ordinary matters, such as buying a bicycle or a car, asking for a raise, or sharing a holiday dinner with certain relatives.

In getting ready for a such events, the most appropriate or useful meditative practice might depend on your current state of mind, the nature of the situation, the other participants, and your experience with mindfulness

Meditation on the breath or body could promote calm. Depending upon your level of experience and comfort with the other meditations, you might wish to extend your focus to thoughts and emotions or to practice open awareness. Such meditations should help you manage your emotions, think less about yourself and more about others, and focus better.

I am not suggesting that, during such meditations, you deliberately think about the conflict or situation. But during formal meditation, insights often arise without any special effort.[4] You cannot anticipate what might enter your mind while it seems at rest. For instance, Steven Schwartz, head of a public-interest disability law firm, says that mindfulness meditation helps him think creatively.[5] Sometimes, when he is meditating—simply observing body sensations, thoughts, and emotions—solutions to practical problems occur to him; on occasion, when he meditates in this way just before he sits down to write a "brief"—an argument to submit to a court—the outline of the entire brief will come to him, and, he says, "It is sublimely, precisely correct."[6]

And consider Kim, a lawyer whose clients—all of them—are appealing their death-penalty sentences, which means that Kim almost always loses the appeals, and Kim's clients almost always remain on death row, or worse. She and other lawyers in her office had developed particularly difficult relations with several judges on the highest court of the jurisdiction in which they practiced. Loud, bitter interactions frequently arose during Kim's court appearances. Then Kim learned about mindfulness and meditated before a court session, to calm her mind and body; it "changed everything," she said. Kim was no longer angry and felt at ease. The harsh arguments morphed into "conversations"; and, from time to time, Kim's clients got better outcomes.

You might send loving kindness to participants in difficult events, such as negotiations or mediations, especially if you feel antipathy or other negative emotions toward them. That could prepare you to focus on the task at hand and the needs of others more than on your own egocentric wants and needs, which otherwise could distract you or dominate your mental processes. A full-time mediator whom I know routinely sends loving-kindness to all the participants before each session, even those they do not know.

I find it especially useful to meditate during a break or shortly after a significant activity, such as a negotiation, for two reasons: First, meditation can help us during the transition to decompress or detach so that we can be present with whatever happens next. Second, sometimes our minds will automatically generate insights about what happened and why. We may get ideas about what to do next or how, if at all, to deal with mistakes.[7]

* * *

But mindfulness comes and goes. People who achieve a state of mindful awareness cannot maintain it consistently or indefinitely. Even advanced practitioners frequently lose it—if only temporarily—as circumstances overwhelm their skills.[8] In the words of Pir Vilyat Khan, leader of the Sufi order in the West, " 'Of so many great teachers I've met in India and Asia, if you were to bring them to America, get them a house, two cars, a spouse, three kids, a job, insurance, and taxes . . . they would all have a hard time.' "[9]

And, as you have already noticed, it's easy to lose our mindful awareness during formal meditation.

Luckily, semiformal and informal mindfulness practices and tools, which I explain below, can help us quicky establish, maintain, or sustain mindfulness and loving-kindness.

Semiformal Mindfulness Practices

What I call semiformal mindfulness practices usually have explicit structures and purposes, like formal practices, but people tend to devote less time to semiformal practices.

RAIN

RAIN has a more specific objective than the formal meditations in Chapter 6. It is meant to help us deal with certain kinds of internal processes or experiences that we find especially unpleasant or hard to manage; they often include or produce anxiety or other difficult emotions. The acronym, RAIN, as presented by Tara Brach, stands for Recognize, Allow, Investigate, and Nurture.

Box B-12. RAIN Meditation—Instructions

Sit quietly and in a position that allows you to be alert and relaxed.

- Take three or four deep breaths, pausing for a moment after each inhalation and each exhalation.

- Bring to mind—or notice—something that has bothered you or is currently bothering you. It might be a conflict or difficult situation that leads to anxiety, despair, or fear. Once you have that in mind, put yourself mentally back into the situation or how you experience it. Then follow these steps:

Recognize what is going on within you.

You may, notice anxiety or fear, worry, or negative thoughts about yourself or others, for example.

Accept or allow whatever is happening.

Instead of wishing or trying to change whatever internal phenomena you notice, welcome them. Acknowledge that they are actually present and that that is ok.

Investigate with kindly curiosity.

Carefully and closely observe the internal phenomena and how they might interact, staying present with them. Locate the area(s) in your body where you most strongly experience whatever is happening. You may want to gently note body sensations, emotions, thoughts, or other phenomena. For instance, you might note "thinking," "worrying," or "feeling." Try to see such phenomena not as inherent aspects of you. Instead acknowledge that the thoughts are just thoughts; the body sensations are just body sensations; and the emotions are just emotions.

Nurture.

Move toward the difficult phenomena, rather than denying or trying to get away from them. Sense what kind of support these aspects of you need. They may need reassurance, love, appreciation, or other kinds of help. Then try to address such needs. For instance, send them (or yourself, if that is more comfortable) loving-kindness or any of the elements of loving-kindness; or send forms of encouragement that you might convey to a friend, colleague, or client, such as "you will get through this," "you can handle this," "you have dealt with tougher problems before," or "I will be with you every step of the way."

This is my own version of RAIN, which draws primarily on recent work of the meditation teacher, writer, and psychotherapist Tara Brach[10] and of the psychiatrist and mindfulness expert Judson Brewer,[11] as well as my own experience in practice and teaching.

When you notice manifestations of a difficult emotion, such as anxiety—*while you are meditating or in your daily life*—you can do RAIN on the spot. As you gain experience working with RAIN, you can use it without advanced planning, abbreviating and customizing it as appropriate.

* * *

Back to Laura, briefly. For a considerable time before the incident in question, she had been unhappy and angry about her work situation, including her colleagues, at the law firm. If she had been familiar with RAIN and had taken time to practice it shortly before the meeting or during the meeting, she probably would have responded more skillfully.

* * *

Over the past decade or so, Rachel Wohl—mindfulness teacher, lawyer, and mediator—and I have adapted or developed tools that can help you rapidly establish mindfulness, virtually any time, even in the heat of conflict, and to integrate such mindfulness with negotiation or other tasks. We call these tools "STOP," "STOPSI," and "Taking STOCK." We, and others, have used them extensively in courses and workshops on negotiation and mediation.[12]

STOP

STOP can help you quickly establish mindful awareness, arrest the development or slow the escalation of inner or outer conflict, and enhance the ability to think slowly and clearly. Before I say more, please do a STOP, right now, following the instructions in Box B-13.

Box B-13. STOP Instructions

<u>S</u>top

(That is, stop doing whatever you are doing. If you are holding a pen, put it down. If you are looking out the window, stop looking.)

<u>T</u>ake a deliberate breath.

<u>O</u>bserve, without judging, evaluating, or thinking about,

> Body Sensations (about 15 seconds)

> Emotions (about 15 seconds)

> Thoughts (about 15 seconds).

Give a mental "O.K." to whatever you notice. In other words, simply recognize and acknowledge what is happening in the current moment. Do not deliberately think about what you observe or about how to deal with the external aspects of the situation.

<u>P</u>roceed (That is, continue with whatever you were doing, or do something else.)

[This is a modified version of the STOP Exercise developed by the Stress Reduction Clinic at the University of Massachusetts Medical School and formerly used in its training programs.]

Just to be clear, STOP is meant to establish mindfulness, to create a mindful pause, which should foster calmness and clarity. As you will recall, the Triangle of Awareness (Box B-8) depicts the relationships among three major components of human consciousness—body sensations, emotions, and thoughts (BETs)—and it suggests using these as the principal objects of awareness. The BETs interact and can prompt, enhance, or diminish one another. For instance, when Mildred rudely dismissed the large bonus that Laura anticipated, Laura probably experienced unpleasant body sensations, strong destructive emotions, and negative thoughts about everyone in the room—herself included.

These BETs prompted (or resulted from) a fight, flight, or freeze response.[13] During these processes, Laura lost her ability to recall or attend to any of her longer-term interests or core concerns. Had Laura been mindfully aware, she still might have experienced the same or similar body sensations, thoughts, and emotions, but she might have been able to manage them more effectively. Mindfulness can insert a "wedge of awareness" between BETs and behavior. With such awareness, Laura might have recognized and acknowledged the presence of BETs, which could have afforded her some freedom from them.

Imagine that, immediately after Mildred says there will be no bonus, Laura remembers to do a STOP, and that she has practiced enough that she can actually do it. She takes a breath, which interrupts her progress toward the emotional-verbal explosion, and drops her awareness into her body, which brings her into the present moment. Laura may first observe tightness in her jaws, a rapid pulse, pressure in her head, and widespread tension, especially in the abdominal area. Next, she senses her emotions—anger, hatred, and fear—and an impulse to retaliate. Then she notices thoughts: "Those greedy barbarians are screwing me. I hate them. I will quit. I deserve that bonus. No one else in the firm could have gotten that client. I always get taken."

Laura's mindful observation of these phenomena should weaken her sense of identification with them and their influence on her. As Tara Brach puts it, "Non-identification means that your sense of who you are is not fused with or defined by any limited set of emotions, sensations, or stories."[14] We could say that it involves reframing, for instance, from "I am enraged" to "There is rage." This quickly established awareness could allow Laura to more fully appreciate what is going on and to respond more skillfully.

* * *

Practice the STOP exercise frequently, not only to manage your internal processes but also to increase your ability to use STOP almost automatically. Using STOP might be most helpful when you are feeling anxious or when you are about to begin a new activity and do not have time for a more formal meditation. Many of our students use STOP during exams to keep themselves calm and clear, especially when they encounter a question they find challenging or feel otherwise stuck. With practice, you will be able—and sometimes eager—to abridge STOP and do a "short STOP," so that no one will notice that you are doing anything special, which may be especially valuable during interpersonal activities.

Finally, there is no magic about the order in which you observe body sensations, emotions, and thoughts (BETs). You may wish to experiment, or begin with whatever seems most prominent at a particular time.

STOPSI (STOP and Set Intentions)

STOPSI begins with STOP, and then adds a step: Set a clear and simple intention as to how you would like "to be" during the negotiation or other activity. Such an intention is ordinarily different from our substantive goal. And even if we do not achieve our substantive goal, deliberately setting an intention can help align our behavior with our values. Simply setting an intention—for instance, to be kind, to be attentive, or to listen deeply—can take us off auto-pilot and help us consciously monitor and manage ourselves.

Box B-14 sets out instructions for STOPSI.

Box B-14. STOPSI

> **S**top.
>
> **T**ake a breath.
>
> **O**bserve BETS (body sensations, emotions, and thoughts).
>
> **P**roceed to
>
> **S**et a clear and simple
>
> **I**ntention (for how you would like "to be" during this activity or time period).
>
> Record the intention, to help yourself remember it.
>
> © 2022 Leonard L. Riskin and Rachel Wohl

What does it mean to set an intention for how you will "be"? This is hard to explain, so I will offer examples. One comes from meditation teacher and writer Phillip Moffitt, who always holds the intention "to be kind."

> I've chosen this because of the sense of well-being that kindness bestows in all situations. Even when I have to be firm with someone or go against their wishes, I am very clear that I wish to be as kind as possible. I am indiscriminate in my kindness . . . . Nor is my intention of kindness based on pity or wanting to be liked. What happens when I am not kind in a particular moment?

I simply start over, learning from my mistakes as much as possible so that I can be more capable of kindness in the next moment.[15]

The writer George Saunders expresses a similar reason, in his graduation address at Syracuse University: "So here's something I know to be true, although it's a little corny, and I don't quite know what to do with it: What I regret most in my life are failures of kindness."[16] My own experience is exactly the same as Saunders'. Behaving or feeling kindly does more than help you avoid regret. It also can promote happiness in you and others around you.[17]

If Laura had been able to set—and follow—an intention to "be kind," she would not have launched her attack. She might even have experienced glimmers of kindly thoughts and emotions about Mildred and the other partners (and herself). Such thoughts and emotions might have helped her feel better and think more clearly, which could have enabled her to consider underlying interests and core concerns.

But Laura did not set an intention for how she wanted to be during the meeting. In the absence of such a specific intention, she reacted in automatic ways. She might have set intentions about being calm or balanced or respectful. Or, instead, Laura might have set quite different kinds of intentions, such as being strong, ruthless, or, as a colleague described his ambitious nephew, "appropriately ruthless."

We set "clear and simple" intentions because, later, if and when we Take STOCK (the tool introduced next), we can readily determine whether we have been following our intention, and possibly change it. Monitoring complex or multiple intentions would be much more difficult.

Taking STOCK

With the Taking STOCK tool, you begin with STOPSI, establishing mindfulness and setting intentions for how you want to be. You can set intentions at the beginning of a day or before a project or a potentially difficult activity, such as a negotiation or a meeting or a class, regardless of your role in these activities. A person's state of mind or awareness is constantly in flux. Taking STOCK allows you to establish, or re-establish, mindfulness, and to consider whether you have been following the intentions you set. Next, the tool prompts you to deliberately decide on your immediate next step—and then to keep going. Instructions for Taking STOCK appear in Box B-15.

Box B-15. Taking STOCK—Instructions

Before the Activity (e.g., a negotiation, a hearing, or a difficult meeting): STOP and Set Intentions for How You Want "To Be" (STOPSI)

Stop.

Take a breath.

Observe Body Sensations, Thoughts, Emotions.

Proceed to

Set a clear and simple

Intention (or two).

During or after the Activity, Take STOCK:

Stop.

Take a Breath.

Observe Body Sensations, Emotions, Thoughts (BETS).

Consider:

- Have you been following your intention(s)?
- Do you want to change your intention(s)?
- What next?

Keep Going.[18]

© 2013–2022 Leonard L. Riskin & Rachel Wohl

If Laura had been familiar with Taking STOCK and had wanted to use it, she might have deliberately set her intention shortly before the annual review meeting. Let's assume that she set an intention to remain calm, no matter what happened, and that she remembered to Take STOCK immediately after she learned the bonus would not come through—but just before her first angry and crude attack. She would take a breath and then observe her body sensations, emotions, and thoughts. Doing so should sap some of her reactivity. Then she would consider whether she had been following her intention to remain calm and whether she should change this intention, perhaps to something like "be polite" or "be courageous."

In considering "What next?" Laura might decide, for instance, to express her anger, but in a way that honors her intentions. For instance, rather than act out her anger, as she did in the actual meeting, Laura could have told Mildred that she "feels a lot of anger." In that way, she would be describing her anger, rather than enacting it. Perhaps she also could buy time by saying something like, "This is totally unexpected, and I'd like to take a few minutes to think it through before responding."

As you can see, Taking STOCK could have enhanced the likelihood that Laura would have had a more peaceful inner experience, would have behaved more skillfully, and would have achieved an outcome that would better serve her interests.

Informal Mindfulness Practices

"Informal" practices or exercises are brief versions of formal or semiformal practices. You can use them to quickly establish present-moment awareness. The more frequently you do a particular practice of this nature, the more likely it will become a habit and happen automatically.

First, I suggest that you select two or three mindfulness bells, that is, reminders for you to quicky establish present-moment mindful awareness.

Mindfulness "Bells"

- You are waiting—in traffic, in line at a grocery store, or for an important phone call.
- You are cleaning your bathroom sink, or something else.
- You are taking a shower.
- You are taking an exam.
- You are about to give a presentation.
- You just heard the sound of an actual bell, perhaps a bell from a clock, a church, or smart phone app.
- You are walking.

Informal Mindfulness Exercises

- Take one, two, or three deliberate breaths.
- Take one, two, or three deep, slow breaths. When you complete an inbreath, pause for a few seconds before you exhale. Likewise, when complete an outbreath, pause before you exhale.
- Direct your awareness toward sensations of breathing or other body sensations, emotions, or thoughts.
- Direct your awareness to sensations in your hands or feet, or to sounds.

Even when you are *not* agitated, these techniques can bring you into the present moment and help you develop a habit of briefly inducing present-moment awareness several or many times each day.

Informal Loving-Kindness Practices

During your daily life and activities, look for opportunities to briefly send good wishes to others who come into your awareness. They could be people with whom you are familiar at any level, as well as strangers you might pass by chance. Try sending good wishes, in the moment, to people you see on the sidewalk, in an airport, or in other settings: a cashier at the grocery store, a postal service delivery person, your students (if you teach), your teachers (if you are a student). Notice thoughts, emotions, and body sensations that arise before, during, and after you send such wishes.[19]

Also, try sending loving-kindness to yourself regularly, and especially when you need it, using brief versions of the instructions set forth in Box B-7 in Chapter 6.

REVIEW OF SECTION B

Section B offers a sunny response to the dreary claim at the end of Section A. The dreary claim is that even people who are well trained in negotiation—based on positions, interests, and core concerns—often have trouble negotiating skillfully because of one or more of five obstacles: insufficient awareness or management of emotions; excessively self-centered perspectives; automatic, habitual ways of thinking, feeling, and behaving; insufficient social skills; and inadequate focus. Section B's optimistic response is that mindfulness, a method of paying attention without judgment to our present-moment experience, can help us overcome those obstacles, and, as a result, negotiate more wisely. To support this claim, I presented mindfulness, its mechanisms, and its potential benefits, along with instructions for cultivating and deploying it through formal, semiformal, and informal practices.

Yet mindfulness itself is vulnerable to the same five obstacles that it can overcome. Thus, for instance, sometimes the present moment—full of thoughts, body sensations, and emotions—can overpower our ability to notice when we have lost our mindfulness.

So, what to do? First, take heart. Negotiation knowledge and skill can support mindfulness, as you will see in the Review of Sections A, B, and C; and Internal Family Systems (IFS) (the third domain) can support both mindfulness and negotiation, as Section D explains.

Second, even a little mindfulness knowledge and practice can produce benefits and set the groundwork for more. Research supports this. And many of my students report the benefits of mindfulness during and long after their courses and workshops. For instance, Katherine Larkin-Wong, then an associate at the Latham & Watkins law firm in San Francisco, described her experience with mindfulness, STOP, and Taking STOCK (which she learned in my Conflict Management in the Legal Profession course at Northwestern Law in 2010) as follows:

> I continue to use STOP exercises to prevent a wandering mind when reading case law. I find that I no longer read multiple pages before realizing that I have not absorbed any of it. STOP exercises help me refocus. Taking STOCK exercises have also been useful in many situations. I use them when going into a tough conversation or sometimes before attending a class where I have struggled to pay attention. I will formulate the intention to stick

with it through the entire class and then take STOCK throughout to make sure I am following my intention.[1]

Frequently students report using one or more of these tools while studying, taking exams, participating in moot court, interviewing for jobs, and—most relevant to this book—paying attention in class. Colleagues at the Center on Negotiation, Mediation, and Restorative Justice at Northwestern Law also use these tools in some of their courses and meetings.

REVIEW OF SECTION B IN LIGHT VERSE

B. MINDFULNESS
The practice of mindful attention
Delivers a different dimension.
For managing conflict, within and without,
It's almost essential, there's nearly no doubt.

It keeps us calm and helps us think
And more, provides a needed link
For using constructs named above,
And doing so with kindly love.

* * *

SECTION C

BACK TO THE FIRST DOMAIN, NEGOTIATION: THE THREE CONVERSATIONS

Remember my negotiation with the carriage driver in Luxor, Egypt? I mentioned it briefly in the Introduction and promised to return to it.

The Luxor Carriage-Fee Negotiation, Egypt (1992)

On the last night of our vacation in Egypt, Casey (my wife), Andrew (our son, age twelve), and I begin a one-mile stroll along the Corniche, a broad boulevard bordering the Nile, to La Mamma's Restaurant in an upscale Sheraton hotel that was reputed to have the best pizza in Luxor. Andrew campaigns to take a horse-drawn carriage. Although I prefer to walk—and to save money—I eventually give in. Then I commence a difficult negotiation over the fare with one of the dozens of carriage drivers searching for customers among the many tourists. We stand at impasse when another carriage driver pulls up and offers what I think is a bargain rate: ten Egyptian pounds (EGP), about three USD—half as much as the first driver demanded. I assume they are colluding, but I accept and climb into the front seat while Casey and Andrew, embarrassed, jump into the back. The driver (I will call him Mr. Hassan) compliments me on my family and says he works long and hard to provide for his wife and six children.

Then, in a series of steps, he blatantly cheats me on the fare. Thirty seconds after the carriage starts moving, he says the fare is 30 EGP—10 EGP per person. I get angry and insist that he stop the carriage so we can get out. But he does not. Gradually, he seems to agree to a total of 10 EGP But when we reach the Sheraton, I discover that I have only a 20 EGP note. I ask if he has change. I think he says yes. So I hand it up to him. Within seconds, he displays a 50 Piaster note (which resembles the 20 EGP note, note but is worth just a tiny fraction), protesting that I had given him only that. I know, at least I am pretty sure, he is trying to cheat me; I had succumbed to a similar scam in another country some years earlier. But I think he is getting angry. I am on his turf, and now I am scared about what may happen to me and my family. Finally, Casey produces a 20 EGP note, which I hand up to him. And he gives me change! But then, in a sparkling demonstration of chutzpah,[1] he

103

extends his hand and asks for baksheesh, a tip. And somehow—perhaps because my fury was supplanted by fear, confusion, and embarrassment—I comply.

As we walk into La Mamma's, my anger rushes back. I fume throughout the dinner and plot to get revenge—or at least to right the imbalance between us. After ruining our meal, I insist that we patrol the Corniche to find and confront Mr. Hassan. When I locate him, he has a sidekick riding with him—doubtless for protection; we exchange long glares across the Corniche, suffused with meaning (at least, in my imagination). Yet I feel a bit like the proverbial dog chasing a car who had never considered what he would do if he caught it. Eventually, I decide that we have reached another stalemate—a stare down, rather than a showdown. Casey, Andrew, and I slouch back to the Marriott.

* * *

This section shows how I could have better (or differently) understood and addressed the Luxor situation through each of the three negotiation focuses we covered previously: positions, interests, and core concerns. It then unveils one more negotiation focus—the three conversations—and one model for implementing it, both from the book *Difficult Conversations: How to Discuss What Matters Most*, by Douglas Stone, Bruce Patton, and Sheila Heen.[2] Next, I explain how this approach might have helped me better manage the Luxor situation, and, finally, I invite you to learn how the three conversations could apply to a conflict of your own.

CHAPTER 9

POSITIONS, INTERESTS, AND CORE CONCERNS IN THE LUXOR CARRIAGE-FEE NEGOTIATION

This chapter examines the Luxor negotiation using the three negotiation focuses that we covered in Section A—positions, interests, and core concerns—and shows how they might have helped me perform better.

Positions and Interests

Notwithstanding my professed devotion to interests, Mr. Hassan and I engaged exclusively in narrow, positional bargaining. As I saw it, he proposed a fare of 10 EGP for all three of us. I accepted. Then he changed his position and said the fare was 10 EGP per person. I asserted the position that we had agreed on 10 EGP total and that I would pay no more.

I did not consider Mr. Hassan's interests or those of his family (which might have included survival needs), Casey or Andrew's interests in avoiding unpleasantness, or even my own deeply submerged interests in having a pleasant time with my family. I did, however, try to foster *some* of my own interests. Strange and humiliating as this seems today, I actually *did* care about saving money. But I focused equally on goals that I could promote only indirectly, as secondary benefits of the negotiation: enhancing or protecting my self-esteem, and teaching Andrew negotiation and survival skills.

Mr. Hassan's behavior threatened my sense of competence and my self-esteem, which were entangled with my identities as a sophisticated negotiator, a man of the world. Although I generally use and promote interests in negotiation, I probably believed that, in this context, my self-esteem depended primarily on my ability to demonstrate skill in adversarial, positional bargaining. I must have assumed, too, that I would get or regain self-esteem in part by looking at myself through the eyes of others—Mr. Hassan, Casey, and Andrew—after I had dazzled them with my negotiation prowess by getting a low fare. I never consciously considered including the other interests I just mentioned. Of course, my strategy and tactics wholly failed to achieve my goals.

I not only ignored most interests, I also failed to use other strategies or tactics listed in the most influential explication of the interest-based model,

Getting to Yes. As you will recall from Chapter 2, this model tells us that, in addition to focusing on interests, we should be hard on the problem and soft on the people, invent options before deciding, insist on objective criteria, and develop our BATNA (best alternative to a negotiated agreement) and measure options against it.

But in Luxor I did not observe any of these guidelines. I did not separate any of the people from the problem—so I was not soft on any of us. I did not seek, let alone insist on, objective criteria. I did not try to generate options. I did not consider my alternatives, which included walking (or limping) away (after leaping from the moving carriage, with or without my family) and finding another carriage.[1]

Under the circumstances, finding objective criteria—let alone agreeing on them—would have been impossible, and generating options would have weakened my already-depleted abilities. But what if I *had* looked, quickly, for other ways to foster some of the interests described above?

I might have told Mr. Hassan that I knew he was trying to cheat me (which, I realize, could have threatened some of his core concerns), but that I wanted to help him take care of his family, so I would pay what he asked. This offer would have fostered both Mr. Hassan's interest in supporting his family and my family's interest in enjoying the evening. It also might have enhanced my self-esteem in two ways. I could have considered this an act of kindness or charity. Mr. Hassan might have reached the same conclusion and realized that I was both sophisticated about negotiation and generous; this could have bolstered my self-esteem and reduced my concern about status or appreciation—had I been aware of it.

I might have paid Mr. Hassan more than he asked, which would have improved my standing with my wife and son.

I might have paid him only the amount on which I thought we had agreed, and then given him a very large tip and said it was for his children. This could have showed Andrew and Casey both my negotiation skill and my generosity, and enhanced my self-esteem.

Once Mr. Hassan made clear that he wanted 10 EGP per person, I could have acknowledged that I might have misunderstood and then offered an intermediate amount.

Had I made any one of these choices, Mr. Hassan might have behaved differently. This may be far-fetched, but he might have reciprocated in some fashion. Perhaps, for instance, if I had paid what he asked, or even more, he would have offered to take us on a specialized tour of Luxor, after dinner—

at a lower rate.[2] That would have given him additional income for his family
and made the evening more pleasant for all concerned.[3]

But I could not have done any of this, principally because I felt too
angry, agitated, fearful, and insecure. But why?

The Core Concerns

The core-concerns model from *Beyond Reason* helps answer that
question. In Luxor, all of my core concerns probably suffered, but I will
explore just three—appreciation, affiliation, and status. As to Mr. Hassan's
core concerns, my comments below are almost sheer speculation. But
perhaps I could have better managed the situation if I had simply entertained
the idea that he had core concerns, too, and that my behavior had impacted
them negatively.

Understanding the Situation Through the Core Concerns

Affiliation

"You have a beautiful family," said Mr. Hassan, just as I sat down next
to him on his bench seat. "I have a family too, a wife and six children. And I
must work very hard to feed them." I assumed that he was trying to establish
or build a connection, but only to get more money. Because of that
assumption, I distrusted and feared him, and I did not want to build
affiliation. So I had to restrain my natural friendliness and curiosity. "The guy
is just trying to manipulate me," I thought. "Besides, if I *really* got to know
him, I might want to give him everything he asks for and more because he
has such a difficult life." Yet I worried about my affiliation with Casey and
Andrew. This event might confirm their suspicion that I *am* a jerk and their
fear of embarrassment whenever they are with me in public.[4]

My assumptions about Mr. Hassan's behavior and motives might have
been incorrect. Perhaps he did prefer to have some kind of human, person-
to-person connection, some glimmer of affiliation, however brief.[5]

Appreciation

My core concern for appreciation really took a beating. I believed that
Mr. Hassan did not appreciate that I was a negotiation expert, a sophisticated
man of the world. He showed no respect for these aspects of my identity,
and he tricked me. He did not understand that my family and I also "needed"
the money. Nor did Casey or Andrew. They probably realized that I meant
to teach Andrew important life skills, but considered my display of hard
bargaining unwise, unkind, and unrealistic.[6]

I am sure that Mr. Hassan supposed I was wealthy—or at least more prosperous than he—and assumed that I did not appreciate (or care) that he needed money for his family and had to scramble for it.

Status

My status concern overlapped with my appreciation concern. *Beyond Reason* distinguishes between general status (a person's standing in the community) and particular status (a person's standing or expertise in a certain area or activity). I probably wanted Mr. Hassan to show respect for what I thought was my high general status and for my particular status as a negotiation expert and an urbane and worldly traveler.

I do not know whether Mr. Hassan experienced a status concern, though he might have wanted recognition of his particular status as an expert on Luxor, or parts of it, and on the local customs about fees for carriage rides. Maybe he was a leader among carriage drivers. I imagine he also did not want to be seen as a cheat, a severe diminishment of his dignity, even if he was trying to squeeze me for more money.

Responding to the Situation Through the Core Concerns

Had I been aware of the possible core concerns in this situation, what might have happened?

I might have understood Mr. Hassan better if I had considered his motivations and emotions. Such understanding would have made it harder for me to dislike him and easier for me to care about his core concerns or other interests. I might have been able to promote positive emotions in each of us by, say, building affiliation, expressing appreciation, or respecting status, as Fisher and Shapiro suggest.[7] For instance, I could have inquired about Mr. Hassan's life and family or about Luxor; maybe this would have met his core concerns for appreciation, affiliation, and status. Perhaps that would have fostered positive or at least congenial interactions that might have led to a nicer evening—and less guilt for me. I might have wound up paying less, but probably not. The resulting positive emotions, however, could have increased the likelihood that either or both of us would have paid more attention to the interests of all concerned. I might have generated options to satisfy my active, unsatisfied core concerns as well as my interests. Finally, perhaps I could have suspended or de-prioritized some of my core concerns—such as appreciation or status—or sought other ways to satisfy them.

Now we have seen how I might have understood and addressed the situation in Luxor through the position-based, interest-based, and core-concerns negotiation models. That prepares us for the three conversations, which the next chapter introduces and applies to the Luxor situation.

CHAPTER 10

THE THREE CONVERSATIONS IN THE LUXOR CARRIAGE-FEE NEGOTIATION

This chapter offers a fourth negotiation focus and model, from the book *Difficult Conversations*.[1] That book provides perspectives and methods for managing conflict that complement and support the skillful use of positions, interests, and core concerns. *Difficult Conversations* proposes that we should view every difficult conversation (which includes many negotiations) as if it were composed of three conversations, which I call the What Happened Conversation,[2] the Emotions Conversation,[3] and the Identity Conversation.[4]

The difficult-conversations model, as I conceptualize it, consists of three primary strategies or tactics:

- Identify and describe, internally, the three conversations that have actually taken place or are taking place.

- Reframe these three conversations, (internally) to develop more realistic or more helpful versions.

- Conduct a "Learning Conversation" in which the participants try to understand, rather than persuade, one another. This should lead to further reframing, which, in turn, should help the participants try to solve the problem that they wish to address.

The first two steps are mainly about understanding—even though they sometimes lead automatically to resolution. You can take these steps on your own, without help from the other party. The third step, the Learning Conversation, includes substantial elements of understanding and responding. It requires that both parties participate.

How might the *Difficult Conversations* model have helped me understand and respond more wisely to the situation in Luxor?

Understanding the Situation Through the Three Conversations

The What Happened Conversation

The What Happened Conversation concerns what the parties think happened and how they understand it.[5] Who did what? Why—or what did they intend? Who is to blame? What *should* they have done?

Identify and Describe (Internally) the What Happened Conversation

Mr. Hassan and I conducted an external conversation about what happened. We disagreed about the fee on which we had agreed; the denomination of the note that I had handed to him; and, of course, whether he had cheated me, or vice versa.

The external and internal aspects of the What Happened Conversation frequently interact. My internal What Happened Conversation *might* have sounded something like this:

> This man is deliberately cheating me, using lies, sleight-of-hand, and intimidation. This proves he behaved badly. I bargain only because it is the custom here. I am spending a fortune on this trip! I can't just pay everyone whatever they ask! Even if he is poor and needs the money, he *shouldn't cheat* me. It's okay to negotiate, but once people reach an agreement, they should stick to it.

Mr. Hassan's internal What Happened Conversation, based on a huge dose of speculation, might have been a near-polar opposite:

> This rich American is selfish and rude. He has money, but he is unwilling to pay a fair price; so in order to support my family, I have to trick him into behaving properly. I do this all the time, as do *all* the other drivers; it is the only way I can survive. Besides, most of our customers like to haggle.

Reframe the What Happened Conversation

Difficult Conversations suggests several ways to achieve a deeper and perhaps more helpful understanding of the facts:

Question the Truth Assumption

In the What Happened Conversation, each participant often thinks that *they* know what happened but the other participant does not. I had such a belief in Luxor and held on to it for decades. In fact, I had never imagined the possibility that I did not know the truth about what happened in Luxor—until recently—when my friend and colleague Professor Melody Daily, who had been reviewing the manuscript for this book, said:

> It's also possible that [Mr. Hassan] was not trying to trick you. Earlier, you said that you "thought" he had agreed to a total fare of 10 EGP, but perhaps the language barrier caused the two of you to have different understandings. It's also possible that you actually

handed him a 50 Piaster note. He might have believed that you
were trying to cheat him.

I was stunned at those suggestions, especially because they might be correct.

Forget Blame and Identify Contributions

In the What Happened Conversation, each party typically blames the
other. *Difficult Conversations* suggests that, instead, we identify
"contributions"—what a person did that in some way made the event
possible, even if they were not blameworthy or culpable. In trying to identify
contributions, we should ignore fault or culpability. Let's say, for instance,
that you are driving through an intersection, observing the rules of the road,
when another driver crosses the intersection and collides with your car,
damaging it severely. In most U.S. trial courts, if you sued the other driver,
they would be deemed negligent and found legally responsible for your
damages. But you also "contributed" to the accident, even though you are
not "at fault," just by being where you were.

In that sense, how did I contribute to the Luxor incident? The answer
is not entirely clear, but here are some possibilities: I insisted on a fare lower
than Mr. Hassan expected, and perhaps below the going rate. I stuck rigidly
to my position and did not propose an intermediate price. I neglected to carry
a variety of Egyptian notes and coins. I gave way to my emotions. If I had
become aware of such contributions, during or shortly after the incident, my
anger at Mr. Hassan might have declined (at least I would like to think so),
and perhaps we all would have had a nicer evening.

Separate Impact and Intent

If you do not receive an invitation to your friend Amina's wedding, you
might assume that she intended to hurt your feelings. *Difficult Conversations*
would urge you to look for other reasons, possibly benign, that might explain
her behavior.[6] Perhaps she gave in to family pressures to invite only relatives.
Or maybe she thought you could not afford the airfare or a gift, and she did
not want to embarrass you or force you to overspend your limited budget.
It's also possible that a mistake—by Amina, a relative, or the post office—
actually prevented an invitation from reaching you.

Similarly, because I felt humiliated and offended by Mr. Hassan's
behavior, I probably assumed that he intended to humiliate and offend me.
As I think of it now, however, he likely had no such purpose, but simply
wanted to collect as much money as he could—a reasonable way for him to
deal with his circumstances.

My negative judgments about Mr. Hassan might have derived from what psychologists call the "fundamental attribution error"—the tendency to attribute the behavior of others to their own internal processes or their character, rather than to the situation, and to attribute our own problematic behavior to circumstances.[7] If you are late for our meeting, for instance, I might think you are lazy or inconsiderate. But when I am late, it is always due to circumstances I cannot control—I stepped into a hole full of wet concrete, or a waiter spilled a tray of pasta on my new suit. Likewise, when Mr. Hassan insisted that I pay him 30 EGP, lied about the denomination of the bill I gave him (or so I believed), and then asked for a tip, I blamed his character, not circumstances (such as his apparent poverty, my apparent wealth, and local custom), for all of that. Implicit bias, discussed in Chapters 4 and 7, may have contributed as well.

The Identity Conversation

The Identity Conversation is primarily internal; it concerns what we think the events in question say about us,[8] and it often incorporates "core identity" questions such as "Am I competent?" "Am I a good person?" "Am I worthy of love?"[9] What we think the events say about us can also impact any of our core concerns, interests, and positions. Obviously, our Identity Conversation depends a good deal on how we understand and interpret the What Happened Conversation.

Recognize and Describe (Internally) the Identity Conversation

My internal Identity Conversation *might* have gone something like this:

> This man does not respect me. He does not realize who and what I am—a distinguished professional, competent and compassionate. How *dare* he treat *me* like that! On the other hand, maybe I am not as good a negotiator as I thought. In fact, I am a big phony, and always have been. Casey and Andrew will now think less of me. Maybe I am not much of a father, either, if I can't show my son how to negotiate in this kind of situation. I can't even teach him how to avoid getting cheated.

Mr. Hassan's Identity Conversation *might* have run along similar lines:

> This man does not respect me. He does not realize who I am—a hard-working father and family man, an expert on Luxor, laboring long hours every day and night to feed my family. It crushes me to constantly haggle with these rich Americans who think they can

come in and control my world. At least I can hold my own at bargaining and show him that, on these streets, I'm the boss.

Reframe the Identity Conversation

In my Identity Conversation, I suddenly doubted my established beliefs about who and what I was, so I lost confidence, composure, and balance. From the *Difficult Conversations* perspective, I had an "identity quake." In particular, I questioned my identities as a capable negotiator and as a father. *Difficult Conversations* suggests that if we have an all-or-nothing view of an identity, it becomes vulnerable to contrary information. If, for instance, you think you are a "fabulous" trapeze artist or baritone, and other people express contrary views (perhaps your superior at the circus or the opera says you are not good enough to stay on the payroll), you may flip to the opposite extreme and think yourself a "terrible" trapeze artist or baritone. You may lose your equilibrium if you have to choose between fabulous and terrible.[10]

In Luxor, I might have recovered my balance by following some of the suggestions in *Difficult Conversations,* the most central of which is to "complexify your identity." Instead of rigidly holding the idea that you are perfect in some area, you should acknowledge—internally and, when appropriate, externally—that you make mistakes. Thus, I might have asked myself questions such as these:

Am I *always* good at negotiating? What about the time I paid $200 for a handmade vase that I could have gotten for $20, and which I did not like?

Do I *always* behave gracefully abroad? What about the time in British Columbia when I locked myself out of my hotel room at 2:00 a.m.—wearing only undershorts and a T-shirt?

Do I *always* behave as a good father would? What about my callous willingness to embarrass my adolescent son in Brussels in order to keep my head warm and maintain my sense of style;[11] my self-righteous refusal to follow sports;[12] my preoccupation with time during Andrew's childhood?[13]

The idea here is to accept that you are neither perfect nor completely incompetent in any sphere—nor is anyone else—and that you make mistakes. If you can do this, you will have less need to protect your identities, and you will become more receptive to feedback, regardless of whether you requested it. In daily life, we see many examples of people who forfeit opportunities because they are strongly attached to certain identities and go to great lengths to maintain them: the employee who does not ask for help in dealing with a problem; the boss who will not brook any suggestion that his opinion is incorrect; or the seventy-five-year-old who cheats at golf—even though his companions know it.

If I had perceived my identities more realistically, I might have suffered a much less forceful identity quake—or none at all. And had my thinking slowed down enough, I might have considered *why* I cared so much about what Mr. Hassan thought of me. Then I could have decided to stop worrying about maintaining what I thought were my identities.

We also should complexify our sense of the other person. For instance, I might have thought cheating me was bad behavior, and so Mr. Hassan was a bad person. It was a huge leap from bad behavior to the bad-person label (even if I thought that concept was useful, which I do not). I could have reframed my understanding of Mr. Hassan by, say, recognizing that he had his own three conversations as well as interests and core concerns.

The Emotions Conversation

The Emotions Conversation, as you might suspect, consists of the emotions that the negotiators experience. These emotions frequently result from the negotiators' interpretation of events in the What Happened Conversation and the Identity Conversation.[14]

Identify and Describe (Internally) the Emotions Conversation

My emotions included anger, frustration, embarrassment, sadness, fear, and perhaps even a smattering of hatred.

I assume, without much confidence, that Mr. Hassan also experienced anger, or at least annoyance, and perhaps some of the other emotions I felt. Perhaps he also had some fun or satisfaction in teasing and manipulating me, as well as some joy and satisfaction in "winning." And I realize that Mr. Hassan, as a general matter, probably lacked the time, energy, or inclination to worry about such things. He struggled to earn a living, while I enjoyed a luxurious life that allowed me to obsess and write about my emotions and the like.

Reframe the Emotions Conversation

Difficult Conversations suggests several methods to reframe the Emotions Conversations and so understand them differently. The first is to acknowledge the strong feelings that you are experiencing, whether positive or negative, and try to imagine the feelings of your counterpart, as illustrated above. Then look for sources of these emotions.

In Luxor, my What Happened and Identity Conversations combined to produce strong negative emotions. These emotions torpedoed my curiosity and ability to notice or care about interests and core concerns. As a result, I blamed Mr. Hassan, attributed bad intentions to him, and, perhaps, assumed that he was a bad person. All of that pushed me toward positional adversarial negotiation.

Responding to the Luxor Situation Through the Three Conversations and the Learning Conversation

The final steps in the *Difficult Conversations* model include preparing for and, if appropriate, conducting a "Learning Conversation." Preparation consists of trying to understand and reframe the three conversations, as shown above, and then planning what you would do in an actual Learning Conversation, were you to have one.

The Learning Conversation

In a Learning Conversation, the parties do not try to persuade. Instead, they endeavor to understand, primarily by listening, deeply and openly, to each other and to themselves. The actual conversation can help you and your counterpart more thoroughly comprehend what has happened, internally and externally, and, as a result, negotiate more wisely.

Difficult Conversations puts forward a batch of thoughtful suggestions about how to engage in a Learning Conversation, and I urge you to consult them.[15] Here are a few high points:

- Begin with the "third story," the kind a mediator might tell, from a neutral perspective.
- Jointly review the three conversations; listen carefully and openly.
- Problem solve: reframe, develop options to meet interests and concerns, use objective standards.

It would not have been feasible or appropriate, however, to actually conduct a Learning Conversation about the Luxor incident. A Learning Conversation requires both parties' involvement and takes some time, so it is more frequently suitable in conflicts between people with important, long-term, intense, or complex relationships, such as Pedro and Billy in the *Shoe-Dog Split.*

Preparing for a Learning Conversation in a Conflict of Your Own

To give yourself a better understanding of the three-conversations approach and how you might use its focus and model, bring to mind a conflict in which you have been involved in the past or in which you are currently engaged. The conflict should be meaningful to you, should primarily concern you and one other person, and should include a significant emotional aspect. Then complete Appendix Exercise C-1, the *Difficult Conversations* Preparation Worksheet.

REVIEW OF SECTION C IN LIGHT VERSE

C. BACK TO NEGOTIATION: THE THREE CONVERSATIONS

For more insight on tough situations,
Consider the three conversations.
Facts and feelings, you can see.
The third one is identity.

This model's for helping you learn
From those you might otherwise spurn,
To avoid attributions erroneous,
And seek some solutions harmonious.

REVIEW OF SECTIONS A, B, AND C

Sections A, B, and C present negotiation and mindfulness and explain how mindfulness can improve our capacity to negotiate skillfully.

Negotiation

Section A introduced negotiation focuses based on positions, interests, and core concerns. Section C added the Three-Conversations focus. These four negotiation approaches are related in several ways. Box C-1 presents them in their order of accessibility.

Box C-1. The Pyramid of Negotiation Focuses

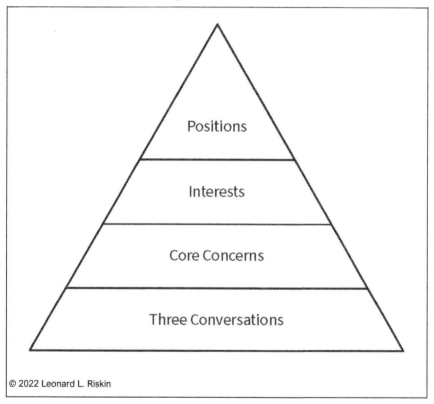

Positions

Interests

Core Concerns

Three Conversations

© 2022 Leonard L. Riskin

It typically is easiest for us to be aware of positions, then interests, then core concerns, and then the three conversations. In real life, of course, we may perceive them in different orders at various times.

Depicting the relationships is tough, in part because they overlap and sometimes are not distinct. In Luxor, for instance, I had an *interest* in being treated fairly. We also could call that a *core concern*, such as status or autonomy. And my *identity conversation* probably was entangled with my *positions*, *interests*, and *core concerns*.

Box C-2 displays the same four negotiation focuses and models, with their strategies and tactics for understanding and for responding to conflict.

Box C-2. Positions, Interests, Core-Concerns & Three-Conversations in Negotiation

Level & Focus	A Specific Model	Model's Components for Understanding Conflict	Model's Components for Responding to Conflict
Level 1 **Positions**	Model: Position-based (Extreme)	Focus on positions, rather than interests. Define the problem to be addressed narrowly. Assume that any gain for one party means a loss for the other.	Mislead other side as to your bottom line and situation. *Examples:* • Learn other side's bottom line and situation. • Use anchoring through extreme demands. • Assert positions; undermine the other's positions. • Make few and small concessions. • Persuade other side to compromise or to agree with your position. • Walk away or threaten to do so.
Level 2 **Interests**	Model: Getting to Yes	Focus on interests rather than positions. Be soft on the people but hard on the problem. Understand "the problem" broadly. Expand the pie.	Seek to accommodate the interests of both parties. Be soft on people and hard on problem. Generate options before deciding. Use objective standards.

Level & Focus	A Specific Model	Model's Components for Understanding Conflict	Model's Components for Responding to Conflict
			Develop your BATNA and measure proposed agreements against it.
Level 3 Core Concerns	Model: Beyond Reason	Observe both parties' behaviors and emotions. Trace your emotions to the core concerns—appreciation, affiliation, autonomy, status, and role—that may have produced those emotions. Trace your counterpart's emotions to the core concerns—appreciation, affiliation, autonomy, status, and role—that may have produced those emotions.	Address unsatisfied core concerns in order to promote positive emotions in the other party; for example, express appreciation, build affiliation, foster autonomy, acknowledge status, and create fulfilling roles. Address your own unsatisfied core concerns by, for instance, helping your counterpart understand them or by reframing them. With the benefit of positive emotions, negotiate, using core concerns and interests.
Level 4 Three Conversations	Model: Difficult Conversations	Understand the three conversations that took place: about facts, emotions and identity. Reframe these three conversations, or at least your own three conversations. Prepare for a learning conversation.	Conduct a learning conversation with the other party, if feasible and appropriate. Jointly review the three conversations. Listen carefully and openly. Problem-solve: Reframe, develop options to meet interests and concerns, use objective standards.

© 2022 Leonard L. Riskin

Mindfulness and Negotiation

After presenting negotiation focuses and models based on positions, interests, and core concerns, Section A informs us that—even if you master all of its concepts, strategies, tactics, and skills—sometimes you may be unable to use them wisely or effectively. This inability may result from any of five obstacles: automatic, habitual ways of thinking, feeling, and behaving; self-centered perspectives; inability to manage emotions; inadequate social skills; and inability to manage your focus and awareness. Section B explains mindfulness, and shows how it can help us overcome the five obstacles to skillful negotiation. Section C serves up a fourth negotiation approach, based on the three conversations. Although I did not mention this in Section C, the same five obstacles threaten our ability to use that approach, and mindfulness can help us transcend these obstacles in that context as well.

But mindfulness itself is vulnerable to the same five obstacles that it can overcome.

Fortunately, however, negotiation knowledge and skills can support mindfulness in many ways. I will deal with a small sample. To begin, knowledge of negotiation theory and practices can help us better understand ourselves and others. Such understanding allows us to feel compassion, empathy, and concern for ourselves and others. Negotiation also provides methods to act on such compassion and empathy and concern, for instance, by using appropriate elements of the four negotiation focuses or their models.

Negotiation theory and practice also can help us understand what's going on by giving or offering different lenses through which to view aspects of the situation or problem and possibilities for improving the situation. Such ideas make whatever is going on seem more interesting and potentially useful; as a result, we can pay attention more easily.

Those same lenses can help us gain insights that can promote certain other aspects or aspirations of mindfulness. Consider the Shoe-Dog Split, the dispute between Pedro and Billy. If Pedro sees that situation through the lens of positions, he might get stuck on Billy's position that he will not leave the firm unless Pedro pays him an amount that any fair-minded person would find outrageous. That might intensify Pedro's disdain for Billy. On the other hand, if Pedro understands the idea of underlying interests in negotiation, he might see Billy's need for connection with his clients (in part because he is lonely) as reasonable. Similarly, if Pedro could realize that Billy's position and interest were supported by core concerns for affiliation, appreciation, and status, his antipathy toward Billy might diminish, which might help foster the compassion and caring for others that are elements of mindfulness. Pedro might also notice the role of his own core concerns in this situation.[1] And if Pedro could see Billy's behavior through the lens of the three conversations, he might reconsider some of his beliefs and assumptions about Billy. Simply being aware of the idea of three conversations might help Pedro develop understanding and compassion for Billy.

Positions, Interests, Core Concerns, and Three Conversations in a Conflict of Your Own

To get a better sense of the interrelationships among the four negotiation focuses and their models, bring to mind a meaningful conflict in which you are or were involved. It should be primarily between you and one other person and should include a significant emotional aspect. It could be one of the conflicts you worked with in Exercises A-1, A-2, or A-3 in the Appendix. Then complete the form Appendix Exercise C-2, Understanding Positions, Interests, Core Concerns and Three Conversations in a Conflict of Your Own.

The four negotiation focuses have many links and synergies that may not fit neatly into the chart in Exercise C-2. We could consider these relationships in a linear fashion. In Luxor, for instance, my *position* about the fees was based on my *interests* in educating my son, enhancing my own self-esteem, and saving money; these *interests* might have arisen from my *core concerns*; and these *core concerns* might have emanated from my *three conversations*. But in fact, any of these phenomena could interact with any of the others, in any order. For instance, any of the *three conversations* can activate—or result from—*positions*, *interests*, or *core concerns*. My internal identity conversation, in which I thought Mr. Hassan had no respect for me, impaired my *core concern* for appreciation. So, I wanted to earn appreciation—from Mr. Hassan and from my wife and son. I mistakenly assumed that I could do so by defeating him, in some sense, and that the best way to do that was to assert inflexible positions and stick with them. Of course, most of these thoughts, emotions, and behaviors resulted from fast thinking or automatic reactions. And, at the time, I did not understand much, if any, of this.

Understanding such complex thoughts, behaviors, and emotions in your own difficult negotiations or problematic situations should help you avoid rigidly following a certain model, and, instead, consider what is most appropriate or wise in the precise circumstances. And remember that, in some situations, you will be better off drawing on strategies and tactics of more than one model. "If you understand something only in one way, then you don't really understand it at all," said the late MIT cognitive scientist Marvin Minsky. "The secret of what anything means to us depends on how we've connected it to all other things we know."[2]

INTERNAL FAMILY SYSTEMS (IFS), THE THIRD DOMAIN

Well, that was easy! You have now learned a good deal about the first two domains of mindful conflict management—negotiation and mindfulness—and how they can reinforce and support one another.

This section presents the third domain, Internal Family Systems (IFS), and shows its synergies with negotiation and mindfulness. Before you plunge in, I suggest that you take a deep breath and open your mind. You might also benefit from watching the movie, *Inside Out*, or at least a trailer,[1] which will give you a partial sense of IFS—as well as abundant opportunities to laugh.

IFS differs from the four negotiation focuses and their models in two general ways. First, it deals more extensively and rigorously with internal aspects of conflict. Second, and more fundamentally, it rests on a different understanding of the nature of the human mind or psyche. All four negotiation approaches and their models generally regard a person as a unit, what some psychologists call a "unitary self." IFS, instead, is grounded on a "multiplicity" concept, specifically, the idea that the mind or psyche contains two fundamentally different kinds of entities—Parts (a.k.a. Sub-Personalities) and a Self—and that these entities interact as a system and influence or manage aspects of internal conflict and their relationship with external conflict.

CHAPTER 11

INTERNAL FAMILY SYSTEMS: THE BASICS

Previous sections have dealt primarily with conflicts (or problematic situations) involving two or more individual human beings—that is, external conflicts. In such contexts, it is ordinarily easy to identify the participants. But if we wish to imagine such processes operating *within* an individual human being, recognizing the players is not so simple. Who or what is in conflict with whom or what? Who or what is negotiating, mediating, or adjudicating? To answer such questions, we need a theory of the mind or psyche that includes components that could engage with one another in negotiations or other conflict-management processes.[1]

Countless theories, concepts, and models of the mind or psyche or self include some idea of multiplicity. This chapter briefly surveys a few of them and then presents Internal Family Systems (IFS), the model that I have found most useful.

Multiplicity of Selves, Minds, or Personalities

The idea that a person might have more than one self, mind, or personality is ingrained in common parlance and everyday life.[2] Most people feel and behave differently in different settings, of course. The late John Haynes, a pioneer in family mediation, described an experience with this phenomenon. When he was in his fifties, he flew from the U.S. to London to accept an international award for his contributions to mediation. As he received the award before a large crowd and basked in the praise, he became quite pleased with himself; he felt big, powerful, mature, and important. After the conference, Haynes rented a car and drove to Wales to visit his mother. During the drive, he felt as though his size and age steadily diminished until, when he pulled up at his mother's home, he felt about four years old and three feet tall.

Consider whether your own feelings and behavior vary depending on whether you are attending a holiday dinner with your in-laws, updating classmates at your high school reunion, watching football in a bar, strolling through an art museum, or dancing at a rock concert. Such variations may become even more frequent when we communicate on social media, where we may present more varied and elaborate online identities.

The notion of multiple selves finds expression in many fields, including poetry, literature, philosophy, religion,[3] and neuroscience.[4] Here are a few examples from economics and psychology.

Quite a number of economists have embraced—or at least discussed—versions of the multiple selves idea. Adam Smith, for instance, talked about resolving conflict between "two selves": one governed by "the passions," the other acting as an "impartial spectator."[5] Other economists have employed the notion of different selves at different times in our lives. Does our eighteen-year-old self (who wants to party more than study) have an obligation to our eighty-one-year-old self (who would like to have a substantial pension)? This concept of intertemporal selves has led to discussions about how someone's "present self" can "bind" a "future self" by eliminating or reducing temptations or the possibility of indulging in them.[6]

Western psychology has provided a large and sophisticated array of models that include units of the self or personality that might be capable of negotiation-like interactions.[7] Many of these models are ancestors, cousins, or more distant relatives of IFS. Here is a small sample, in roughly chronological order: Freud's psychoanalytic model of the mind describes tugs between the Id (which consists of the basic drives of hostility, aggression, and sex) and the Superego (the strict, internalized conscience). The Ego mediates such conflicts.[8] Carl Jung describes "human figures" that appear in one's dreams, such as "the *shadow*, the *wise old man*, the *child* (including the child hero), and the *mother* ('Primordial Mother' and 'Earth Mother')."[9] The Italian psychoanalyst Roberto Assagioli developed "psychosynthesis," a model that includes a self and subpersonalities.[10]

It would not be much of a stretch to suggest that cognitive-behavioral therapy (CBT)—as elaborated in the work of Albert Ellis and Aaron Beck—implies disagreement between or among various cognitions in a person's mind, with CBT replacing negative thoughts and schemas[11] with healthier, more adaptive ones. Thus, we could say that CBT deals with multiple cognitive parts of the mind.[12] Steven Pinker refers to "Inner Demons"[13] and to the "Better Angels of Our Nature," using Abraham Lincoln's term.[14] Psychologist Daniel Kahneman speaks of the "remembering self" and the "experiencing self."[15] Max Bazerman and his colleagues have described the difference between the "want self" and the "should self,"[16] and, because of the power of the "want self," they suggest dealing with internal conflict through a negotiation framework.[17]

Many other potentially useful multiplicity models of the mind have been proposed. These include structural metaphors other than a family, such as a parliament;[18] a jury;[19] an orchestra;[20] a computer, its software, and its operator;[21] an organization;[22] a committee;[23] and a "team of rivals."[24]

Internal Family Systems (IFS), developed by the family therapist Richard C. Schwartz, is one of the primary contemporary models of marital and family therapy,[25] and it is taught in graduate programs in that field; thousands of practicing therapists have trained in or studied it. It has been employed in a variety of other arenas,[26] including elementary education,[27] corrections,[28] organizational change consultation,[29] conflict management between and within ethnic groups,[30] and medicine and health care (e.g., making medical decisions,[31] managing arthritis,[32] healing trauma,[33] administering medication,[34] managing pain,[35] and doing breathwork[36]). In recent years, IFS has also been introduced into training, practice, and scholarship in negotiation[37] and mediation.[38]

Internal Family Systems (IFS): Components and Structure

Schwartz based *Internal* Family Systems Therapy on *Family* Systems Therapy, which rests on the idea that individuals are constrained by their external family systems, and, accordingly, that a therapist must frequently work with such systems.[39] In creating IFS, Schwartz integrated Family Systems Therapy with his own multiplicity model of the mind. In fact, he developed the notion of IFS from what his clients told him during Family Systems Therapy. It's easy to confuse or conflate the two.[40] Schwartz describes IFS as both a "theory of mind and an approach to psychotherapy."[41]

The IFS model of the mind or psyche contains two principal kinds of components: "Parts," of which there are many; and a "Self," of which there is just one. IFS regards the Self and the Parts as an internal family system.

Box D-1. Internal Family Systems (IFS) Model of the Mind: Self and Parts

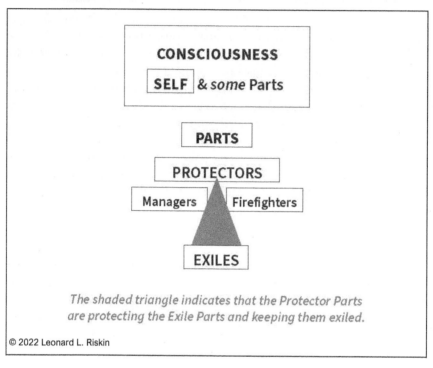

CONSCIOUSNESS

SELF *& some* Parts

PARTS

PROTECTORS

Managers   Firefighters

EXILES

The shaded triangle indicates that the Protector Parts are protecting the Exile Parts and keeping them exiled.

© 2022 Leonard L. Riskin

Consciousness controls how a person understands and deals with conflict (and just about everything else). And the processes of understanding and responding to conflict are determined by who or what is in Consciousness at a given time.

Self is always in Consciousness—at least to some extent—and one or more Parts are almost always in Consciousness, although which Parts are present at a particular time varies. The Self is not a Part. The Self's principal qualities are curiosity, calm, confidence, connectedness, clarity, creativity, courage and compassion.[42] My Self does not prefer me to you, and vice versa. The goal of IFS therapy is Self-Leadership—that the Self should lead the Parts—as that would yield the best processes and outcomes.

Parts are like little people inside us, with their own personalities, preferences, and values; they want to benefit the person and generally think they have specific responsibilities. My Parts typically prefer me to you; your Parts typically prefer you to me.

Protector Parts are akin to high-level managers in large human organizations, such as corporations, foundations, and government agencies.

Some have responsibilities for one or more functions, such as protecting the person's health or reputation or security.

Exile Parts are sheltered from certain kinds of information and excluded from consciousness by Protectors, for reasons explained below.

Now for some details.

Let's begin with Parts, which are easier to explain and to understand, and turn to the Self later.

Parts

Psychologist John Rowan defines Subpersonalities (another name for Parts) as "[s]emi-permanent and semi-autonomous regions of the personality capable of acting as a person."[43] Parts "are best considered internal people of different ages, talents, and temperaments," says Richard Schwartz.[44] I have Parts, for example, that I call "Professor," "Befuddled," "Inner Critic," "Cheerleader," "Warrior," "Worrier,"[45] and, believe it or not, "James Bond, 007"—though this one has been quiet for decades.

Schwartz identifies and explains two kinds of Parts: Protectors and Exiles. The Protectors maintain our internal narratives about our identities. And each has a particular function or responsibility. Protectors will "exile" other Parts in order to limit their influence or their access to certain kinds of information or activities.

Parts are "partial" in two senses of the word. First, as mentioned, they typically intend to benefit "their" person: speaking generally, my Parts favor me, and yours favor you. Second, they are incomplete: they operate on limited and frequently out-of-date information about the person's age, abilities, and situation. This is because Parts come with us into the world and are present at birth, either manifest or dormant, and are there to help us survive and thrive. In other words, it's the nature of the mind to have Parts from birth.

Traumas and difficult situations, however, can freeze some Parts in time, inject them with extreme beliefs and emotions (burdens), including the notion that they must run things because Self didn't protect the system. All of these events force them out of their naturally valuable states into roles that they're not designed for and, while these roles might have been needed during the trauma, later they are anachronistically extreme and sometimes destructive. To clarify, these Parts are "forced" into these roles or states in the same sense that children in dysfunctional external families are "forced" to take on parentified roles—such as caring for or feeding younger children—because the actual parents are not fulfilling these functions. Most of the young Parts who feel the emotional pain or shame or terror of the trauma become the Exiles who are contained and protected by the Protectors.

Each Part itself has many characteristics of an individual person—attitudes, beliefs, goals, aversions, and even an age. Parts can conflict or collaborate with each other, just as individual people do. They can learn, grow, and change, and they all want useful roles. As we will see below, Parts can have positions, interests, and core concerns; they can engage in the three conversations; they can argue; and they can negotiate.

Each Protector Part usually has responsibility for protecting or containing one or more specific Exile Parts.[46]

IFS divides Protectors into two categories: "Managers" and "Firefighters." The Manager Parts are analogous to "managers" in many human organizations, such as corporations, government agencies, and universities. In such organizations, managers are responsible for various functions that are necessary for the organization to stay afloat and pursue its goals. In a large business organization, for instance, these functions would include marketing, sales, production, distribution, finance, human resources, law, and security.

IFS Managers have comparable responsibilities. "[M]anagers ... monitor how you're coming across to parents, bosses, and others you depend on," Schwartz explains.

> They scan for cracks in your masks of invulnerability, friendliness, and perfection, and compare you unfavorably to cultural icons or to the Joneses next door or in the next office. Managers interpret the world to you and create the narratives you live by. They are the authors and enforcers of the story you have about yourself that is called your identity. Managers are your reality makers .... Your Managers suck in the emotions and beliefs of significant others and the culture at large. They are what some psychotherapies call your "false self" and what some spiritual traditions refer to as your "ego that keeps you attached to the world."[47]

As this illustrates, IFS Managers ordinarily plan ahead to avoid, prevent, or manage problems. In contrast, Firefighters in your Internal Family System, like firefighters in most communities, take action primarily after a problem has already arisen, and frequently resort to desperate measures. But in large organizations, the missions of management and firefighting often are carried out by the same management organization or individuals.

Some Exiles come into being when Protectors exclude other Parts from certain activities and from Consciousness in order to limit their awareness, influence, or power. And the Protectors do this for two primary reasons: to shield those Exiles from whatever they most fear (and which might prompt them to panic and take control), and to protect the person from dangers that would result if the Exile did exercise control. Within human organizations, some individuals are treated in similar fashion for similar reasons.

In Box D-1, between the Protectors (Managers and Firefighters) and Exiles, you will notice a shaded triangle: it signifies that the Managers and Firefighters try to control and protect the Exiles. But they act in different circumstances, using different strategies and tactics. Managers tend to intervene *before* the Exile is aroused. If the Exile is nonetheless aroused, however, it may create an emergency situation, that is, one that endangers the person or an identity that is supported by one or more Parts. Firefighters respond to emergencies, usually becoming active only *after* the Exile (or something else) has created one, and so they may push for extreme behavior, such as excessive drinking or self-abuse. In short, Managers are proactive; if a healthy Manager is concerned about an Exile who has a desperate fear of rejection, it might direct the person to prepare extra hard for a job interview. A Firefighter, however, tries to protect or restrain the Exile, once it is aroused, at almost any cost. A Firefighter might, for instance, press the person to avoid the interview by, say, developing a psychosomatic illness, watching a movie, or getting drunk.[48]

Each Part has distinctive perspectives and functions, usually associated with a specific role or need. One or more Parts can take over at a particular time, often without our awareness or consent. In a given situation, it is important that the most appropriate Parts have the most influence. For instance, your Trial Lawyer Part (and you need not be a lawyer to have one) might do well in settings that call for advocacy. But when you go home to your actual four-year-old child, who had a rough day at preschool and needs comforting, a compassionate Part would do a better job.

Similarly, when you negotiate with a Subaru dealer for a new Outback, it *may* be wise to recruit an assertive Part, assuming it would work hard to get a low price—and that's what you want. But if you are negotiating with your fiancée over how much to spend for wedding invitations, as did the George Costanza character in the TV situation comedy *Seinfeld*,[49] another Part might be more suitable. (George bought the cheapest invitations available, which turned out to have toxic glue on their envelope flaps; his fiancée, Susan, licked the glue on the envelopes while preparing to mail them. She died as a result; and George mourned, but only when he learned that he would miss out on a life of great wealth and luxury, including a Manhattan town house.)

The decision to buy the cheapest cards came from a stingy, short-sighted Part of George.

Parts often polarize while attempting to protect the person or to exile or protect other Parts. People experiencing such inner conflicts feel both timid and brave, introverted and extroverted, stingy and generous. A person might have Parts that are racist and others that are anti-racist.[50] Polarizations can become so intense that people experience dissociative identity disorders (DID), formerly known as multiple personality disorders).[51]

The "Self"

The Self is of a wholly different nature than the Parts. It is essentially impartial, and characterized by "compassion, calmness, clarity, curiosity, confidence, courage, creativity and connectedness."[52] It "comes fully equipped to lead and does not have to develop through stages,"[53] says Schwartz, who also suggests it is the "true self." It is a center of awareness, which—if sufficiently present in consciousness—can observe the Parts and help them work together for the welfare of the person and others. The Self does not prefer one Part over another, nor does it prefer one person over another. My Self does not care more about me than about you, and vice versa. For that reason, Parts frequently fear that the Self will not do what is best for the person.

In IFS, the entities that are present in Consciousness at any given time control the person's perceptions, thoughts, and behaviors. The Self is essentially always present in Consciousness. Usually, however, one or more Parts are also present in Consciousness. In such situations, the Self[54] and one or more Parts are "blended,"[55] and the Part or Parts usually lead.

To the extent that the Self is in charge, the person sees the world through the perspective of the Self, and the Self is theoretically able to influence the behavior of the Parts. Such leadership *should* produce harmony among the Parts, foster appropriate behavior, and reduce suffering. Self has the *capacity* to know which Part or Parts are, or wish to be, in control at a given time and—at least in theory, although not at every moment—to affect the degree and nature of the influence that a Part or Parts exert.[56]

In order to get along, sometimes Parts need extra assistance, of the kind that a mediator, counselor, or leader might provide to people in conflict.[57] In other words, the Self might be able to provide mediation (facilitated negotiation), counseling, or similar services. If not enough of the Self is "present," a Self-like Part or an "outside" third party—such as a psychotherapist or coach—could do so. For example, a psychotherapist could work with Parts, sometimes directly and sometimes through the client.

CHAPTER 12

MANAGING THE LUXOR CARRIAGE SITUATION WITH IFS

If I had been skilled in IFS and able to use it, I might have understood and responded to the situation in Luxor more wisely and left all concerned happier.

Understanding the Situation Retrospectively Through IFS: What Happened and Why?

Several aspects of "me" *might have* engaged in relevant internal processes. In addition to the Self, certain Protector Parts and the Exiles they sought to shelter were theoretically available, in the sense that they would have cared or worried about this situation:

- **Gandhi, a Compassionate Manager Part**

Gandhi cares about and feels connected with other people and with me. This is a "healthy" Part, and it *tends* to embrace many of the qualities of the Self; in other words, it is a Self-like Part.

- **Big Shot, a law-professor-man-of-the-world-expert-on-negotiation Manager Part**

Big Shot wants to protect this storyline about one of my identities. In Luxor he was protecting **Tiny**, a very insecure Exile who *was burdened*, when I was young, with beliefs that I am incompetent, inferior, and vulnerable.

- **Mr. Stingy, a security-oriented Manager Part**

Mr. Stingy believes that his principal responsibility or interest is building and maintaining financial security for my family and me. He also was trying to protect **Penny Pincher.**

- **Penny Pincher, an Exile Part**

Penny Pincher, who fears poverty, is even stingier than Mr. Stingy and would give *nothing* to anyone unless it seemed absolutely necessary. Penny Pincher developed when I was young; my parents, who had suffered during the Great Depression, worried a lot about not having enough money.

- **Good Dad, a Manager Part**

This Part wants to prepare my son Andrew to survive in the world, and, in this situation, steered me to do so by teaching him how to negotiate. This Part has a secondary concern: to earn Andrew's admiration for my negotiation expertise. Good Dad also was trying to protect **Scaredy Cat**, an Exile who is extremely frightened about *any* risk to my family or me.

- ### Good Time Charlie, an Exile Part

This Part encourages me to relax and enjoy life; other Manager Parts consider that a threat to my well-being and therefore have exiled him.

Box D-2. illustrates these and other relationships between and among Protector Parts and Exile Parts

Box D-2. Understanding the Luxor Situation Through IFS: Which of My Parts Participated or Might Have Been Concerned?

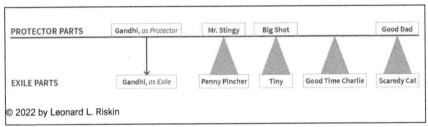

© 2022 by Leonard L. Riskin

Box D-2 identifies the relevant individual Protector and Exile Parts. Protectors—Gandhi, Mr. Stingy, Big Shot, and Good Dad—appear at the top; I have not divided them into Managers and Firefighters. Exiles—Penny Pincher, Tiny, Good Time Charlie, and Scaredy Cat—appear at the bottom. The shaded triangles indicate that the Protectors, at the top, are sheltering certain Exiles. Thus, we see that Mr. Stingy protects Penny Pincher; Big Shot protects Tiny; Good Dad protects Scaredy Cat; and *all* of the Protectors confine and shield Good Time Charlie.

In Luxor, Big Shot dominated; he joined forces with Good Dad and Mr. Stingy to form the "Coalition of the Small-Minded," which took charge. The Coalition did not trust the Self or Gandhi to manage this situation, fearing that either might induce me to give Mr. Hassan too much for my own good. So the Coalition put the Self under house arrest,[1] confining it to a small corner of Consciousness.[2] For similar reasons, the Coalition exiled the Protector Gandhi.

My chronological reconstruction: When Mr. Hassan said, "I have six children and must work very hard to support them," I heard an internal voice, which must have been Gandhi, saying, "That *poor* family, you *really* should *help* them." "Shut up!" Big Shot snapped at Gandhi, and then told me that Mr. Hassan was trying to manipulate me, was unfair, and did not recognize my standing. That's when the Coalition exiled Gandhi and launched its *coup d'état*, endeavoring to protect me.

The Coalition tried to protect me in other ways as well. It wanted to stop existing Exiles from getting so upset that they would exert influence. Remember the Exile Tiny, who feels incompetent, inferior, and vulnerable? If Tiny breaks out of control, he might induce me to do something more extreme and unwise; I could, for instance, refuse to go on *any* carriage ride, retreat to the hotel room for the evening, or scream or cry or otherwise have a tantrum. Good Dad wanted to avoid anything like that. And Mr. Stingy sought to protect Penny Pincher, another fragile Exile who desperately feared I would give away too much money and become destitute. Penny Pincher was already rattled because we had spent a lot of money on this trip—and especially worried because I had squandered money on a vase that I did not much like. The entire Coalition exiled and was trying to protect Good Time Charlie, so that he would not lead me to spend even more money in trying to have a good time.

Recall that, when I described and analyzed the Luxor incident, in Chapters 9 and 10, I treated each person involved—Mr. Hassan, my wife, my son, and myself—as a single entity. I referred to *my* positions, *my* interests, *my* core concerns, and *my* three conversations. But from the IFS perspective, they were not exactly "mine"; rather, they belonged to the Coalition or its member Parts. IFS could have enabled me to realize that these Parts caused or influenced some of my internal experiences and interpretations—and resulting behaviors.

Let's look at "my" core concerns,[3] for example. The *appreciation* concerns of the Coalition members and the *autonomy* concern of my Big Shot Part suffered. To the extent that I worried about my *affiliation* with Casey and Andrew, it was the *affiliation* concerns of Big Shot and Good Dad that were imperiled or damaged. Likewise, the *status* and *role* concerns of several Parts went unfulfilled. These unsatisfied core concerns brought about anger and fear; and those emotions, of course, pushed me further toward positional, adversarial negotiation strategies and tactics.

My three conversations nudged me in the same direction. My internal What Happened Conversation—in which only members of the ruling Coalition exercised influence—produced this interpretation: Mr. Hassan was deliberately cheating *me*, which was "wrong," and, therefore, he did not deserve the amount he sought. This interpretation prompted my negative feelings toward him.[4] The Coalition decided that I had already spent so much money on this trip that I could not "afford" to pay Mr. Hassan what he asked. That belief, combined with the idea that Mr. Hassan was cheating me, further encouraged and "justified" my adversarial perspectives, strategies, and tactics.

Technically, the external process was a negotiation between me and Mr. Hassan. But my internal processes included neither negotiation, mediation, nor adjudication. Instead, as I have suggested, certain Parts—the Coalition of the Small-Minded—staged a semi-secret *coup d'état*, took control, and kept it. Fast thinking produced all of my decisions, and that sheltered me from experiencing difficult internal identity conversations (as explained in Section C).

Despite my active Parts' desires to protect and otherwise benefit me (the person), neither the process nor the outcome fostered that goal. The process was infused with and influence by anxiety, anger, and fear, which led to adversarial behavior, which led—from "my" point of view—to other mainly negative outcomes. I spent much more money than I had intended. No one admired my negotiation skills or me. I suffered "identity quakes"—which inclined me to question whether I am "a good person," "competent," or "worthy of love"[5]—and destructive emotions. My active core concerns went unsatisfied. In short, my family and I had a very unpleasant evening. Over the ensuing years, I have experienced guilt and shame about my performance during this event. (On the other hand, I have published several pieces about this incident, which enhanced my professional resume—if not my personal reputation.)

As you can see, my positional, adversarial strategy was over-determined, that is, caused by multiple factors: my own IFS processes—along with the interpretations, narratives, and emotions associated with the three conversations and core concerns—compelled and reinforced it.[6] I am pretty sure that my Self exerted no influence.[7] In IFS terms, I was "Parts-led" rather than "Self-led."

From another perspective, my ability to negotiate wisely in Luxor was stymied by all five of the obstacles to skillful negotiation that appear in Chapter 4: automatic, habitual ways of thinking, feeling, or behaving; excessively self-centered perspectives; inadequate management of emotions; insufficient social skills; and inadequate management of awareness and focus.

How Might IFS Have Helped Me Manage the Situation More Wisely: Transcending the Five Obstacles to Skillful Negotiation

IFS might have helped me manage the situation more wisely. It would have given me unique access to internal processes and unique tools for dealing with them. These could have enabled me to transcend the five obstacles to skillful negotiation. Trauma may lead to create or strengthen any or all of the barriers.[8] And IFS-based interventions can help a person overcome such obstacles, as described below.[9]

Developing Awareness of—and Distance and Freedom from—Automatic, Habitual Ways of Thinking, Feeling, and Behaving

If I had grasped—and kept in mind—IFS and my own internal family system, I might have quickly realized which of my Parts were active at specific times and which produced the thoughts and emotions that controlled my interpretations and behaviors. That might have broken the automaticity between the thoughts and emotions emanating from these Parts and my responses and might have allowed me to decide whether to follow or accept their interpretations and advice. If I decided not to do so, I might have been able to simply ignore their perspectives. Or I could have chosen to work with these Parts, to understand, counsel, or heal them.

Diminishing Self-Centered Perspectives or Their Influence

Working with IFS might have changed my conception of what or who I am. Simply being aware of my Parts and their perceptions and goals would have helped me separate or disidentify from them, which would have made room for the Self to appear.

Most of us routinely think of ourselves and others as units—even though each person might harbor a range of preferences, perspectives, beliefs, affiliations, and identities, and consequently behave quite differently in various situations. Working with IFS gives us much more complex and nuanced perceptions of ourselves, which can lead to more complex and nuanced perceptions of others—such as Mr. Hassan. I could have performed better in our actual encounter if I had not felt angry, insulted, and fearful, and if I had not demonized Mr. Hassan—or if I had had some distance and freedom from these phenomena. Knowledge of IFS should have enabled me to consider or believe that Mr. Hassan's behavior emanated from one or more of his Parts, not from him.

As such new understandings unfolded, I might have developed empathy for Mr. Hassan, which could have led to compassion, which might have inclined me to help him and his family. The conflict might not have developed at all or might have dissipated or disappeared.

Enhancing Emotional Awareness and Management

As mentioned above, knowledge of IFS and of my own internal family system would have enabled me to identify the Part or Parts that were active.

That, in turn, would have given me the opportunity to deal with them and the emotions they were producing, if and as appropriate, in ways described below.

Improving Social Skills

Improved social skills could have resulted from my enhanced abilities to engage in slow thinking, to understand and manage my emotions, and to recognize emotions in others.[10]

Enhancing Ability to Manage Focus and Awareness

We have an easier time focusing on what we find pleasant, as opposed to unpleasant or neutral. An IFS perspective leads to perceptions that most of us would find pleasant, which could mean interesting or potentially helpful. So we are more able to stay attentive. Knowledge of IFS and my own internal family system would have given me a lot to which I could attach my focus in order to understand and respond to the circumstances.

What I Could Have Done in Order to Actually Use IFS in Dealing with This Situation

If IFS had enabled me to overcome these five obstacles, I would have been able to skillfully use negotiation strategies and tactics such as those covered in Sections A and C. That's the theory.

But in practice, what might I have done to enhance my chances of reaping such potential insights and benefits?

IFS has four basic goals:

"Liberate Parts from the roles they have been forced into, so they can be who they're designed to be."

"Restore trust in the Self and Self-leadership."

"Reharmonize the inner system."

"Become more Self-led in your dealings with the world."[11]

IFS includes many insights, strategies, and tactics for helping a person realize these goals, some of which I might have been able to use almost automatically in Luxor. And we shall see examples below.

Using IFS Insights and Behaviors Automatically or Naturally

If I had had sufficient study, practice, and perhaps therapy, some negotiation and IFS components and perspectives might have joined my collection of automatic and habitual thoughts, emotions, and behaviors. Holding the IFS perspective might even have become a trait, rather than a more temporary state of mind.[12] While I was interacting with Mr. Hassan, for instance, or thinking about the situation, insights based on IFS could have arisen automatically—even when I was not intentionally focusing on IFS. Perhaps I would have automatically recognized that some of my beliefs or behaviors or tendencies came from one or more specific Parts. I might even have realized that certain of my Parts had staged a *coup d'état* and these Parts, not my Self or other potentially interested Parts, were dictating how I interpreted events, felt, and behaved.

More specifically, I might have understood that these Parts were pushing me toward highly positional behavior that ignored important goals of my Self, of my Gandhi Part, of my wife and son, and of Mr. Hassan; that they intended to shield certain Exiles, in order to protect me from those Exiles; that my Big Shot Part felt most insulted and exerted the greatest influence.

Such insights could have allowed me to consider whether I wanted to follow Big Shot's perspectives and instructions in this situation and, perhaps, to wonder why I cared about appearing to be a big shot in these circumstances

I also might have developed insights related to Mr. Hassan: for example, that his circumstances—which brought out certain of his Parts (and their interpretations, interests, core concerns, and the like)—inclined him toward behavior that produced more income and that matched national and local industry custom; that, although my Parts-in-charge thought Mr. Hassan was cheating me, *he* likely believed he was doing nothing wrong; that other of my Parts, such as Gandhi, wanted to help Mr. Hassan help his family; that Mr. Hassan had not singled me out for special treatment; rather, he had dealt with me as he generally dealt with other customers who did not readily agree to the fee he requested.

With such insights, I might not have perceived a serious conflict or could have seen easy ways to avoid or deal with it. Perhaps I would have felt compassion for Mr. Hassan and his family. My Self or a kindly Protector Part might have leapt into action. Maybe I would have followed Gandhi's advice: "That *poor* family, you *really* should *help* them." Maybe my emotions would have stopped raging—or never started. I might have understood and managed the situation wisely, using an appropriate mix of the four basic negotiation focuses and models.

For these events to have happened, I would have needed some freedom from certain of my habitual negotiation patterns. With such freedom, perhaps I could have recognized that whatever fare I paid for a one-mile carriage ride could not affect my family's well-being; that carriage drivers on the Corniche doubtless needed the money more than we did; and that a carriage ride could be fun, and a warm family memory, *if* I stopped worrying about money and stopped deferring to the ruling Coalition.[13]

Using IFS More Deliberately

Let's assume that I had been familiar at the time with IFS and with some of my Parts and how to work with them, but not so familiar that IFS perspectives and skills would have automatically come to mind during my encounter with Mr. Hassan. What could I have done to enable myself to use IFS in hiring a carriage that night in Luxor and, perhaps, in other situations that might provoke similar internal and external conflicts?

I could have prepared.

Let's also assume that, before we left the hotel, I had a session with my Self and Parts to get ready for the evening. To make that assumption seem almost reasonable, imagine that I had an even bigger problem than I actually had: during this and previous travels (and preparations for them), I had frequently behaved in inappropriate ways that resembled my conduct in Luxor; when financial issues arose—such as choices about flights and other modes of travel, hotels, restaurants, tours, and tourist and cultural attractions—I had tried to skimp and became upset when I thought we were spending too much money. This had undermined a good deal of the potential joy in these trips. I wanted to change my behavior in this regard, but much of it seemed automatic, and I had little control. That is why I wanted to conduct an IFS preparation session. In such preparation, I might have drawn upon IFS and conflict management in a number of ways.

In the IFS perspective, as you will recall, at any given time, you are either "in Self"—which means that the Self is exerting a strong influence in your Consciousness, that is, you are "Self-led—or a Part or Parts are blended with the Self and both occupy the seat of Consciousness. In the latter circumstance, the blended Part or Parts usually exercise the most control; in other words, they are "driving the bus." If the Self and a Part (or Parts) are blended, in order for the Self to increase its influence, it may have to persuade the Part (or Parts) that it is safe to separate from the Self, at least to some extent.

The Self inherently knows how to relate to both Parts and people in a way that creates harmony and healing. Thus, although it is rare for Parts to totally separate from the Self, ideally the Self can be sufficiently present that it can exercise leadership. Making that happen can be challenging. Generally, a person is unaware at a particular time that a Part is in control; sometimes a Part with power may not know the Self or know that there is such a thing as Self, or may even believe that *it* is the Self.[14]

In Luxor, several active Parts blocked the Self from coming forward, through their voices, emotions, and pushy advocacy. These Parts did not want the Self to exercise influence because they did not trust the Self to protect "me" or what they believed were "my" interests. In order to get access to the Self, I might have had to get those Parts to "open space inside"—so that the Self could step forward.[15] IFS provides numerous methods for doing that, while also dealing kindly with the Parts involved.

Here are a few specific strategies, processes, and techniques—from IFS and external conflict management—that I might have used, separately or together, during preparation or, in abbreviated form, during the actual incident, as time and circumstances allowed.

First, after I (that is, my Self) gathered the potentially relevant parts, including Gandhi, I could have explained the problem and told them that I needed their help. Specifically, I wanted them to agree that, when I got into circumstances of this nature, they would "step back" and allow the Self to come forward and manage the situation. Next, I might have facilitated a discussion, or asked the Parts to present their arguments, or encouraged them to negotiate with one another.

I also might have mediated, that is, facilitated a negotiation between Parts on all sorts of issues. If time were very short, I could have simply tried to focus on their positions and reach for a quick, narrow compromise—in Luxor, for example, about how much money I would spend. But I would have tried to understand the underlying interests of the Parts, whether such interests were really at stake in this situation, and whether the positions that the Parts asserted were the best ways to protect these interests. Similarly, I could have tried to identify their core concerns and three conversations, and how these influenced the Parts' behavior.

In addition, I could have carefully considered following various approaches to mediation,[16] as well as similar processes that have evolved for external conflict involving multiple parties, such as public-policy mediation[17] and negotiated rulemaking.[18]

In the course of carrying out some of these processes, I might have healed some of the traumatized or exiled Parts or helped them unblend from the Self.

Let's say that I wanted to work with Mr. Stingy. Here is a sample dialogue for such a process.

Me: What would you like me to know about you? (Or: what are you worried about? Or: what do you worry about most in this context? Or: what is your job?)

Mr. Stingy: My job is to make sure that you have enough money to support your family and yourself.

Me: What do you think would happen if you did not do this job?

Mr. Stingy: That you would spend money that you cannot afford because you do not know how to manage money and you do not have very much.

Me: I appreciate your concern for me and my family. Do you like your job?

Mr. Stingy: No.

Me: Why?

Mr. Stingy: It seems impossible to stop you from blowing money. I constantly worry about and struggle with this. I feel like a failure.

Me: If I did not need you or any other Part to do this job, how would you feel?

Mr. Stingy: Relieved.

Me: If you did not have to do this job, what would you most like to do instead?

Mr. Stingy: I don't know.

Me: How old do you think I am?

Mr. Stingy: Nine.

Me: Actually, I am forty-eight. I can see why you would be so worried if you think I am only nine. Also, my wife and I have had good jobs for about twenty years, and we have been careful and saved a lot of money, so we are financially secure.

Mr. Stingy: That's a big relief for me.

Me: Would you agree to step back from this or similar situations?

Mr. Stingy: Yes

Me: How can I help you going forward?

Depending on Mr. Stingy's response I probably would try to find out what kind of job or responsibility he would like to have, if he could give up this one.[19]

I might have depolarized some Parts. Gandhi was polarized with one or more Parts that made up the Coalition that exiled Gandhi. My Self, if I were sufficiently skillful, could facilitate a dialogue in order to help my polarized

Parts stop viewing each other as enemies, and instead, notice one another's positive qualities, learn to trust each other, and figure out how to collaborate. This depolarization process could resemble an interest-oriented negotiation or mediation, and in it, perhaps, I (my Self) could draw upon what I have learned by working with such processes in connection with external conflict, such as generating options.[20] If I were not sufficiently skillful to do that, an IFS psychotherapist or coach could work directly with some of my Parts in a similar fashion.

At some point along the way, I might have adjudicated, using a process akin to what typically happens in court and arbitration proceedings: the relevant Parts present their arguments,[21] my Self deliberates, and my Self decides the outcome.[22] A comparable process in IFS would have included the Self taking care of Parts "that lost out in the decision."[23] Processes of this nature also are commonly used in all sorts of decision-making and management situations.

In these and other ways, I could have worked with relevant Parts to improve internal (and then external) processes by educating or calming them, and showing affection, understanding, and appreciation. I also might have helped them comprehend the differences between their positions and their interests. I might have used other strategies and tactics from the core-concerns and three-conversations approaches (covered in Section A). I could have helped the Parts that were fixated on saving money realize that my financial condition had changed over the years, that we had enough money, and that anything I spent this evening—and even in Paris the following day— could not possibly have a significant impact on the family's financial situation. Such "updating" processes are part of what Schwartz calls "unburdening" the Parts[24]—freeing them from certain strongly felt obligations.

I might have been able to persuade another Part, Big Shot, that we could satisfy his need for recognition in other ways, say, by negotiating a low fare and then voluntarily paying a higher one. I could have thanked him for his efforts and concerns and persuaded him that I did not need the recognition. Perhaps I could have offered similar suggestions to Good Dad and proposed that interest-oriented negotiation moves, along with generosity, would provide a better model of behavior for my son.[25] Such strategies and tactics could have fostered internal harmony and wise decision-making that could continue into the future.

These kinds of steps could have prepared me for Self-leadership in the Luxor carriage situation and in similar circumstances. And, just to be clear, as this or similar situations unfolded, I could have improvised, using brief versions of the processes I just suggested. For instance, if time were short, I might have asked or ordered these Parts to step back, or just ignored them. Obviously, tactics of this nature also come in handy in many aspects of life. Think of the head of a unit within a large organization who may take over a negotiation from one of their subordinates—or the center fielder (in American baseball) who signals the left fielder to let them catch a fly ball by saying, "I've got it."

Of course, this kind of tactic does not always succeed. Like some employees in large organizations and some baseball players, internal Parts can be strongly attached to their perceived responsibilities and believe that no one else, especially the Self, can handle the situation at hand. So they will be reluctant to follow such requests or orders.

Using IFS to Deal with Racism (and Other Biases)

We live in an age of heightened conflict over race, gender, equity, and inclusion. Among other manifestations of this situation, many people in the U.S. classify themselves and others—publicly or privately—as "racist" or "anti-racist" or "not racist."

Looking back at the Luxor incident, I believe that some of my interpretations, perspectives, and behaviors derived from (hopefully unconscious) racist beliefs or perspectives that emanated from racist Parts. From the IFS perspective, there is no such thing as a person who is "racist," "anti-racist," or "not racist," but the vast bulk of human beings have racist Parts. In Schwartz's words,

> [Y]ou can't grow up in the US or other countries with a long history of racism and not carry that legacy burden (although I do find that people from some countries don't carry it). No matter what your race is, no matter how much anti-racism work you've done, it's still likely that there's a part of you that still carries that burden.[26]

Racist Parts sometimes influence the person's perspectives and behaviors, leading the person to regard and treat themselves or others in negative or destructive ways. And yet, "all parts are welcome" is the IFS motto.[27] In Schwartz' words, "racism is in all of us. And if we respond to . . . [a racist] part by shaming it into exile, we just create more implicit racism, which means even more blind spots and keeping the larger system of racism spinning."[28]

Schwartz recommends that we "understand and love our racist Parts and help them to heal and to change their functions."[29] Most racist Parts "hate their jobs," he tells us,[30] and "parts cannot change parts; only Self can do that."[31]

Many racist Parts are Protectors, formed in order to protect us (and certain of our possibly racist Exiles) from perceived or possible risks. If I could have recognized such Parts, I might have been able to ignore their advice or, if time allowed, to educate and heal them. And that might have enabled or encouraged me to treat Mr. Hassan and his family more charitably.

CHAPTER 13

MANAGING YOUR OWN
CONFLICTS WITH IFS

Enough about me. How might IFS help *you* deal more wisely with your own conflicts or problematic situations? This chapter should enable you to answer that question.

Understanding Your Own Internal Family System: In General

Box D-3 will help you get a general sense of your own Internal Family System. Before you begin that exercise, get a light-colored file folder and about five crayons of various colors. If this is not feasible, improvise with paper and pen or pencil or with other tools or devices that suit you better.

Box D-3. Mapping Your Internal Family System: In General

Sit in a comfortable position, in which you can be relaxed and alert.

- Do the following version of the STOPSI exercise.

    Stop.

    Take two or three deliberate breaths.

    Observe BETs (Body Sensations, Emotions, Thoughts).

    Set Intentions

    o   to be relaxed and alert

    o   to follow the instructions

Identify Your Parts and (Perhaps) Notice Self

- Relax and see what comes to mind.

    o   It may be helpful to find and follow "trailheads" or leads. Trailheads could include the three objects of attention in mindfulness—body sensations, emotions, and thoughts—as well as other manifestations of core concerns or internal conversations.

    o   As you contemplate your Parts, notice how they look or feel, and what they do or say.

    o   You also may notice manifestations of your Self—the core of your being, a center of attention—which is calm, clear, compassionate, and wise.

Depict Your Parts

- When you are ready (or after about 15 minutes):

  Open the folder and begin to draw whatever you have envisioned—and whatever you might envision while drawing. As you do this, continue to contemplate. Pause whenever you wish. Your images of your internal system likely to change as you draw.

  No two people would produce the same drawing. The drawing can be as abstract or representational as you like. Don't fret about getting this just right. But if you do experience such worries, try to identify the Part or Parts from which they arise. In other words, treat these concerns as trailheads that could lead you to a Part.

  After you have drawn for a bit—say 15–20 minutes, but longer is okay—consider naming some of the Parts. You might name a Part after its principal characteristic (say, generous or stingy) or with the name of a particular person or animal that seems appropriate. Also, if you are so inclined, consider which Parts might be Protectors (Managers or Firefighters) or Exiles (covered in Chapter 12). If such categories seem to apply to any of the Parts you identify, you may wish to indicate that.

*   A portion of these instructions was inspired by an exercise led by Center for Self-Leadership Senior Trainer Paul Ginter at an IFS Conference in Oak Brook, IL in October 2010.

Notice that these instructions begin with establishing mindfulness, specifically by using STOP and STOPSI instructions that are similar to instructions set forth in Section B, Chapter 8.

I have used versions of this exercise many times to introduce IFS to people from countless walks of life: executives, law students, lawyers, judges, mediators, professors, engineers, real estate agents, and K–12 and higher education administrators and teachers. To my surprise and delight, virtually everyone was able to do it, and most seemed to find it enlivening.[1] The exercise should give you a general picture of your own internal family system. And each time you work with IFS, you may develop additional or different understandings of your Parts and their relationships.

We all have many identities, a good proportion of which derive from our work, religion, ethnic group, politics, values, and the like. We get attached to or identified with some of them. For instance, the University of Florida, where I used to teach, has a mascot (as do most U.S. universities)—a "Gator," short for alligator, many of which actually live on campus in Lake Alice, a nature preserve. With great pride, many students and alumni refer to themselves as Gators. During a class in which we studied IFS, I asked the law students, "How many consider yourselves a Gator?" Most raised their hands. "Is that the *real* you?" About 40 percent said yes.[2] "So when you die, if there

is an afterlife, will you still be a Gator?" At least half of the self-declared
Gators thought so. Over the next few days, several students came to my
office, visibly upset, and told me that I "just do not understand what a great
university this is."

Understanding a Conflict or Problematic Situation of Your Own Through IFS

Now that you are familiar with your principal Parts, let's consider how
IFS might assist you in managing (understanding and responding to) a
specific conflict or difficult situation or decision of your own. The exercise
in Box D-4 will help you map elements of your internal family system that
are or might be interested in a particular conflict of your own.

Before doing that exercise, get a light-colored file folder and about five
crayons of various colors. If this is not feasible, improvise with paper and
pen or pencil, or use other tools or devices that suit you better.

Box D-4. Mapping Your Internal Family System in Relation to a Conflict or Problematic Situation of Your Own

Sit in a comfortable position, in which you can be relaxed and alert.

- Do the following version of the STOPSI exercise.

  Stop.

  Take two or three deliberate breaths.

  Observe BETs (Body Sensations, Emotions, Thoughts).

- Set Intentions to

  o   be relaxed and alert

  o   follow the instructions

Then:

Follow the instructions below for identifying and depicting your Parts, Self,
and Internal Family System in relation to the conflict or problematic situation
you have selected.

Finding Parts and the Self

- Bring to mind a difficult conflict in which you were recently or are
  currently engaged, or which you are worried about. It should involve
  strong emotions and, ideally, take place principally between you and
  one other person.

- Recall a specific incident, event, or time period related to this conflict.
  Put yourself mentally back into that time, as best you can. Notice what
  is happening, what you and others are doing.

- Observe your (BETs)—body sensations, emotions, and thoughts—as they arise. Some of these may emanate from a Part, and so could serve as trailheads, and lead you to that Part.

- Follow an individual trail until you identify a Part to which it leads.

- In less formal ways, also try to identify Parts to which body sensations, emotions, thoughts, and desires are connected.

- Observe what various Parts are doing, saying, or feeling.

- Notice how these Parts relate to one another.

- You may observe the presence of Self. When you are "in Self," your awareness will be clear, compassionate, curious, and without judgment.

Depicting Parts and the Self

- When you feel ready, open the manila-colored file folder and, with several crayons of different colors (if you have them) draw the components of your internal family system in relation to this conflict or problematic situation As you draw, feel free to pause when you wish and return to the meditative state just described.

---

* A portion of these instructions was inspired by my recollections of an exercise led by Center for Self-Leadership Senior Trainer Paul Ginter at an IFS conference in Oak Brook IL in October 2010.

To understand more about what happened, consider the following questions, and then complete Appendix Exercise D-1 Understanding a Conflict of Your Own Using IFS and Negotiation.

1. Which Parts of my internal family system participated or might have been concerned?

2. What did these Parts do?

3. Did the Self participate?

4. What was the nature of interactions between or among Parts or between the Self and Parts?

   Did any of their interactions include or resemble components of external conflict-management processes—such as negotiation, mediation, or adjudication?

5. Was your understanding or performance hindered by any of the five obstacles to wise negotiation?

   Automatic, habitual ways of thinking, feeling, or behaving

   Excessively self-centered perspectives

   Inadequate management of emotions

   Insufficient social skills

Inadequate management of awareness and focus

Responding to the Conflict or Situation

With your knowledge of IFS (and negotiation and mindfulness), consider how IFS might have helped you respond better to this situation or how it still might help you to deal with it. In order to do that, you might want to revisit the treatment of IFS and the Luxor situation in Chapter 12.

CHAPTER 14

SYNERGIES BETWEEN IFS AND NEGOTIATION (AND MEDIATION)

Chapters 12 and 13 described specific ways in which IFS and the four negotiation focuses and models—emphasizing positions, interests, core concerns, and the three conversations—could support and enhance one another. This chapter sets out such interactions more broadly.

IFS can bolster our performance in negotiating about both internal aspects and external aspects of conflict in several ways. First, simply understanding IFS can enable us to accept the idea that we, as well as our negotiation counterparts, may be governed by different Parts at various times and circumstances. We might understand that crucial aspects of a conflict or problematic situation occur within each person's internal family systems and between the parties' respective internal family systems.

Thus, IFS gives us another perspective through which to comprehend positions, interests, core concerns, and three conversations—and their relationships. Imagine that you ask your normally polite boss for a raise, and they say, "A raise? You are lucky I haven't fired you. You don't deserve this job, and you sure don't know how to behave." IFS could enable you to reframe your understanding of this event, to see that such behavior emanates, not exactly from your boss, but from their momentarily most influential Parts, and that these Parts are trying to protect your boss—from something. That insight could prevent you from automatically assuming that that your boss intended to treat you cruelly, and this could enable you to deal wisely with the situation.

IFS also can offer new variations on strategies and tactics for dealing with clients or counterparts in a conflict or problematic situation. I have, for instance, picked up a great deal about working with clients as a lawyer and mediator by studying IFS and watching video and live demonstrations of IFS therapists or coaches getting acquainted with a client's Parts, learning what they need, and helping them become better members of the internal family, and thus happier.

IFS gives us special insights about our internal processes and their impact on decision-making. Such perceptions, along with IFS tools, provide us opportunities to decide whether to accept a Part's recommendations or impulses or, instead, intervene to change the process or outcome, which, if time allowed, might even include educating and healing relevant Parts. In the Luxor situation, had I previously developed knowledge and skills in IFS, I might have realized that Parts that belonged to the Ruling Coalition were pushing me toward parsimonious interpretations and behaviors, and that perhaps these Parts were not the wisest advisors in that situation. And I might have been able to calm my Parts, if necessary, and consciously decide what would be best for all concerned. My wisdom in dealing with my Parts—and in trying to understand and influence Mr. Hassan's Parts—might have been strengthened by considering their positions, interests, core concerns, and how these might have made my interaction with Mr. Hassan so difficult.

Lawyer-mediator David Hoffman explains another benefit that IFS could afford mediators and mediation participants:

> [T]he concept of internal "parts" provides mediators with a linguistic tool for managing ambivalence and resistance. The parties in a mediation are sometimes prone to exaggerated statements of their views. The mediator can deescalate such commitments, using the language suggested by IFS, by reframing them: "So, I hear you saying that a *part* of you is very angry and wants vindication." This statement has a significantly different meaning than the same statement without the concept of "parts" (viz. "I hear you saying that you are very angry and want vindication"). The concept of parts allows the mediator to inquire as to whether there are *other* parts, with differing goals and agendas—thus providing the parties with a psychologically safer way to express the full range of emotions they may be experiencing, and to consider loosening their commitment to strongly held positions.[1]

Although Hoffman is discussing the benefits of IFS for mediators—who facilitate negotiation between others—these tools are equally valuable to negotiators, whether they are representing themselves or others. In the Shoe-Dog split case (in Section A), for instance, had Pedro been familiar with IFS, he might have asked Billy whether he had a Part that wanted to be friends.

Similarly, concepts, strategies, and tactics for dealing with external conflict—in negotiation and other dispute management processes—can support and enhance the use of IFS. Negotiation concepts such as positions, interests, core concerns, and three conversations, as well as strategies and tactics associated with their models, could enable a person using IFS to better understand and manage their own internal family systems and influence the internal family systems, or at least some Parts, of others. IFS practitioners might also benefit from employing ideas from other dispute management processes. External mediation is the most obvious because it is essentially negotiation that is facilitated by a third party; in IFS, internal (among and between Parts) mediation is one of the Self's primary tools of Self-leadership. Some external mediation approaches and models might work particularly well in mediation among and between a person's Parts. These include Understanding-Based Mediation,[2] Transformative Mediation,[3] and Civic Fusion.[4]

CHAPTER 15

SYNERGIES BETWEEN IFS AND MINDFULNESS

IFS and mindfulness can reinforce and support one another because aspects of the two are similar or complementary.

Both mindfulness and IFS can help us transcend the five obstacles to skillful negotiation. As we have seen, mindfulness and IFS can do this in similar fashion, by developing awareness of (and distance and freedom from) automatic, habitual ways of thinking, feeling, and behaving; by diminishing attention to self-centered perspectives; by enhancing emotional awareness and management; by improving social skills; and by strengthening the ability to focus.[1]

Mindfulness and IFS share important concepts, goals, and potential outcomes. These include reducing suffering, promoting peace of mind, and fostering compassion and kindness toward oneself and others, along with a sense of connection. In the IFS framework, a person can achieve these goals through being "in Self," and thereby exercising "Self-Leadership," that is, dealing with their own inner and outer worlds through the perspective of Self. Some Buddhist traditions stress the importance of realizing "no-self" and seeing your internal and external worlds from that perspective.

You might assume that "Self" in IFS and "no-self "in Buddhist thought are opposites, and you would have plenty of company. But ever since I began working with IFS, I have been struck by their similarities.

Perhaps both terms point to the same phenomenon or state of mind. Some experts say so. The Buddhist scholar Jack Engler and the psychologist Paul Fulton, for example, assert that "[t]he term *Self* as used in IFS denotes the same reality as *anatta* or *no-self* in Buddhist thought: a state that is not motivated by or organized around a separate, inherently existing agentic self."[2] Similarly, IFS founder Richard Schwartz believes that the Self in IFS is called by other names in other traditions, names such as "the spirit, Buddha Nature, or soul."[3]

IFS and mindfulness include other similar or identical concepts, terminology, and processes.

The perspective that a person's mind, psyche, or personality is composed of Parts is central to IFS, where it carries a specific meaning that includes what Parts are and do; how they come about, develop and change; and how they interact with one another and with the Self. IFS provides extensive elaborations and instructions on how to understand and work with Parts.

Some mindfulness literature, teachings, and trainings also include elements that resemble or might overlap with IFS Parts but typically are less specific and less developed. For instance, the late Thich Nhat Hanh—Vietnamese Buddhist monk, mindfulness teacher, and global spiritual leader—refers to "parts of ourselves."

> If we face our unpleasant feelings with care, affection, and nonviolence, we can transform them into the kind of energy that is healthy and has the capacity to nourish us. By the work of mindful observation, our unpleasant feelings can illuminate so much for us, offering us insight and understanding into ourselves and society . . . . Instead of acting as if we can dispose of *parts of ourselves*, we should learn the art of transformation. We can transform our anger, for example, into something more wholesome, like understanding. . . .This is peacemaking. . . . You calm your feeling just by being with it, like a mother's tenderness, the baby will calm down and stop crying.[4]

Tara Brach offers suggestions about how to work with "parts of yourself" in RAIN meditation (covered in Chapter 6). The goals, strategies, and tactics that she describes resemble their IFS counterparts, but they are less detailed and specific, as are the parts to which she refers.[5]

Mindfulness and IFS complement one another. IFS provides a unique set of tools and language to understand and work with internal and external conflict-related processes and behaviors. Mindfulness can strengthen our nonjudgmental awareness and focus while working with IFS. It can help a person gain and sustain awareness of their IFS Parts and Self. For example, mindfulness (in the sense of moment-to-moment nonjudgmental awareness), can help someone identify trailheads[6] or leads—which can include thoughts, emotions, and sensations; follow such trailheads to a particular Part; and maintain attention while working with a Part or Parts using IFS methods. Similarly, mindfulness can help a person notice manifestations of the Self's presence.

Both being in-Self in IFS and achieving no-self in Buddhist thought are difficult to sustain and typically short-lived. The IFS Self is usually blended with a Part or Parts. When it separates from such Parts, the Self is in control, and we are said to be "in Self." These periods, however—like periods of selfless awareness that are associated with mindfulness—usually do not last long; the Self and Parts will re-blend naturally, and mindfulness disappears. We do not usually notice the shifts occurring, and we may not gain such awareness for some time, if ever.

As I have explained, mindfulness can help us stabilize our awareness of IFS-related phenomena. Reciprocally, IFS can strengthen our ability to sustain mindful awareness of our own moment-to-moment experience. It is easier to maintain focus and awareness—and curiosity—when we find the "objects" of that awareness interesting, potentially useful, or pleasant; IFS can imbue the objects of mindfulness with these qualities. And IFS perspectives and skills provide additional methods of accessing, understanding, and dealing with conflict and problematic situations within and between ourselves and others.

I suspect that many people who work with both IFS and mindfulness tend to integrate concepts, strategies, and techniques from these domains, deliberately or automatically. I certainly do. During mindfulness meditation, for instance, I sometimes observe objects of awareness from or through the perspective of the IFS Self or a specific Part. And recently, while doing a RAIN exercise presented online by Tara Brach, I began to notice the presence of a few of my IFS Parts, though she did not suggest that. In certain of the instructions in Section D, I have included concepts, strategies, and tactics from both mindfulness and IFS.

Flint Sparks—a Zen Buddhist priest, psychologist, and psychotherapist who uses IFS in his practice—considers IFS "an essential and very skillful bridge between psychological work and contemplative practice"[7] and a skillful means of achieving goals of Buddhism and of mindfulness practice that are expressed in the Four Noble Truths and the Noble Eightfold Path.[8]

REVIEW OF SECTION D

Previous sections introduced four negotiation focuses and a model for each—based on positions, interests, core concerns, and the three conversations—as well as obstacles to using them skillfully. These focuses and models generally regard an individual person as a unit, a so-called unitary self. IFS, however, rests on a fundamentally different conception of the mind or psyche; it includes two wholly different kinds of entities—one Self and numerous Parts—that interact as a system, much as do humans in a family or other group. Section D shows how IFS, combined with negotiation knowledge and skill, could have helped me better understand and respond to the Luxor carriage-fee negotiation, as well as other problematic situations. It also illustrates how you might understand and work with your own internal family systems, combined with negotiation, and thereby better handle conflict.

REVIEW OF SECTION D IN LIGHT VERSE

D. INTERNAL FAMILY SYSTEMS

Considering conflict within,
it's hard to know how to begin.
When you're deciding what to do,
Query: Who (or what) is "you"?

To deal with that, I now suggest
a model known as IFS.
It can highlight your subpersonalities,
so the "Self" might undo their dualities·

and help you manage more inside,
less controlled by Parts that plied.
Profoundly perplexed about an offer?
IFS could be the best that I can proffer.

MINDFUL CONFLICT MANAGEMENT

We have come a long way together, and I am glad you are still here. This Section reviews the book and offers practical advice about how to enhance your ability to mindfully manage conflict—inside out and outside in—using the three-domains approach.

REVIEW OF THE BOOK

The thesis of *Managing Conflict Mindfully* is that we can better manage conflict and problematic situations if we can appropriately employ elements of three domains—negotiation, mindfulness, and Internal Family Systems. Each of these domains can support and draw support from the others.

Box E-1 presents the essence of MCM in a Venn diagram, which you also saw in the Introduction.

Box E-1. The Venn of Mindful Conflict Management: Negotiation, Mindfulness, and Internal Family Systems (Revisited)

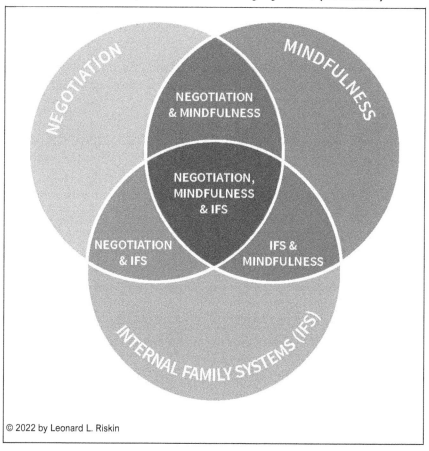

© 2022 by Leonard L. Riskin

The large circles represent the three domains. The zones of overlap (smaller and darker) show that we are able to draw on more than one domain to manage the same situation. When that happens, the domains involved can reinforce or support one another. As a result, we should have a better chance to skillfully understand and respond to the conflict or conflicts at issue. When our mind is in the central zone (the darkest color), we can use tools from any or all of the three domains to understand and address conflict, that is, we can use MCM.

Each of the three domains, alone, can help individuals understand and address conflict or other problematic situations and enhance their abilities— and tendencies—to behave with wisdom, compassion, and kindness toward themselves and others. Each domain offers unique ways of understanding and responding to conflict. Each has vulnerabilities. And each can both support and draw support from the others to help a person deal better with conflict and problematic situations, both within themselves and between themselves and others.

This claim has three components.

- **Negotiation and mindfulness can support and enhance one another.**

  This interplay is explained in Section B and in the Review of Sections A, B, and C. On the Venn of MCM (Box E-1), it is depicted by the area of overlap labeled Negotiation and Mindfulness, in the upper portion of the overlapping areas.

- **Negotiation and IFS can support and enhance one another.**

  This is explained in Section D, Chapter 14. On the Venn of MCM (Box E-1), it is depicted by the area of overlap labeled Negotiation and IFS.

- **Mindfulness and IFS can support and enhance one another.**

  This is explained in Section D, Chapter 15. On the Venn of MCM, it is depicted by the area of overlap labeled IFS and Mindfulness.

* * *

Box E-2 displays a step-by-step version of this thesis.

Box E-2. The Road to (and Through) Mindful Conflict Management, Step-by-Step

Problems/Challenges	Causes	Methods of Addressing the Problems or Causes
1. Many people do not negotiate (or deal with) "external" conflict well.	2. Deficiencies in knowledge or skill in managing external conflict.	3. Learn to understand and employ tools for managing conflict, such as negotiation focuses—on positions, interests, core concerns, and three conversations—and their models.
4. BUT, people who master such tools for managing conflict frequently fail to use them appropriately.	5. Their ability to use these tools appropriately is overcome by strong, usually negative, emotions, which often arise because a person's core concerns—appreciation, autonomy, affiliation, status, and role—are not sufficiently satisfied.	6. Learn to use emotions in negotiation through the core-concerns focus and model.
7. BUT, some people who learn the core-concerns system frequently do not use it well.	8. Deficiencies in self-awareness and self-management that are associated with automatic, habitual ways of thinking, feeling, or behaving; excessively self-centered perspectives; inadequate management of emotions; insufficient social skills; inadequate management of awareness and focus.	9. Learn and practice mindfulness, which can help a person overcome these obstacles.
10. BUT, mindfulness is difficult to sustain, especially in challenging situations.	11. Mindfulness is vulnerable to the same obstacles that it can address. (See row 3 in this column, directly above.)	12. To strengthen the ability to create and sustain mindfulness, practice formal, semiformal, and informal mindfulness exercises frequently.

Problems/Challenges	Causes	Methods of Addressing the Problems or Causes
		Use negotiation knowledge to sustain mindfulness.
13. BUT even those who have followed the suggestions above often will fail to negotiate wisely.	14. Inadequate ability to understand and manage their own internal processes.	15. Learn and practice internal family systems (IFS), which can help you better understand and manage internal processes.
16. BUT it is difficult to use IFS in this way.	17. Insufficient mindfulness or inadequate understanding and skill with negotiation approaches and models.	18. Use Mindful Conflict Management (MCM) to combine and strengthen the three domains.
19. BUT some people will be unable to skillfully use MCM.	20. It's difficult.	21. Practice MCM and learn to use it appropriately.
© 2022 Leonard L. Riskin		

MCM IN PRACTICE: HOW TO ACTUALLY USE MINDFUL CONFLICT MANAGEMENT

So far, Section E has presented primarily theory. Now for the practice: How can you actually manage conflict mindfully, using this framework?

Our main task here is to acquire the ability to access and use elements of each domain, as appropriate, in order to wisely manage negotiations and other problematic situations. To do that, I offer two suggestions:

- **Enhance your foundational competencies and skills in each of the three domains.**

To the extent that you improve your understanding and skill in each domain, you should more effectively use all three—alone or together. Resources for enhancing your understanding and competence in each of the domains are abundant and include books and articles, training programs, courses of study and practice (with or without credit toward a degree or certificate). More information on some of these resources appears at https://tinyurl.com/ManagingConflictMindfully.

- **Learn, invent, and practice methods for accessing the three domains and calling upon their components, separately or together, as helpful and appropriate.**

The more you practice or use any of the domains, the more easily or more automatically you will be able to employ them, alone or in combination.

* * *

You can use MCM, or any of its components, to understand a conflict or problematic situation and to plan for how to manage it. But do not commit to using that plan. As the situation evolves, you may need to improvise. Likewise, do not rigidly attach yourself to the MCM system as a whole or to any of the individual principles, concepts, and models it presents. If you follow the two suggestions above, you will (and should) customize, combine, draw upon, or ignore the MCM system and any of the principles, concepts, or models that fall within it. You will feel more comfortable or capable with some elements than with others. In real life, the situations you face will almost never quite match the situations presented in this book (or most other books).

So, remember your principles and goals, and be flexible about the manner in which you serve them. Be kind to yourself and others. And finally, don't believe everything you think.

REVIEW OF *MANAGING CONFLICT MINDFULLY* IN LIGHT VERSE[*]

————

A.   NEGOTIATION

A mountain serves as metaphor,
which helps convey a little more.
This mountain has levels without and within,
and at the top we will begin.

Positions

Near the peak's where we seek our positions,
which we find there in any conditions.
As for mine, I am quick to proclaim them.
And for yours, I will claim to disdain them.

Sometimes, when our outlook's positional,
our counterpart seems oppositional.
Discussions, therefore, might get stuck
and then, of course, we're out of luck,

---

[*]   Portions of this poem appear at the end of Sections A, B, C, and D of this book. For an earlier—and fully footnoted—version of the poem, see Leonard L. Riskin, *Negotiation, Outside-In and Inside-Out: On the Level or Thereabout*, Kormendy Lecture, 43 Ohio Northern Univ. Law Rev. 399 (2017).

Interests

unless we look beneath positions,
there to find our deeper missions.
Practicing prospecting underground
can yield discoveries quite profound.

As the pathway for getting to yes,
Roger Fisher et al. clearly stress
attending to interests, more than positions,
so to foster ripe conditions

in which you can generate options
and evaluate them for adoptions,
which could lead to agreement success—
Pareto-ly optimal, which they say is the best.

And although "You can't
always get what you want,"
should wisdom succeed in exceeding greed,
perhaps you will want no more than you need.

Core Concerns

Sources of interests and positions
may include our dispositions.
When core concerns are unfulfilled
our spirits get distinctly chilled.

You see, we need appreciation,
recognition of our station,
freedom, belonging, a meaningful role—
these will soothe a tender soul.

And so, each person's heart does burn
to satisfy a core concern.

Else they may feel emotions negative,
and may require a calming sedative.

So if you're soaked with negativity—
although that's not your prime proclivity—
it could come from some core concern,
or several, for which you yearn.

Unmet concerns, if they're galore,
can leave you looking like a boor.
You may appear, well, too competitive,
and use language too loud and too repetitive.

Besides, your judgment goes kerplunk,
so others wonder what you thunk,
and you can't get your interests met.
You may not try, but just forget.

B.   MINDFULNESS

The practice of mindful attention
delivers a different dimension.
For managing conflict, within and without,
it's almost essential, there's nearly no doubt.

It keeps us calm and helps us think
and more, provides a needed link
for using constructs named above,
and doing so with kindly love.

C.   BACK TO NEGOTIATION: THE THREE CONVERSATIONS

For more insight on tough situations,
consider the three conversations.
Facts and feelings, you can see.
The third one is identity.

This model's for helping you learn
from those you might otherwise spurn,
to avoid attributions erroneous,
and seek some solutions harmonious.

D.   INTERNAL FAMILY SYSTEMS

Considering conflict within,
it's hard to know how to begin.
When you're deciding what to do,
Query: Who (or what) is "you"?

To deal with that, I now suggest
a model known as IFS.
It can highlight your subpersonalities,
so the "Self" might undo their dualities

and help you manage more inside,
less controlled by Parts that plied.
Profoundly perplexed about an offer?
IFS could be the best that I can proffer.

Appendix

Table of Contents for Exercises in Appendix

Exercise A-1. Positions and Interests in a Conflict of Your Own

To ground your understanding of positions and interests, try this: Call to mind a conflict that was or is significant to you in any aspect of your life. It could have happened in the past or it might be ongoing. It should have an emotional element, and if it occurred in the past, it should still bother you. The exercise works best if the conflict concerns mainly you and just one other person.

Once you have such a situation in mind, close your eyes, and recall a particular event, moment, or time period associated with it.

Out of all that, try to identify positions and interests, yours and the other person's.

Then complete the form on the next page.

Exercise A-1, continued

Identify the conflict (for your own reference):			
My positions	**My interests**	**Their Positions**	**Their Interests**

If you had achieved your positions, would your interests have been satisfied?
If they had achieved their positions, would their interests have been satisfied?

© 2022 by Leonard L. Riskin

Exercise A-2. Core Concerns in a Conflict of Your Own

To get a better sense of the core concerns, bring to mind a conflict in which you are or were involved, primarily with one other person, that has or had a significant emotional component. This conflict could be the one you used in Appendix Exercise A-1. Once you have selected a conflict, recall a particular moment, event, or time period during the conflict. Put yourself into it mentally. Notice who is present and what they are doing or saying. Observe any of your emotions, body sensations, or thoughts, as best you can. Next try to trace them to core concerns that were significant for you and for the other person. Then complete the form on the next page.

Exercise A-2, continued

Core Concerns	What are some ways this core concern is unmet in me?	What are some ways this core concern might be unmet in the other?	What might I do to address my core concern?	What might I do to address the other's core concern?
Appreciation				
Autonomy				
Affiliation				

Exercise A-2, continued

Core Concerns	What are some ways this core concern is unmet in me?	What are some ways this core concern might be unmet in the other?	What might I do to address my core concern?	What might I do to address the other's core concern?
Status				
Role				

Exercise A-3. Obstacles to Skillful Negotiation in a Conflict of Your Own

To get a better sense of these obstacles, recall a conflict of your own, and put yourself, mentally, into that particular event or time period. Consider whether any of these obstacles were present in you and whether or how they might have affected your understanding or behavior. Then complete the form below.

Identify the Conflict (for your own purposes):

Obstacle	Present? Y or N? Examples?	Impact on your understanding or behavior
Automatic, habitual ways of thinking, feeling, or behaving		
Excessively self-centered perspectives		
Inadequate awareness or management of emotions		

Obstacle	Present? Y or N? Examples?	Impact on your understanding or behavior
Insufficient social skills		
Inadequate management of focus or awareness		

Exercise C-1. Difficult Conversations Preparation Worksheet

TRIAD Difficult Conversations™ Preparation Worksheet

1. Understand "What Happened?"

▶ **Stories:**

What is the problem from my point of view?

What is the problem from their point of view?

What data is behind my story?

What data makes their story make sense?

What are my relevant past experiences?

What past experiences are relevant?

▶ **Contributions:**

How have I contributed to the current situation?

How have they contributed to the current situation?

▶ **Impact and Intentions:**

What impact has the situation had on me?

What were their intentions?

What were my intentions?

What impact might this situation have had on them?

TRIAD · CONSULTING GROUP   Difficult Conversations™ Preparation Worksheet

2. Feelings

How do I feel about this situation?

What might they be feeling?

Which feelings make sense to share?

3. Identity

What do I fear this situation says about me?

What might they think the situation says about them?

What is true about this?

What is not?

4. Purpose

What is my purpose for having this conversation?

Circle the purposes that are 1) in your control, and 2) Helpful to you.

Used with permission. © 2022, Triad Consulting Group. This chart is based on material in Difficult Conversations: How to Discuss What Matters Most (Penguin, 2010, 2nd Ed.), by Douglas Stone, Bruce Patton, and Sheila Heen. An easier-to-use copy is available at https://www.triadconsultinggroup.com/learning-resources.

Exercise C-2. Understanding Positions, Interests, Core Concerns and Three Conversations in a Conflict of Your Own

To get a better sense of the interrelationships among the four negotiation focuses and their models, bring to mind a meaningful conflict in which you are or were involved. It should be primarily between you and one other person and should include a significant emotional aspect. It could be one of the conflicts you worked with in Exercises A-1, A-2, or A-3 in the Appendix. Then complete the form on the next page.

Exercise C-2, continued

Identify the conflict (for our own reference):

Issue(s)	My Positions	My Interests	My Core Concerns	My Facts Convers.	My Emotions Conv.	My Identity Conv.
			Appreciation?			
			Affiliation?			

Exercise C-2, continued

Issue(s)	My Positions	My Interests	My Core Concerns	My Facts Convers.	My Emotions Conv.	My Identity Conv.
			Autonomy?			
			Status?			
			Role?			

Exercise C-2, continued

What relationships do you see between your positions, interests, core concerns, and three conversations?

Exercise C-2, continued

Issue(s)	Their Positions	Their Interests	Their Core Concerns	Their Facts Conversation	Their Emotions Conversation	Their Identity Conversation
			Appreciation?			
			Affiliation?			
			Autonomy?			

Exercise C-2, continued

Issue(s)	Their Positions	Their Interests	Their Core Concerns	Their Facts Conversation	Their Emotions Conversation	Their Identity Conversation
			Status?			
			Role?			

Exercise C-2, continued

What relationships do you see between **their** positions, interests, core concerns, and three conversations?

What insights or ideas about how to deal with situation do you have?

**Exercise D-1. Understanding a Conflict of Your Own Using IFS and
        Negotiation**

To understand more about what happened, consider the following
questions and then complete Exercise D-1 Understanding a Conflict of
Your Own Using IFS and Negotiation, in the Appendix.

1.   Which Parts of my internal family system participated or
     might have been concerned?

2.   What did these Parts do?

3.   Did the Self participate?

4.   What was the nature of interactions between or among
     Parts or between the Self and Parts?

     Did any of their interactions include or resemble
     components of external conflict-management processes—
     such as negotiation, mediation, or adjudication?

5.   Was your understanding or performance hindered by any
     of the five obstacles to wise negotiation?

     Automatic, habitual ways of thinking, feeling, or behaving

     Excessively self-centered perspectives

     Inadequate management of emotions

     Insufficient social skills

     Inadequate management of awareness and focus

Exercise D-1, continued

Question	Answer	Comment
1. Which components of my internal family system participated or might have been concerned?		
2. What did the Parts or the Self do?		
3. What was the nature of these interactions or processes? Or Did any of their interactions include or resemble components or elements of external conflict-management processes—such as adjudication, negotiation, or mediation?		

Exercise D-1, continued

Question	Answer	Comment
4. What was the quality of the processes and outcomes? Or How beneficial or detrimental were the processes and outcomes?		
5. Was your understanding or performance hindered by any of the five obstacles? Automatic, habitual ways of thinking, feeling, or behaving. Excessively self-centered perspectives. Inadequate management of emotions. Insufficient social skills. Inadequate management of awareness and focus.		

* * *

INDEX

References are to Pages

ENDNOTES

The citation format used in these endnotes derives from *The Bluebook: A Uniform System of Citation* (Columbia Law Rev. Ass'n et al. eds., 21st ed. 2020), which is widely used in legal writing. In these endnotes, sources are only cited in full one time; subsequent citations to the source, if any, start with a shortened version of the source author and name, followed by the page(s) in the source where the cited material can be found, followed in parentheses by a cross-reference to the chapter endnote in this book where the full citation can be found.

Introduction (pp. 1–6)

    1   Leonard L. Riskin, *Negotiation and Self-Esteem*, in *Proceedings of the Carl A. Warns Institute on Labor Law*, Univ. of Louisville School of Law 8 (William F. Dolson & Janice M. Theriot eds., 1999); Leonard L. Riskin, *Managing Inner and Outer Conflict: Selves, Subpersonalities, and Internal Family Systems*, 18 Harvard Negotiation Law Rev. 1, 3–4 (2013).

    2   Such evidence shows my callous willingness to embarrass my adolescent son in order to keep my head warm and maintain my sense of style (Leonard L. Riskin, *The Cat in the Hat*, Atlantic Monthly 30 (July 1995)); my self-righteous refusal to follow sports (Leonard L. Riskin, *Unsportsmanlike Conduct*, NY Times Mag. 14–16 (Jan. 22, 1989)); my excessive preoccupation with comfort (Leonard L. Riskin, *Andrew in Monet's Garden*, Washington Post E1 (Oct. 6, 1996)); and my tendency to devote too much time and energy to finding bargains on foreign travels (Leonard L. Riskin, *A Couple Abroad: Tomayto vs. Tomahto*, Newsday (Travel Section) 10 (Dec. 27, 1992)).

    3   From *You Can't Always Get What You Want*, by the Rolling Stones (Olympic Studios 1969). The lyrics are available on numerous websites, including Genius.com, https://genius.com/The-rolling-stones-you-cant-always-get-what-you-want-lyrics (last visited Mar. 10, 2022).

    4   A trailer for *Inside Out* is available on You Tube: https://www.youtube.com/watch?v=seMwpP0yeu4 (last visited Mar. 10, 2022). The full movie is available, as of the time of this book's publication, for fee-based streaming on the Disney+ site. Disney+, *Inside Out*, https://www.disneyplus.com/movies/inside-out/uzQ2ycVDi2IE (last visited Mar. 10, 2022).

Roadmap and Guide (pp. 7–9)

    1   G.E.P. Box, *Robustness in the Strategy of Scientific Model Building*, in *Robustness in Statistics* 201, 202 (Robert L. Launer & Graham N. Wilkinson eds., 1979). I also agree with the common assertion that every category is both underinclusive and overinclusive. And sometimes categories can limit our creativity.

    2   For thoughtful comments about the uses of models in scientific literature—and in conflict resolution—see Michael Colatrella, *True Enough*, in *Discussions in Dispute Resolution* 183 (Art Hinshaw, Andrea Kupfer Schneider & Sara Rudolph Cole eds., Oxford Univ. Press 2021).

Section A. Negotiation, the First Domain (pp. 11–53)

    1   See Emeran Mayer, *The Mind-Gut Connection: How the Hidden Conversation Within Our Bodies Impacts Our Mood, Our Choices, and Our Overall Health* (Harper Wave, an Imprint of HarperCollins Publishers 2016); Peter Andre Smith, *Can the Bacteria in Your Gut Explain Your*

Mood?, NY Times Mag. (June 23, 2015), https://www.nytimes.com/2015/06/28/magazine/can-the-bacteria-in-your-gut-explain-your-mood.html.

 2 For information about possible origins of this saying, see *Quote Investigator, Tracing Quotations*, https://quoteinvestigator.com/2013/10/20/no-predict/ (last visited Jan. 24, 2022).

 3 Daniel Gilbert, *Stumbling on Happiness, passim* (Vintage Books/Random House 2005).

Chapter 1. Conflict and Conflict-Management Processes (pp. 13–16)

 1 See Phil Knight, *Shoe Dog: A Memoir by the Creator of NIKE* (Scribner/Simon & Schuster Paperback ed. 2018).

 2 Inspired by *The Corporate Divorce Mediation Roleplay*, © 1992 by J. Michael Keating, Jr. (modified by Leonard Riskin, 2006, 2011, 2017, and 2018). Used with permission of J. Michael Keating, Jr.

 3 See Bernard Mayer, *The Dynamics of Conflict Resolution: A Practitioner's Guide* 3 (Jossey-Bass 2000) [subsequently, Mayer, *Dynamics*].

 4 See Dean Pruitt, *Social Conflict: Some Basic Principles*, 2007 J. Dispute Resolution 152, 152 (2007).

 5 See Mayer, *Dynamics*, pp. 4–8 (fully cited in Chap. 1 endnote 3).

 6 Id. at 89–108.

Chapter 2. Negotiation Basics: Positions and Interests (pp. 17–31)

 1 Leonard L Riskin, Chris Guthrie, Richard C. Reuben, Jennifer K. Robbennolt, Nancy A. Welsh & Art Hinshaw, *Dispute Resolution and Lawyers: A Contemporary Approach* 127 (6th ed., West Academic 2019) [subsequently, Riskin et al., *DRL 6th*]. For other ways to understand the term negotiation, see Robert H. Mnookin, *When Not to Negotiate: A Negotiation Imperialist Reflects on Appropriate Limits*, 74 Univ. of Colorado Law Rev. 1077, 1079–82 (2003) [subsequently, Mnookin, *When Not*]; Alexandra Carter, *Ask for More: 10 Questions to Negotiate Anything* 4–5 (Simon & Schuster 2021).

 2 *Negotiate*, Dictionary.com, https://www.dictionary.com/browse/negotiate (last visited Jan. 24, 2022).

 3 In this book, I have separated the three conversations from the first three negotiation focuses by inserting "Section B. Mindfulness, The Second Domain" between Section A and Section C. When teaching this material, I have learned that this arrangement enhances learning.

 4 The distinction I draw between focuses and models in negotiation resembles the distinction in law between standards and rules, which is explained in Duncan Kennedy, *Form and Substance in Private Law Adjudication*, 89 Harvard Law Rev. 1685 (1976).

Models have the advantage of providing specific guidance. But such guidance is sometimes based on unstated assumptions about the situation. And if these assumptions are incorrect, it may be unwise to follow some of the instructions. For example, what if the traffic lights in a particular situation are not working, or if a corner crossing is not possible because of a traffic accident, construction, or a water leak?

 5 Of course, you could use other models of negotiation in working with Mindful Conflict Management.

 6 Roger Fisher, William Ury & Bruce Patton, *Getting to Yes: Negotiating Agreement Without Giving In* 40–42 (2d ed., Penguin Books 1991) [subsequently, "Fisher et al., *Getting to Yes 2d*"].

 7 Id.

 8 Mike Ewers, Cartoon, in Ronald B. Adler, Russell F. Proctor II & Neil Towne, *Looking Out, Looking In* 27 (Thomson/Wadsworth 2005).

[9] Note that, although their positions seem far apart, some of their interests overlap. These overlaps allow opportunities to reach creative agreements that address both of their interests, as we will see below.

[10] I am trying to make this simple, but confusion, disagreement, and ambiguity about negotiation models abound. See John Lande, *A Framework for Advancing Negotiation Theory: Implications from a Study of How Lawyers Reach Agreement in Pretrial Litigation*, 16 Cardozo J. Conflict Resolution 1, *passim* (2014).

[11] See Art Hinshaw, Alyson Carrel, Leonard L. Riskin, Chris Guthrie, Richard C. Reuben, Jennifer K. Robbennolt & Nancy A. Welsh, *Negotiation and Lawyers* 92–93 (West Academic 2021) [subsequently, Hinshaw et al., *Negotiation and Lawyers*]. See also Binyamin Cooper, Christopher R. Giordano, Amir Erez, Trevor A. Foulk, Heather Reed & Kent B. Berg, *Trapped by a First Hypothesis: How Rudeness Leads to Anchoring*, J. Applied Psychology (Mar. 2021), https://www.researchgate.net/publication/349928920_Trapped_by_A_First_Hypothesis_How_Rudeness_Leads_to_Anchoring.

[12] See Lande, *Framework*, pp. 27–28 (fully cited in Chap. 2 endnote 10). See also James K. Sebenius, *Why a Behavioral Theory of Labor Negotiations Remains a Triumph at Fifty but the Labels Distributive and Integrative Should be Retired*, 31 Negotiation J. 335 (2015); Bruce Patton, *Managing the Value and Dangers of Dualities*, 31 Negotiation J. 349 (2015).

[13] Finding and agreeing upon objective criteria is frequently very challenging. Note that objective criteria tend to be even more important when dealing with positions, such as those concerning the value of an item.

[14] For fuller explanations of the idea of problem-definition as it applies in mediation, see Leonard L. Riskin & Nancy A. Welsh, *Is That All There Is?: "The Problem" in Court-Oriented Mediation*, 15 George Mason Law Rev. 863, 884–97 (2008) [subsequently, Riskin & Welsh, *The Problem*]; Leonard L. Riskin, *Understanding Mediators' Orientations, Strategies, and Techniques: A Grid for the Perplexed*, 1 Harvard Negotiation Law Rev. 7, 18–23, 42–44 (1996).

[15] See Donald A. Schon, *The Reflective Practitioner: How Professionals Think in Action* 18–19, 40–41, passim (Basic Books 1983).

[16] Leonard L. Riskin, *Mediation and Lawyers*, 43 Ohio St. Law J. 29, 44–45 (1982).

[17] Howard J. Aibel, *ITT Mini-Trial Settles Long-Pending Expensive Damage Suit for Market Share Loss*, 3 Alternatives to the High Cost of Litigation 6 (Jan. 1985).

[18] Guy Olivier Faure, *Negotiating in the Orient: Encounters in the Peshawar Bazaar, Pakistan*, 7 Negotiation J. 279 (1991).

[19] Many writers agree. See, for instance, Robert H. Mnookin, Scott R. Peppet & Andrew S. Tulumello, *Beyond Winning: Negotiating to Create Value in Deals and Disputes* 9–96 (The Belknap Press of Harvard Univ. Press 2000) [subsequently, Mnookin et al., *Beyond Winning*].

[20] See David Lax & James Sebenius, *The Manager as Negotiator: Bargaining for Cooperation and Competitive Gain* 29–30, 32–35 (Free Press 1986) [subsequently, Lax & Sebenius, *Manager as Negotiator*]. Mnookin, Peppet, and Tulumello recommend that, in order to deal with this problem, lawyer-negotiators should deliberately separate their trial preparation and their efforts to settle the matter. See Mnookin et al., *Beyond Winning*, pp. 225–71 (cited in Chap. 2 endnote 19). Similarly, law firms or their clients sometimes assign each of the tasks to a separate team of lawyers; one is preparing for trial, the other for settlement. See Jim Golden, H. Abigail Moy & Adam Lyons, *The Negotiation Counsel Model: An Empathetic Model for Settling Catastrophic Personal Injury Cases*, 13 Harvard Negotiation Law Rev. 211 (2008).

Mediators also can help someone deal with this tension. A party can tell the mediator certain of their interests, with instructions not to disclose them but instead to keep them in mind in case that knowledge might help reach or improve a settlement. See Jennifer Gerarda Brown & Ian Ayres, *Economic Rationales for Mediation*, 80 Virginia Law Rev. 323 (1994).

[21] Lax & Sebenius, *Manager as Negotiator*, pp. 29–35 (fully cited in Chap. 2 endnote 20).

22   Mnookin, Peppet, and Tulumello describe three tensions that arise in negotiations in which lawyers represent clients: between creating and distributing value (as discussed above); between empathy and assertiveness; and between principals and agents. Mnookin et al., *Beyond Winning* (fully cited in Chap. 2 endnote 19). Their problem-solving approach appears at pages 173–269 of their book.

23   This hypothetical was inspired by the "Prisoner's Dilemma." For more on that, see Robert Axelrod, *The Evolution of Cooperation* 7–19, *passim* (Basic Books 1984).

Chapter 3. Emotions and the Core Concerns (pp. 33–43)

1   Authorities frequently distinguish emotions, feelings, and moods. For purposes of this book, I will not elaborate on the differences. For a discussion of the impact of mood on negotiation, see Daniel Kahneman, Olivier Sibony & Cass R. Sunstein, *Noise: A Flaw in Human Judgment* 86–90 (Little, Brown Spark 2021) [subsequently, Kahneman et al., *Noise*]. See generally *Noise* for the distinction between noise and bias.

2   Thanks to Professor Nancy Welsh for introducing me to this term. See Riskin & Welsh, *The Problem*, p. 863 (fully cited in Chap. 2 endnote 14).

3   It should be obvious that these emotions do not stand alone. They are intricately interrelated with thoughts and body sensations, important influences that the next chapter addresses. For simplicity and clarity, I will continue to focus on emotions for the moment.

4   Examples include the tort of intentional infliction of mental suffering (or distress) and a variety of personal injury claims in which emotional suffering can be an element of damages.

5   For a description of a person with this kind of limitation, see Daniel J. Siegel, *The Mindful Brain: Reflection and Attunement in the Cultivation of Well-Being* 300–04, 307–08 (W.W. Norton & Co., Inc. 2007) [subsequently, Siegel, *Mindful Brain*].

6   See Fisher et al., *Getting to Yes 2d*, *passim* (fully cited in Chap. 2 endnote 6); Carrie Menkel-Meadow, *Toward Another View of Legal Negotiation: The Structure of Problem Solving*, 31 UCLA L. Rev. 754, *passim* (1984).

7   Daniel Shapiro, *Negotiating Emotions*, 20 Conflict Resolution Quarterly 67, 67–68 (2002).

8   See Riskin & Welsh, *The Problem*, pp. 877–94 (fully cited in Chap. 2 endnote 14)(describing a particular case in which the professionals systematically ignored some of the plaintiff's obvious core concerns). Recall Bernard Mayer's ideas in *Dynamics* that we should understand conflict along three dimensions—behavioral, cognitive, and emotional—and that full resolution requires resolution along all three dimensions. See Chap. 1, note 3 and accompanying text.

9   See Roger Fisher & Daniel Shapiro, *Beyond Reason: Using Emotions as You Negotiate* (Penguin Pub. Grp. 2005) [subsequently, Fisher & Shapiro, *Beyond Reason*].

10   Id. at 5–6.

11   Id. at 12–14.

12   Id. at 11.

13   Henry Wadsworth Longfellow, *Driftwood* (1857), quoted in John Bartlett, *Bartlett's Familiar Quotations* 467 (Justin Kaplan ed., 17th ed. 2002).

14   In commenting on a draft of this book, the psychologist Professor Daniel Shapiro said, "The mere act of labeling our emotional experiences using the core concerns can placate strong negative emotion, similar to the way in which the healing power of psychotherapy seems to derive, at least in part, from the act of putting to words one's emotional experiences. More generally, once the 'message' of an emotion is understood, we can exhale some of its intensity."

[15] Fisher & Shapiro, *Beyond Reason*, pp. 25–140 (fully cited in Chap. 3 endnote 9). Professor Clark Freshman has described situations in which trying to satisfy a negotiation partner's core concerns might not work. See Clark Freshman, *Yes, and: Core Concerns, Internal Mindfulness, and External Mindfulness for Emotional Balance, Lie Detection, and Successful Negotiation*, 10 Nevada Law J. 365 (2010) [subsequently, Freshman, *Yes*].

[16] See Fisher & Shapiro, *Beyond Reason*, pp. 52–68 (fully cited in Chap. 3 endnote 9).

[17] See id. at 94–102.

[18] See id. at 117–18.

[19] See id. at 49.

[20] See id. at 75–82.

[21] See id. at 50.

[22] See id. at 105–06.

[23] For a consideration of circumstances in which trying to satisfy a negotiation counterpart's core concerns might not benefit the negotiation, see Freshman, *Yes* (fully cited in Chap. 3 endnote 15).

Chapter 4. Five Obstacles to Skillfully Using the Core Concerns (and Positions and Interests) (pp. 45–50)

[1] See Daniel Kahneman, *Thinking, Fast and Slow* (Farrar, Straus and Giroux 2011) [subsequently, Kahneman, *Thinking*]. He also calls them System 1 and System 2, familiar terms in psychology.

[2] Id. at 13.

[3] Id. at 24–25.

[4] Id. at 30.

[5] Here I use "top down" in the sense in which psychiatrist Daniel Siegel does: to mean "how engrained brain states can impinge on emerging neural circuit activations and thus shape our awareness of ongoing experience in the present moment." Siegel, *The Mindful Brain*, p. 135 (fully cited in Chap. 3 endnote 5). The term is used in various other ways, too. Id. at 134–37.

[6] For fuller explanations of explicit and implicit biases, see Jerry Kang, *Implicit Bias: A Primer for Courts* (2009) (prepared for the National Center for State Courts), available at both JerryKang.net/research/2009-implicit-bias-primer-for-courts/ and http://wp.jerrykang.net. s110363.gridserver.com/wp-content/uploads/2010/10/kang-Implicit-Bias-Primer-for-courts-09.pdf; Jerry Kang, Mark Bennett, Devon Carbado, Pam Casey & Justin Levinson, *Implicit Bias in the Courtroom*, 59 UCLA Law Rev. 1124 (2012); Donald Gifford & Robert Rhee, *Legal Negotiation: Theory and Practice* (3rd ed., West Academic 2017); Mark B. Baer, *The Amplification of Bias in Family Law and Its Impact*, 32 J. American Academy of Matrimonial Lawyers 305 (2020).

[7] Yoona Kang, Jeremy R. Gray & John F. Dovidio, *The Nondiscriminating Heart: Loving-Kindness Meditation Training Decreases Implicit Intergroup Bias*, 143 J. Experimental Psychology: General 1306, 1306–1313 (2015).

[8] Marianne Bertrand & Sendhil Mullainathan, *Are Emily and Greg More Employable than Lakisha and Jamal? A Field Experiment on Labor Market Discrimination*, 94 American Economic Rev. 991, 992 (2004).

[9] Adam Lueke & Bryan Gibson, *Mindfulness Meditation Reduces Implicit Age and Race Bias: The Role of Reducing Automaticity of Responding*, 6 Social Psychological & Personality Sci. 284 (2015).

[10] See Jean R. Sternlight & Jennifer Robbennolt, *Good Lawyers Should Be Good Psychologists: Insights for Interviewing and Counseling Clients*, 23 Ohio St. J. Dispute Resolution 437, 462 (2008).

11 See Robert H. Mnookin, *Why Negotiations Fail*, 8 Ohio St. J. Dispute Resolution 235, 246–47 (1993). See also Lee Ross, *Reactive Devaluation in Negotiation and Conflict Resolution*, in *Barriers to Conflict Resolution* 26 (Kenneth J. Arrow, Robert H. Mnookin, Lee Ross, Amos Tversky & Robert J. Wilson eds., W.W. Norton & Co. 1995) [book subsequently cited as *Barriers to Conflict Resolution*].

12 See Daniel Kahneman & Amos Tversky, *Conflict Resolution: A Cognitive Perspective*, in *Barriers to Conflict Resolution*, pp. 44, 46–50 (book fully cited in Chap. 4 endnote 11); Jennifer A. Robbennolt & Jean R. Sternlight, *Psychology for Lawyers: Understanding the Human Factors in Negotiation, Litigation, and Decision Making* 88, 93 (2nd ed., American Bar Assoc. 2021).

13 Ambrose Bierce, *The Unabridged Devil's Dictionary* 63 (David E. Schultz & S.T. Joshi eds., 2000).

14 Professor Leigh Thompson has identified egocentrism—"the tendency for people to view their experiences in a way that is flattering or fulfilling for themselves"—as a principal cause of ineffective negotiation. Leigh L. Thompson, *The Mind and Heart of the Negotiator* 6 (4th ed. 2009).

15 Shel Silverstein, *Point of View*, in Shel Silverstein, *Where the Sidewalk Ends* 98 (New York: Harper & Row 1974).

Review of Section A (p. 51)

1 Condoleezza Rice, *Opinion: George Shultz will be remembered as one of the most influential secretaries of state in our history*, Washington Post (Feb. 7, 2021), https://www.washingtonpost.com/opinions/condi-rice-george-shultz-appreciation/2021/02/07/1c0a8efa-6972-11eb-9ead-673168d5b874_story.html.

Section B. Mindfulness, the Second Domain (pp. 55–102)

Chapter 5. Mindfulness: Its Nature and Potential Benefits (pp. 57–62)

1 In the words of Jon Kabat-Zinn, "Mindfulness can be thought of as moment-to-moment, nonjudgmental awareness, cultivated by paying attention in a specific way, that is, in the present moment, and as non-reactively, as non-judgmentally, and as openheartedly as possible." Jon Kabat-Zinn, *Coming to Our Senses: Healing Ourselves and the World Through Mindfulness* 108 (Hyperion 2005) [subsequently, Kabat-Zinn, *Coming to*]. See also Jon Kabat-Zinn, *Wherever You Go, There You Are: Mindfulness Meditation in Everyday Life* 3–7, *passim* (Hyperion 1994) [subsequently, Kabat-Zinn, *Wherever You Go*].

The word mindfulness carries other meanings. For the range of meanings in scientific literature, see Simon B. Goldberg, Kevin M. Riordan, Shufang Sun & Richard J. Davidson, *The Empirical Status of Mindfulness-Based Interventions: A Systematic Review of 44 Meta-Analyses or Randomized Control Trials*, 17 Perspectives on Psychological Sci. 108 (2022) [subsequently, Goldberg et al., *Empirical Status of Mindfulness*].

Another meaning is based on the form of mindfulness studied, described, and popularized by the social psychologist Professor Ellen Langer. "When we are mindful," Langer tells us, "we implicitly or explicitly (1) view a situation from several perspectives, (2) see information presented in the situation as novel, (3) attend to the context in which we are perceiving the information, and eventually (4) create new categories through which this information may be understood." Ellen J. Langer, *The Power of Mindful Learning* 111 (Perseus Books, 1997). See more generally *The Wiley Blackwell Handbook of Mindfulness*, vol. I (Amanda Ie, Christelle T. Ngnoumen & Ellen J. Langer eds., Wiley Blackwell 2014). [subsequently, Ie et al., *Handbook*].

In common parlance, to be mindful means to be conscious or aware of something. When I was a child, for instance, my mother told me to "mind your manners when you visit Cousin Ernst." Likewise, when you drive from Toronto to Toledo for the first time, you should be very mindful of the road signs—even, or especially—if you have a GPS. And restaurateurs should be aware of what belongs in their food; in this spirit, "A More Mindful Burger" graces the awnings of all six Epic Burger restaurants in Chicago.

The three principal forms of mindfulness—the one defined by Jon Kabat-Zinn, which I call Eastern-derived; the one described by Ellen Langer; and the one used in common parlance—overlap a bit and share some practices and goals. But to unpack these relationships would take the rest of this book. See Leonard L. Riskin, *Two (or More) Concepts of Mindfulness in Law and Conflict Resolution*, in Ie et al., *Handbook*, p. 458 (fully cited earlier in this endnote). So, henceforth, when I say mindfulness, I intend the first, Eastern-derived, meaning set out in this note.

² See Phil Jackson & Hugh Delehanty, *Sacred Hoops: Spiritual Lessons of a Hardwood Warrior* (Hyperion 1995).

³ See Chade-Meng Tan, *Search Inside Yourself: The Unexpected Path to Achieving Success, Happiness (and World Peace)* (2012) (a guide as well as an explanation of the Google program). See also David Gelles, *Mindful Work: How Meditation is Changing Business from the Inside Out* (Eamon Dolan 2016).

⁴ See Dan Hurley, *Breathing Out v. Spacing Out*, NY Times Mag. 14 (Jan. 19, 2014) (describing a mindfulness program for the U.S. Marines).

⁵ See the book by U.S. Congressman Tim Ryan of Ohio: Tim Ryan, *A Mindful Nation: How a Simple Practice Can Help Us Reduce Stress, Improve Performance, and Capture the American Spirit* (Hayhouse 2012).

⁶ Id.

⁷ See *Mindfulness in Education* (Kenneth Tobin ed., Routledge 2019). See also the website of the Association for Contemplative Mind in Higher Education: contemplativemind.org (last visited Feb. 17, 2023).

⁸ See *Mindfulness and Psychotherapy* (Christopher K. Germer, Ronald D. Siegel & Paul R. Fulton eds., 2nd ed., The Guilford Press 2013).

⁹ See the *Mindful Leader* website: https://www.mindfulleader.org/blog/55916-is-mbsr-evidence-based (last visited Jan. 9, 2022).

¹⁰ See Nathalie Martin, *Lawyering from the Inside Out: Learning Professional Development through Mindfulness and Emotional Intelligence* (Cambridge Univ. Press 2018); Scott Rogers, *Mindfulness for Law Students: Using the Power of Mindfulness to Achieve Balance and Success in Law School* (Paperback ed., Mindful Living Press 2009); Scott Rogers, *The Mindful Law Student* (Edward Elgar Publishing 2022). See generally Leonard L. Riskin, *The Contemplative Lawyer: On the Potential Contributions of Mindfulness Meditation to Law Students, Lawyers, and their Clients*, 7 Harvard Negotiation Law Rev. 1 (2002) [subsequently, Riskin, *Contemplative Lawyer*]; the *Mindfulness in Law Society* website: https://www.mindfulnessinlawsociety.org/ (last visited Dec. 31, 2021).

¹¹ See Joseph Goldstein, *Insight Meditation: The Practice of Freedom* 5 (Shambhala Publics. 1994) [subsequently, Goldstein, *Insight Meditation*].

¹² This sentence is my own summary of The Four Noble Truths, which is fundamental to Buddhist thought. See Matthew Flickstein, *Swallowing the River Ganges: A Practice Guide to the Path of Purification* 7–10 (Wisdom Publics. 2001) [subsequently, Flickstein, *River Ganges*]; Joseph Goldstein, *The Experience of Insight: A Simple and Direct Guide to Buddhist Meditation* 7 (Shambhala 1987) [subsequently, Goldstein, *Experience of Insight*]; U Silananda, *The Four Foundations of Mindfulness* 159–66 (Wisdom Publics., 1990); *Mahasatipatthana Sutta*, in *The Long Discourses of the Buddha: A Translation of the Digha Nikaya* 335, 348–50 (Maurice Walshe trans., Wisdom Publics. 1995) [subsequently, Walshe, *Digha Nikaya*]. "Suffering" is the most common

English translation of the ancient Pali word "dukkha," but it is not adequate. See Walshe, *Digha Nikaya,* p. 20 (fully cited earlier in this endnote). Matthew Flickstein uses "unsatisfactoriness." Flickstein, *River Ganges,* pp. 117, *passim* (fully cited earlier in this endnote). Stephen Batchelor uses "anguish." Steven Batchelor, *Buddhism Without Beliefs, passim* (Riverhead Books, 1997) [subsequently, Batchelor, *Buddhism Without*].

13 Healthy and unhealthy (or destructive) emotions in Buddhist thought correspond or overlap, to a significant extent, with positive and negative emotions. See Daniel Goleman, *Destructive Emotions: A Scientific Dialogue with the Dalai Lama* 45–115, *passim* (Bantam Dell 2003) [subsequently, Goleman, *Destructive Emotions*].

14 Quoted on the website *Forbes Quotes: Thoughts on the Business of Life,* https://www.forbes.com/quotes/7186/.

15 The Buddha set forth the Noble Eight-Fold Path as a way to end the suffering associated with craving and delusion. The Path consists of Right View, Right Intentions, Right Speech, Right Action, Right Livelihood, Right Effort, Right Mindfulness, and Right Concentration. See Flickstein, *River Ganges,* pp. 7–10, 113–43 (fully cited in Chap. 5 endnote 12); Bhikkhu Bodhi, *The Noble Eightfold Path: The Way to the End of Suffering* (BPS Pariyatti Editions 2006), and its table of contents (https://www.accesstoinsight.org/lib/authors/bodhi/waytoend.html) (last visited Jan. 9, 2022).

16 Batchelor, *Buddhism Without,* p. 19 (fully cited in Chap. 5 endnote 12).

17 See, e.g., Joseph Goldstein, *The Science and Art of Meditation,* in *Voices of Insight: Teachers of Buddhism in the West Share their Wisdom, Stories, and Experiences of Insight Meditation* 118, 121 (Sharon Salzberg ed., Shambhala 2000) (quoting Saint Francis de Sales, a 17th Century Bishop, who said, about prayer: "If the heart wanders or is distracted, bring it back to the point quite gently. And even if you did nothing during the whole of the hour but bring your heart back, though it went away every time you brought it back, your hour would be very well employed."). Aspects of Christian centering prayer resemble the concentration aspects of mindfulness meditation. Thomas Keating's guidelines for centering prayer focus on meditating on a sacred word, and therefore are primarily a concentration form of meditation; they include the following: "When you become aware of thoughts, return ever so gently to the sacred word." Thomas Keating, *Appendix: The Method of Centering Prayer,* in *Centering Prayer in Daily Life and Ministry* 129, 130–31 (Gustave Reininger ed., Bloomsbury Academic & Professional 1998).

18 See, for example, Alan Lew, *One God Clapping: The Spiritual Path of a Zen Rabbi* 62–68, 205, *passim* (Jewish Lights Publishing, 2001). The Institute for Jewish Spirituality offers a variety of programs that include mindfulness. See https://www.jewishspirituality.org/ (Last visited Feb. 16, 2022).

19 Batchelor, *Buddhism Without,* pp. 19, *passim* (fully cited in Chap. 5 endnote 12).

20 Id. at 19.

21 Kabat-Zinn, *Coming to,* p. 24 (fully cited in Chap. 5 endnote 1).

22 See Daniel Goleman, *Focus: The Hidden Driver of Excellence* 224–25 (HarperCollins Publishers 2013).

23 Katherine A. MacLean et al., *Intensive Meditation Training Leads to Improvements in Perceptual Discrimination and Sustained Attention,* 21 Psychological Sci. 820 (2010).

24 See Richard Davidson et al., *Alterations in Brain and Immune Function Produced by Mindfulness Meditation,* 65 Psychosomatic Med. 564 (2003) [subsequently, Davidson et al., *Alterations*].

25 Id.

26 Kenneth D. Kaplan et al., *The Impact of a Meditation-Based Stress Reduction Program on Fibromyalgia,* 35 Gen. Hosp. Psychiatry 284 (1993).

[27] John J. Miller et al., *Three-year Follow-up and Clinical Implications of a Mindfulness Meditation-Based Stress Reduction Intervention in the Treatment of Anxiety Disorders*, 7 Gen. Hosp. Psychiatry 192 (1995).

[28] See Michael D. Mrazek et al., *Mindfulness Training Improves Working Memory Capacity and GRE Performance While Reducing Mind Wandering*, 24 Psychological Sci. 776 (2013) [subsequently, Mrazek, *Mindfulness Training*.]; Richard C. Reuben & Kennon M. Sheldon, *Can Mindfulness Help Law Students with Stress, Focus, and Well-being? An Empirical Study of 1Ls at a Midwestern Law School*, 48 Southwestern Law Rev. 241 (2019).

[29] See Mrazek, *Mindfulness Training* (fully cited in Chap. 5 endnote 28).

[30] Britta Holzel et al., *Mindfulness Practice Leads to Increases in Regional Brain Gray Matter Density*, 191 Psychiatry Res. 36 (Jan. 30, 2011).

[31] See Robin Ortiz & Erica M. Sibinga, *The Role of Mindfulness in Reducing the Adverse Effects of Childhood Stress and Trauma*, 4 Children 16 (Mar. 2017), https://www.ncbi.nlm.nih.gov/pmc/articles/PMC5368427/. See also Bessel van der Kolk, *The Body Keeps the Score: Brain, Mind, and Body in the Healing of Trauma* 210–12 (Penguin Books 2014) [subsequently, van der Kolk, *The Body Keeps the Score*]; David A. Treleaven, *Trauma-Sensitive Mindfulness: Practices for Safe and Transformative Healing* (W.W. Norton & Co. 2018).

[32] See note 39 below and accompanying text concerning Brewer's work addressing smoking.

[33] For an comprehensive look at "Buddhist truths" and a carefully documented argument that "Buddhism's diagnosis of the human predicament is fundamentally correct, and that its prescription is deeply valid and urgently important," see Robert Wright, *Why Buddhism is True: The Science and Philosophy of Meditation and Enlightenment* xii, *passim* (Simon & Schuster 2017).

[34] Daniel Goleman & Richard J. Davidson, *Altered Traits: Science Reveals How Meditation Can Change Your Mind, Brain, and Body* (Avery, an imprint of Random House LLC 2017) [subsequently, Goleman & Davidson, *Altered Traits*].

[35] Id.

[36] Id. at 273.

[37] Id. at 273–74.

[38] Id. at 274. For another perspective on the empirical research on the effects of mindfulness-based interventions, see Goldberg et al., *Empirical Status of Mindfulness* (fully cited in Chap. 5 endnote 1).

[39] See Judson Brewer, *The Craving Mind: From Cigarettes to Smart Phones to Love—Why We Get Hooked & How We Can Break Bad Habits* 32–35 (Yale Univ. Press 2017) [subsequently, Brewer, *Craving Mind*.] Conventional treatment tries to reduce the craving. But Brewer concluded that mindfulness, in contrast, breaks the connection between craving and behavior. The successful subjects (those who quit through mindfulness) still craved cigarettes but did not act upon that craving. Id. at 22.

[40] Id. at 33.

Chapter 6. Formal Mindfulness and Loving-Kindness Meditation (pp. 63–75)

[1] As Krishnamurti put it, "Meditation is not a means to an end. It is both the means and the end." Surya Das, *Buddha is as Buddha Does: The Ten Original Practices for Enlightened Living* 136 (Harper San Francisco, A Division of HarperCollins Publishers 2007).

[2] See Chap. 5 endnote 39 concerning Brewer's work addressing the smoking habit.

[3] Mindfulness-Based Stress Reduction (MBSR) is a specific, evidence-based program developed in 1979 by Jon Kabat-Zinn at the University of Massachusetts Medical School.

MBSR programs are offered world-wide by medical and other organizations. For descriptions of MBSR, see Jon Kabat-Zinn, *Full-Catastrophe Living: How to Cope with Stress, Pain, and Illness Using Mindfulness Meditation* (rev. ed., Piatkus 2013).

4 See Larry Rosenberg, *Breath by Breath: The Liberating Practice of Insight Meditation* 170 (Shambhala 2004) [subsequently Rosenberg, *Breath by Breath*].

5 For a deeper and more extensive explanation of meditation on the breath, see id.

6 Joseph Goldstein, *One Dharma: The Emerging Western Buddhism* 83 (HarperSanFrancisco 2002).

7 See Charles Fernyhough, *The Voices Within: The History and Science of How We Talk to Ourselves* 12 (Basic Books 2016).

8 We also have opportunities to assess the truth of a particular thought or train of thought, although such assessment is not part of mindfulness itself, and I am not encouraging you to assess or evaluate anything during this meditation. For an example of this ability in the negotiation context, see Andrea K. Schneider, *Effective Responses to Offensive Comments*, 10 Negotiation J. 107 (1994). In later chapters, we will work with other exercises or tools that include such assessments.

9 For further information on walking meditation, which means being present or mindful while walking, see Goldstein, *Insight Meditation*, pp. 136–37 (fully cited in Chap. 5 endnote 11) and Flickstein, *River Ganges*, pp. 78–82 (fully cited in Chap. 5 endnote 12).

10 See Sharon Salzberg, *Loving-kindness: The Revolutionary Art of Happiness* (Shambhala 1995) [subsequently, Salzberg, *Loving-kindness*].

11 As is the case with all the meditations described in this chapter, loving-kindness meditations come in a wide variety of formulations. For more on loving-kindness, see generally id. and Sharon Salzberg, *Real Love: The Art of Mindful Connection* (Flatiron Books 2017) [subsequently, Salzberg, *Real Love*].

12 *Prose Works of Henry Wadsworth Longfellow*, vol. 1, Chapter: *Drift Wood: A Collection of Essays*, Section: *Table-Talk* 452 (Ticknor and Fields 1857). For a history of this quote, its variations, and (apparently improper) attributions to others, see *Quote Investigator: Tracing Quotations*, https://quoteinvestigator.com/2019/08/19/secret-history/ (last visited Feb. 15, 2022).

13 See generally Kabat-Zinn, *Coming to* (fully cited in Chap. 5 endnote 1).

Chapter 7. How Mindfulness and Loving-Kindness Can Help You Negotiate and Manage Problematic Situations More Wisely (pp. 77–86)

1 The quote is commonly and probably erroneously attributed to Viktor Frankl, the renowned Austrian neurologist, in his book, *Man's Search for Meaning*.

Steven Covey recalls reading that language and thinking it described Frankl's beliefs, but he did not remember the author or title of the book in which it appeared. See Viktor Frankl Institut, *Alleged Quote*, https://www.univie.ac.at/logotherapy/quote_stimulus.html.

2 In 2008, Darshan Brach explained how mindfulness could help a person work more wisely with interest-based negotiation. See Darshan Brach, *A Logic for the Magic of Mindful Negotiation*, 24 Negotiation J. 25 (Jan. 2008) [subsequently, Darshan Brach, *Magic of Mindful Negotiation*]. I agree with everything she said.

3 The extent of practice experience has a linear correlation with changes in awareness and related neuroplastic changes in the brain. For an overview of this issue, see Sharon Begley, *Train Your Mind, Change Your Brain: How a New Science Reveals Our Extraordinary Potential to Transform Ourselves* 233–39 (Ballantine Books 2007) [subsequently, Begley, *Change Your Brain*].

4 Any or all of the barriers may be erected or strengthened through trauma. See van der Kolk, *The Body Keeps the Score, passim* (fully cited in Chap. 5 endnote 31).

5 Adam Lueke & Bryan Gibson, *Mindfulness Meditation Reduces Implicit Age and Race Bias: The Role of Reducing Automaticity of Responding*, 6 Social Psychological and Personality Sci. 284 (2015).

6 Yoona Kang, Jeremy R. Gray & John F. Dovidio, *The Nondiscriminating Heart: Loving-Kindness Meditation Training Decreases Implicit Intergroup Bias*, 143 J. Experimental Psychology: General 1306, 1306–1313 (2015).

7 Goleman & Davidson, *Altered Traits*, p. 121 (fully cited in Chap. 5 endnote 34).

8 Rhonda V. Magee, *The Inner Work of Racial Justice: Healing Ourselves and Transforming Our Communities Through Mindfulness* (Tarcher Perigee, an imprint of Penguin Random House 2019) [subsequently, Magee, *Inner Work*]

9 See Tara Brach, *Radical Compassion: Learning to Love Yourself and Your World with the Practice of RAIN* 200–01 (Viking Life 2019) [subsequently, Tara Brach, *Radical Compassion*].

10 This is a modified version of the Triangle of Awareness developed by the Stress Reduction Clinic at the University of Massachusetts Medical School and formerly used in its training programs.

11 For explanations of the fight, flight, or freeze reaction or instinct, see Brewer, *Unwinding Anxiety*, pp. 21, 94–96 (fully cited in Chap. 5 endnote 39).

12 See Shauna L. Shapiro & Linda E. Carlson, *The Art and Science of Mindfulness: Integrating Mindfulness Into Psychology and the Helping Profession* 99 (2nd ed., American Psychological Assoc. 2017) [subsequently, Shapiro & Carlson, *Art and Science*].

13 Authorship of this quote is disputed. Some have attributed it to C.S. Lewis, but the C.S. Lewis Foundation website lists the quote as a misattribution to Lewis, and instead attributes it to either Rick Warren, in his *The Purpose Driven Life: What on Earth am I Here For?*, or Rich Howard and Jamie Lash in their *This Was Your Life: Preparing to Meet God Face to Face*. See C.S. Lewis Foundation, *Quotes Misattributed to C.S. Lewis*, https://www.cslewis.org/aboutus/faq/quotes-misattributed/. See also GoodReads, https://www.goodreads.com/quotes/201236-true-humility-is-not-thinking-less-of-yourself-it-is (last visited Feb. 15, 2022) (attributing to Rick Warren); Aaron Armstrong, What C.S. Lewis wrote is more powerful than what he didn't, https://bloggingtheologically.com/2015/12/11/what-cs-lewis-wrote-is-better-than-what-he-didnt/ (last visited Feb. 15, 2022) (attributing to Rick Warren).

14 James H. Austin, *Selfless Insight: Zen and the Meditative Transformations of Consciousness* 53–56 (MIT Press 2009) [subsequently, Austin, *Selfless Insight*].

15 Author Interview with James H. Austin, M.D., Dep't of Neurology, Univ. of Mo. Sch. of Med., in Gainesville, Fla. (Mar. 7, 2009) [subsequently, Austin Interview with Author]; Letter with attachments from James H. Austin, M.D., Clinical Professor of Neurology, Univ. of Mo. Sch. of Med., Columbia, Mo., to author (Aug. 20, 2009) [subsequently, Austin Letter to Author].

16 See Austin, *Selfless Insight*, pp. 103–12 (fully cited in Chap. 7 endnote 14); Austin Letter to Author, Attachment (fully cited in Chap. 7 endnote 15); Austin Interview with Author (fully cited in Chap. 7 endnote 15).

17 See Austin Letter to Author, Attachment (fully cited in Chap. 7 endnote 15).

18 Id.

19 Id.

20 Austin, *Selfless Insight*, pp. 153–58, 199–204 (fully cited in Chap. 7 endnote 14); Austin Interview with Author (fully cited in Chap. 7 endnote 15).

21 *See* Austin, *Selfless Insight*, pp. 156–57, *passim* (fully cited in Chap. 7 endnote 14).

²² Austin Interview with Author (fully cited in Chap. 7 endnote 15). For fuller explanations, see James H. Austin, *Zen-Brain Reflections: Reviewing Recent Developments in Meditation and States of Consciousness* 197–200 (MIT Press 2006); Austin, *Selfless Insight*, pp. 103–112, 187–88 (fully cited in Chap. 7 endnote 14).

²³ An important recent study found that, for treating adults with anxiety disorders, Mindfulness-Based Stress Reduction was "non-inferior" to Escitalopram (a first-line medication for treating anxiety disorders). Elizabeth A. Hoge, et al., Mindfulness-Based Stress Reduction vs. Escitalopram for the Treatment of Adults With Anxiety Disorders: A Randomized Clinical Trial, JAMA Psychiatry doi:10:1001/Published on line, Nov. 9, 2022/.

²⁴ See Shauna L. Shapiro et al., *Effects of Mindfulness-Based Stress Reduction on Medical and Pre-Medical Students*, 21 J. Behavioral Med. 581, 589–94 (1998). See generally Shauna L. Shapiro et al., *Toward the Integration of Meditation into Higher Education: A Review of Research Evidence*, 113 Teachers College Record 14 (2008) [subsequently, Shapiro, *Meditation in Higher Ed*].

²⁵ See Rimma Teper, Zindel V. Segal & Michael Inzlicht, *Inside the Mindful Mind: How Mindfulness Enhances Emotion Regulation Through Improvements in Executive Control*, 22 Current Directions in Psychological Sci. 449 (2013).

²⁶ See Shauna Shapiro et al., *Meditation in Higher Ed*, pp. 16–18 (fully cited in Chap. 7, endnote 24)(citing and discussing studies).

²⁷ *See* Zindel V. Segal, J. Mark G. Williams, John D. Teasdale, *Mindfulness-Based Cognitive Therapy for Depression: A New Approach to Preventing Relapse* 244–68 (The Guilford Press 2001).

²⁸ Richard Davidson and his colleagues gave a mindfulness-based stress reduction course to high tech executives with no previous experience in meditation. One result was an increase in neural activity in the left prefrontal cortex, which is associated with happiness. Davidson et al., *Alterations*, p. 569 (fully cited in Chap. 5 endnote 24).

²⁹ Shapiro et al., *Meditation in Higher Ed*, pp. 22–23 (fully cited in Chap. 5 endnote 24).

³⁰ Id. at 21–22.

³¹ See id. at 22–23 (proposing, among other things, that meditation practice over an extended period of time may sensitize the brain's limbic circuitry, which is essential to empathy and compassion).

³² Professor Clark Freshman writes that "[m]indfulness promotes happiness in at least three ways":

First, as new research continues to show, mindfulness itself increases happiness and the predisposition to happiness. Second, internal mindfulness lets us learn what puts us in a good mood. Chocolate may put Columbia [Missouri] doctors in a good mood, but it may put those of us predisposed to migraines in a rather foul mood. Third, internal mindfulness lets us know when our emotions may be efficient for negotiating. Awareness of our own positive emotions may tell us we are in a kind of sweet spot, much as the sweet spot of a tennis racket is the best place for many shots. And awareness of our negative emotions may reveal what Ekman calls a "hot spot" of negative emotions or strained thinking. This is often not the best time to act, or even to take our thoughts too seriously.

Clark Freshman, *After Basic Mindfulness Meditation: External Mindfulness, Emotional Truthfulness, and Lie Detection in Dispute Resolution*, 2006 J. Dispute Resolution 511, 515.

³³ See generally Salzberg, *Loving-kindness*, pp. 119–35 (fully cited in Chap. 6 endnote 10).

³⁴ See Goleman & Davidson, *Altered States*, pp. 113–18 (fully cited in Chap. 5 endnote 34).

³⁵ *See* Begley, *Change Your Brain*, pp. 238–40 (fully cited in Chap. 7 endnote 3).

³⁶ Researchers have documented or suggested that happiness benefits performance in a wide variety of activities. See Peter H. Huang & Rick Swedloff, *Authentic Happiness & Meaning*

at Law Firms, 58 Syracuse Law Rev. 335, 335–37 (2008) (briefly surveying the research and citing studies). See also Barbara L. Frederickson, *Positivity: Groundbreaking Research Reveals How to Embrace the Hidden Strength of Positive Emotions, Overcome Negativity, and Thrive* (2009). See generally Martin E.P. Seligman, *Authentic Happiness: Using the New Positive Psychology to Realize Your Potential for Lasting Fulfillment* (2002).

[37] See Carolina Herrando & Efthmios Constantinides, *Emotional Contagion, a Brief Overview and Future Directions*, Frontiers in Psychology/Emotion Science (July 16, 2021), https://doi.org/10.3389/fpsyg.2021.712606.

[38] *See* Riskin, *Contemplative Lawyer*, pp. 47–48 (fully cited in Chap. 5 endnote 10).

[39] The term "emotional intelligence" was first used in Peter Salovey & John D. Mayer, *Emotional Intelligence*, 9 Imagination, Cognition & Personality 185 (1990). Daniel Goleman developed a particular version of emotional intelligence, which he popularized in a series of books, including Daniel Goleman, *Emotional Intelligence: Why It Can Matter More than IQ* (Bantam Books 1995) and Daniel Goleman, *Working with Emotional Intelligence* (Bantam Books 1998) [hereinafter, Goleman, *Working with EI*]. In 2006, he developed the idea of "Social Intelligence," which he divided into "Social Awareness" and "Social Facility." Daniel Goleman, *Social Intelligence: The New Science of Human Relationships* 84 (Bantam Books 2006).

[40] Goleman, *Working With EI*, p. 55 (fully cited in Chap. 7 endnote 39).

[41] See Riskin, *Contemplative Lawyer*, pp. 46–47 (fully cited in Chap. 5 endnote 10).

[42] See id. at 48. See also Shauna Shapiro et al., *Meditation in Higher Ed*, pp. 20–21 (fully cited in Chap. 7 endnote 24)(discussing research findings on the impact of meditation on interpersonal skills).

[43] See Amishi P. Jha et al., *Mindfulness Training Modifies Subsystems of Attention*, 7 Cognitive, Affective & Behav. Neurosci. 109, 116–17 (2007) (using performance-based measures of cognitive functions). See Shauna Shapiro et al., *Meditation in Higher Ed*, pp. 9–12 (fully cited in Chap. 7 endnote 24).

[44] William James, *The Principles of Psychology*, vol. 1, 424 (H. Holt & Co. 1918) (1890).

Chapter 8. How to Actually Be Mindful: Formal, Semiformal, and Informal Practices (pp. 87–100)

[1] This derives from the "Lester's Bonus" scenario in Leonard L. Riskin & Rachel Wohl, *Mindfulness in the Heat of Conflict: Taking STOCK*, 20 Harvard Negotiation Law Rev. 121 (2015) [subsequently, Riskin & Wohl, *Taking STOCK*].

[2] Methods for working with interests appear in Section A, Chapter 2; methods for working with core concerns appear in Section A, Chapter 3.

[3] Leonard L. Riskin, *Further Beyond Reason: Mindfulness, Emotions, and the Core Concerns in Negotiation*, 10 Nevada Law J. 289–337 (2010) [subsequently, Riskin, *Further Beyond Reason*]; Riskin & Wohl, *Taking STOCK* (fully cited in Chap. 8 endnote 1).

[4] For instance, while I was meditating toward the end of a meditation teacher training program, after which I was to leave quickly for the airport, I suddenly remembered that I had left nearly all of my clothes in the dresser drawers in my hotel room.

[5] See Steven Keeva, *Transforming Practices: Finding Joy and Satisfaction in the Legal Life* 51 (ABA Journal Books 1999).

[6] Id. at 52.

[7] *See* Daniel Bowling, *Who am I as Mediator? Mindfulness, Reflection and Presence*, 5 ACResolution 12–15 (Fall 2005).

[8] *See* Jack Kornfield, *After the Ecstasy, The Laundry: How the Heart Grows Wise on the Spiritual Path, passim* (Bantam Books 2000) [subsequently, Kornfield, *Laundry*].

⁹   Id. at xxi. With sufficient and continued practice, however, we can become more adept at establishing and sustaining mindfulness. *See* Richard J. Davidson, *On the Buffer*, in *Emotional Awareness: Overcoming the Obstacles to Psychological Balance and Compassion* 93, 93–94 (The Dalai Lama and Paul Ekman, eds., Holt Paperback 2008) (discussing the importance of continued meditation practice).

¹⁰   In the original version of RAIN, developed by the meditation teacher Michelle McDonald, the "N" meant "non-identification" or "no-self," which signified that you should not identify with whatever you observe through Investigation. McDonald's approach, which was very effective and popular, rested on the idea that mindfully observing inner phenomena could lead to realization that they were not "yours," which in turn could allow you more freedom from them. Tara Brach began with that and transformed the "N" into "Nurture." More recently she has added a new element, called "After the RAIN," and developed increasingly advanced, extensive, or particularized versions of RAIN. See Tara Brach, *Radical Compassion* (fully cited in Chap. 7 endnote 9). For a history of RAIN, see id. at 245. For many resources on RAIN see TaraBrach.com.

¹¹   Judson Brewer and his colleagues have used RAIN extensively in their work on habit change, with great success. In their studies on helping people stop smoking, for example the experimental group took the mindfulness-based program (as opposed to the most prominent conventional program, offered by the American Cancer Society). Using mindfulness to change habits, the experimental group performed much better than the conventional group. They quit at twice the rate, and they did not resume smoking. See Brewer, *Craving Mind*, pp. 32–35 (fully cited in Chap. 5 endnote 39). Equally important, RAIN was more significant than other mindfulness practices (which included breath meditation and loving-kindness meditation) in breaking the connection between craving and smoking. Id.

¹²   Rachel Wohl and I previously published an explanation of STOP, STOPSI and Taking STOCK. See Riskin & Wohl, *Taking STOCK* (fully cited in Chap. 8 endnote 1). We developed and refined these exercises primarily in or for *Practical Mindfulness: Clear and Calm in the Heat of Conflict* workshops that we led annually for many years in the Summer Skills Program sponsored by the Straus Institute for Dispute Resolution at Pepperdine University School of Law. My colleagues in the Center for Negotiation and Mediation at Northwestern University Pritzker School of Law—Lynn Cohen, Alyson Carrell, Annie Buth, and Daniel Gandert—and I used them in the annual Advanced Negotiation course. I have also used these exercises extensively in negotiation programs that I lead with Dan Shapiro and in many law school courses.

¹³   See Chap. 7 endnote 11 and accompanying text.

¹⁴   Tara Brach, *True Refuge: Finding Peace and Freedom in Your Own Awakened Heart* (Bantam Books 2013).

¹⁵   Philip Moffitt, *Emotional Chaos to Clarity: How to Live More Skillfully, Make Better Decisions, and Find Purpose in Life* 37 (Hudson Street Press 2012).

¹⁶   George Saunders, *Congratulations, By the Way: Some Thoughts on Kindness* 7 (Random House 2014) (unpaginated book; material referenced here appears on seventh page).

¹⁷   As you may be aware, kindness is not universally supported. See Jamil Zaki, *The War for Kindness: Building Empathy in a Fractured World* (Broadway Books 2019).

¹⁸   While we were developing this exercise, Donna Silverberg suggested that we add "Keep Going," which we greatly appreciate.

¹⁹   Salzberg, *Real Love* (fully cited in Chap. 6 endnote 11).

Review of Section B (pp. 101–102)

[1] See Katherine Larkin-Wong, *A Newbie's Impression: One Student's Mindfulness Lessons*, 61 J. Legal Educ. 665, 667 (2012).

Section C. Back to the First Domain, Negotiation: The Three Conversations (pp. 103–119)

[1] The Merriam-Webster dictionary defines *chutzpah* as "supreme self-confidence," and it suggests *nerve* or *gall* as synonyms. *Chutzpah*, Merriam Webster Dictionary, https://www.merriam-webster.com/dictionary/chutzpah#synonyms (last visited Jan. 26, 2022).

[2] Douglas Stone, Bruce Patton & Sheila Heen, *Difficult Conversations: How to Discuss What Matters Most* (Penguin Books 1999) [subsequently, Stone et al., *Difficult Conversations*].

Chapter 9. Positions, Interests, and Core Concerns in the Luxor Carriage-Fee Negotiation (pp. 105–109)

[1] Other alternatives included walking to the restaurant, switching to a closer restaurant, or returning to the hotel and ordering room service.

[2] Subsequently, I learned that carriage and taxi-ride fees were routinely negotiated unless the passenger accepted the driver's request, at least in parts of Egypt. An American student who had worked in Cairo said that she used the same taxi to get to the office every morning, and every morning, the driver tried to negotiate.

[3] David Owen recounts an episode in which he insisted on paying a taxi driver more than requested, which Owen calls "bargaining up." He believes that this led the driver to provide extra services. Owen had a similar experience with a merchant in a market. See David Owen, *Swinging in Morocco*, The New Yorker 52, 53–54 (May 21, 2001). For a counter example, see Guy Olivier Faure, *Negotiating in the Orient: Encounters in the Peshawar Bazaar, Pakistan*, 7 Negotiation J. 279 (1991).

[4] Shortly before this trip, Andrew's junior high school principal had asked the assembled parents whether they knew "how to embarrass your children?" Her answer: "Be in public, be with your children, and be yourself." She said nothing about embarrassing your spouse.

[5] After reading this text in draft form, Daniel Shapiro commented:

Affiliation is complicated. It may have been that Mr. Hassan did affiliate for financial gain, but also did so to satisfy the need for human connection. Affiliation is not a single strand of connection between individuals, but is more like a braid of strands, some with altruistic intent and others seeking personal gain.

Daniel L. Shapiro, Harvard Medical and Law Schools, Email to author (May 29, 2019).

[6] Some of their own core concerns also were damaged; they always felt embarrassed when I negotiated over the price of anything.

[7] Roger Fisher & Daniel Shapiro, *Beyond Reason: Using Emotions as You Negotiate* 115–40 (Penguin Pub. Grp. 2005) [subsequently, Fisher & Shapiro, *Beyond Reason*]. Chapter 3 in Section A, above, presents the core concerns.

Chapter 10. The Three Conversations in the Luxor Carriage-Fee Negotiation (pp. 111–118)

[1] Stone et al., *Difficult Conversations* (fully cited in Sec. C opener endnote 2).

[2]   *Difficult Conversations* calls this "The 'What Happened?' Conversation." Id. at 23–82. I have omitted the question mark.

[3]   *Difficult Conversations* calls this "The Feelings Conversation." Id. at 83–108.

[4]   *Difficult Conversations* calls this "The Identity Conversation," id. at 109–128, as do I.

[5]   Id. at 23–82.

[6]   Stone et al., *Difficult Conversations*, pp. 44–57 (fully cited in Sec. C opener endnote 2).

[7]   See Jennifer A. Robbennolt & Jean R. Sternlight, *Psychology for Lawyers: Understanding the Human Factors in Negotiation, Litigation, and Decision Making* 18–19 (2nd ed., American Bar Assoc. 2021). The fundamental attribution error also is described in Chapter 4.

[8]   Stone et al., *Difficult Conversations*, p. 112 (fully cited in Sec. C opener endnote 2).

[9]   Id.

[10]   Many of the identities that we sense are unrealistic and simplistic. They give us a sense of who and what we are in the world. We often struggle mightily to maintain them. Section D, below, focuses extensively on identity.

[11]   Leonard L. Riskin, *The Cat in the Hat*, Atlantic Monthly 30 (July 1995).

[12]   Leonard L. Riskin, *Unsportsmanlike Conduct*, NY Times Mag. 14–16 (Jan. 22, 1989).

[13]   Leonard L. Riskin, *Father Time*, Child Mag. (Unpaginated Special Insert) (May 1993).

[14]   Stone et al., *Difficult Conversations*, pp. 12–14, 85–108 (fully cited in Sec. C opener endnote 2).

[15]   Id. at 129–234.

Review of Sections A, B, and C (pp. 121–125)

[1]   Knowledge of the Core Concerns system can help a negotiator, such as Pedro, maintain mindful awareness. When Billy makes a nasty comment, Pedro's knowledge of the Core Concerns System could help him realize that Billy's statement was motivated by Billy's core concerns for appreciation and affiliation. Such a realization should reduce Pedro's anger toward Billy, as I have explained above; this is the same anger that might have derailed Pedro's mindful awareness. Similarly, as Pedro recognizes that his own core concern for appreciation is sparking anger toward Billy, this anger diminishes. Such insights about Billy could further soften Pedro's focus on himself, which could allow for a greater focus on and compassion for Billy to arise. Pedro's knowledge of the core concerns also makes Billy seem more interesting (just as a course in herpetology could enhance my interest in alligators), which makes it easier for Pedro to maintain a focus on Billy, which in turn further reduces his focus on himself. Pedro's ability to recognize the role of certain of his own core concerns could also help him notice the habitual thoughts, emotions, and behaviors that are associated with the core concerns—both as causes and manifestations. Such insights could give him additional distance from these phenomena, which would enhance mindfulness.

In these ways, the Core Concerns System could help Pedro maintain mindful awareness by helping him address obstacles to it.

[2]   The quote here appears in multiple sources, including in an article on the Adobe career resource and annual conference website, 99$\underline{u}$. See Scott Young, *Training Genius: The Learning Secrets of Polyglots and Savants*, 99$\underline{u}$ (July 26, 2011), https://99u.adobe.com/articles/7059/training-genius-the-learning-secrets-of-polyglots-and-savants (last visited Jan. 26, 2022).

Section D. Internal Family Systems (IFS), the Third Domain (pp. 127–167)

1 *Inside Out Official Trailer #2 (2015)*, YouTube, https://www.youtube.com/watch?v=semwpP0yeu4 (last visited Feb. 16, 2022). The full movie is available, as of the time of this book's publication, for fee-based streaming on the Disney+ site. *Inside Out*, Disney+, https://www.disneyplus.com/movies/inside-out/uzQ2ycVDi2IE (link requires a log-in to Disney+).

Chapter 11. Internal Family Systems: The Basics (pp. 129–137)

1 In a 2013 article, I covered IFS in relation to negotiation focuses and models based on positions, interests, and core concerns, but not the three conversations (which are included in this book). I did not include anything about mindfulness or how IFS relates to mindfulness, which are major features of this book. Leonard L. Riskin, *Managing Inner and Outer Conflict: Selves, Subpersonalities, and Internal Family Systems*, 18 Harvard Negotiation Law Rev. 1 (2013) [subsequently, Riskin, *Inner and Outer Conflict*].

2 See John Rowan, *Subpersonalities: The People Inside Us* 26–45 (Routledge 1990) [subsequently, Rowan, *People Inside Us*] (surveying idea of multiplicity of personality from many areas of human endeavor).

3 See Richard C. Schwartz & Robert R. Falconer, *Many Minds, One Self: Evidence for a Radical Shift in Paradigm* 153–264 (Trailheads Publications 2017) [subsequently, Schwartz & Falconer, *Many Minds, One Self*].

4 See Riskin, *Inner and Outer Conflict*, pp. 13–14 & notes 30–34 (fully cited in Chap. 11 endnote 1).

5 Adam Smith, *A Theory of Moral Sentiments* 161–65 (Dugard Stewart ed., Henry G. Bohn 1853) (original public. 1759). Thomas Shelling said, "Maybe it isn't only the family that, on a close look, fails to behave like a single-minded individual because it isn't one. Maybe the ordinary man or woman also doesn't behave like a single-minded individual because he or she isn't one." Thomas Schelling, *The Intimate Contest for Self-Command*, 60 Pub. Interest 94, 96 (1980).

6 See generally *The Multiple Self: Studies in Rationality and Social Change* (Jon Elster ed., Better World Books: North 1986) (including essays by a variety of authors that deal with a range of conceptions of multiple selves); *Ulysses and the Sirens: Studies in Rationality and Irrationality* (Jon Elster ed., Cambridge Univ. Press 1979) (describing Ulysses' method of binding his future self against temptation by the sirens and comparing other methods of self-control with that method). Some economists have recognized the existence of, and possible interaction among, contemporary multiple selves. Some see these selves arranged in a hierarchy, and others see them as equals. Economist Jon Elster advises against taking "the notions of 'several selves' very literally . . . . except in cases of severe pathology." Elster, *The Multiple Self*, p. 30 (fully cited earlier in this endnote). "Yet," he says, "some of the motivational conflicts are so deep-seated and permanent that the language of a divided self almost irresistibly forces itself on us. Although only one person is in charge, he is challenged by semi-autonomous strivings that confront him as 'alien powers.' " Id. at 31.

7 For an overview of approaches to psychotherapy that embrace multiplicity, see Rowan, *People Inside Us*, pp. 5–19 (fully cited in Chap. 11 endnote 2); see also Schwartz & Falconer, *Many Minds, One Self*, pp. 151–264, *passim* (fully cited in Chap. 11 endnote 3).

8 See Sigmund Freud, *The Complete Introductory Lectures on Psychoanalysis* 521–44 (James Strachey ed. & trans., W.W. Norton 1966) [subsequently, Freud, *Complete Introductory Lectures*].

9 C.G. Jung, *The Archetypes and the Collective Unconscious* 183 (2nd ed., Princeton Univ. Press 1969) (original public. 1959) (emphasis in original).

[10] Roberto Assagioli, *Psychosynthesis: A Collection of Basic Writings* (Synthesis Center Ed. 2000) (original public. Hobbs, Dorman & Co. 1965). In Fritz Perls's Gestalt therapy, the "open chair" technique is a way of working with multiplicity; the therapist leads the patient to change seats in order to play different parts of himself or herself. "You invent a script or dialogue between two opponents. This is part of integrating the fragmented parts of your personality, and these usually go in opposites—for instance, top dog and underdog." Frederick S. Perls, *Gestalt Therapy Verbatim* 78 (Real People Press 1969).

[11] Schemas are cognitive frameworks that help a person understand and interpret information.

[12] See Aaron Beck, *The Past and the Future of Cognitive Therapy*, 4 J. Psychotherapy Practice & Res. 276, 276–284 (1997); Albert Ellis, *Overcoming Resistance: A Rational Emotive Behavior Therapy Integrated Approach* 9 (2nd ed., Springer Publishing Co. 2002). I am grateful to Daniel Shapiro for this insight.

[13] Steven Pinker, *The Better Angels of Our Nature: Why Violence Has Declined* 482–570 (Penguin Books 2011).

[14] Id. at 571–670. President Lincoln referred to "the better angels of our nature" near the end of his first inaugural address.

[15] Daniel Kahneman, *Thinking, Fast and Slow* 377–407 (Farrar, Strauss & Giroux 2011) [subsequently, Kahneman, *Thinking*].

[16] Max H. Bazerman, A. E. Tenbrunsel & K.A. Wade-Benzoni, *Negotiating with Yourself and Losing: Understanding and Managing Conflicting Internal Preferences*, 23 Academy of Management Rev. 225, 226 (1998).

[17] Id. at 236–37.

[18] See, e.g., David Eagleman, *Incognito: The Secret Lives of the Brain* 200 (Pantheon 2011) [subsequently, Eagleman, *Secret Lives*] ("Knowing yourself now requires the understanding that the conscious occupies only a small room in the mansion of the brain, and that it has little control over the reality constructed for you."). See generally Michael S. Gazzaniga, *Who's in Charge? Free Will and the Science of the Brain* (Ecco 2011) (examining the issue of free will versus determinism from the perspective of brain science).

[19] See Eagleman, *Secret Lives*, p. 108 (fully cited in Chap. 11 endnote 18).

[20] See Tom Holmes & Lauri Holmes, *Parts Work: An Illustrated Guide to Your Inner Life* 18 (Sharon Eckstein illus., Winged Heart Press 2007) [subsequently, Holmes et al., *Parts Work*].

[21] See id. at 11–14.

[22] See Paul Raimond, *"Negotiating with Yourself and Losing": Further Reflections*, 24 Acad. of Mgm't Rev. 387, 387–88 (1999).

[23] See Phillip Moffitt, *From Emotional Chaos to Clarity: How to Live More Skillfully, Make Better Decisions, and Find Purpose in Life* 18–24 (Hudson Street Press 2012).

[24] See Eagleman, *Secret Lives*, p. 109 (fully cited in Chap. 11 endnote 18).

[25] See Richard C. Schwartz, Founding Developer, Center for Self-Leadership, Email to author (Nov. 1, 2011) [subsequently, Schwartz email, Nov. 1] (on file with author).

[26] For extensive information about IFS programs, support, and research, see the websites of the Foundation for SELF Leadership, https://www.foundationifs.org/ (last visited Feb. 17, 2022), and the IFS Institute, https://ifs-institute.com/ (last visited Feb. 17, 2022).

[27] Gail Tomala has introduced IFS at the CCSU-Naylor Leadership Academy, a pre-K–8 elementary school in Hartford, Connecticut, to students, parents, teachers, and staff. Gail Tomala, M.A., Ph.D., Presentations at Internal Family Systems Conferences (Oct. 15, 2011 & Oct 5, 2012). See also *IFS in Schools*, Foundation for SELF Leadership, https://www. foundationifs.org/news/ifs-in-schools (last visited Feb. 17, 2022).

[28] Steven Spitzer, an emeritus sociology professor at Suffolk University, works with incarcerated men through the Jericho Circle Project, in which he employs IFS concepts. See, IFS and Masculinity and Jericho Circles with Steve Spitzer and Glenn Williams at https://the oneinside.libsyn.com/ifs-and-masculinity-and-jericho-circles-with-steve-spitzer-and-glenn-williams.

[29] Bruce Anspach and Catherine Kelly use IFS in organizational consultation. Bruce Anspach & Catherine Kelly, Presentations at Internal Family Systems Conferences (Oct. 15, 2011 & Oct 5, 2012).

[30] Beyond Words, an Israeli organization devoted to building peace through the empowerment of women, uses IFS and has offered IFS training to a group of Arab and Jewish women. Nitsan Gordon-Giles, Founder and Director, Beyond Words, Presentations at Internal Family Systems Conference (Oct. 13 & 15, 2011). For information on Beyond Words, see http://www.beyondwords.org.il/.

[31] John Livingstone, M.D., and Joanne Gaffney have developed a strategy for teaching health care professionals to use IFS in dealing with patients, particularly to help them make difficult health care and health behavior decisions. This effort is grounded in a model that includes working with the patients' Parts. See John B. Livingstone & Joanne Gaffney, *IFS and Health Coaching: A New Model of Behavior Change and Medical Decision Making*, in *Internal Family Systems Therapy: New Dimensions* 143 (Martha Sweezy & Ellen L. Ziskind eds., Routledge 2013) [subsequently, Livingstone & Gaffney, *Health Coaching*].

[32] Nancy A. Shaddick et al., *A Randomized Controlled Trial of an Internal Family Systems-based Psychotherapeutic Intervention on Outcomes in Rheumatoid Arthritis: A Proof-of-Concept Study*, 40 J. Rheumatology 1831, 1831–36 (2013).

[33] See Bessel van der Kolk, *The Body Keeps the Score: Brain, Mind, and Body in the Healing of Trauma* 225–26, 279–97 (Penguin Books 2015) [subsequently, van der Kolk, *The Body Keeps the Score*]; Gabor Mate with Daniel Mate, *The Myth of Normal: Trauma, Illness & Healing in a Toxic Culture* 393–94 (Avery, An Imprint of Penguin/Random House 2022).

[34] See Frank Guastella Anderson, *"Who's Taking What?": Connecting Neuroscience, Psychopharmacology and Internal Family Systems for Trauma*, in *Internal Family Systems Therapy: New Dimensions* 107 (Martha Sweezy & Ellen L. Ziskind eds., Routledge 2013), [subsequently, Anderson, *Who's Taking What*].

[35] See Nancy Sowell, *The Internal Family System and Adult Health: Changing the Course of Chronic Illness*, in *Internal Family Systems Therapy: New Dimensions* 127 (Martha Sweezy & Ellen L. Ziskind eds., Routledge 2013).

[36] Ted Riskin has integrated IFS and breathwork. See generally Ted Riskin, *A Part of Me Did Not Want to Write this Article*, https://www.tedriskin.com/resources/a-part-of-me-didnt-want-to-write-this-article (2013).

[37] See Riskin, *Inner and Outer Conflict* (fully cited in Chap. 11 endnote 1).

[38] See David A. Hoffman, *Mediation, Multiple Minds, and Managing the Negotiation Within*, 16 Harvard Negotiation Law Rev. 297 (2011) [subsequently, Hoffman, *Mediation, Multiple Minds*]. For information about IFS training programs for mediators (and lawyers) see the training portion of the Boston Law Collaborative website, https://blc.law/training (last visited Feb. 20, 2022).

[39] See Richard C. Schwartz, *Internal Family Systems Therapy* 5–8 (Guilford Press 1995) [subsequently, Schwartz, *IFS Therapy*]. See generally Michael Nichols, *Family Therapy: Concepts and Methods* (11th ed., Pearson 2016).

[40] For a fuller explanation of the relationships between the two, see Richard C. Schwartz & Martha Sweezy, *Internal Family Systems* 3–23 (2nd ed., Guilford Press 2020) [subsequently, Schwartz & Sweezy, *IFS 2nd*].

[41] See Schwartz, *IFS Therapy*, pp. 27–60 (fully cited in Chap. 11 endnote 39). For a more recent (2020) explanation of IFS, see Schwartz & Sweezy, *IFS 2nd* (fully cited in Chap. 11, endnote 40). Still more recently, Schwartz has said that "IFS has morphed over time from being exclusively about psychotherapy to becoming a kind of spiritual practice, although you don't have to define yourself as spiritual in order to practice it." Richard C. Schwartz, *No Bad Parts: Healing Trauma and Restoring Wholeness with the Internal Family Systems Model* 4 (Sounds True 2021) [subsequently, Schwartz, *No Bad Parts*].

[42] See Schwartz & Sweezy, *IFS 2nd* (fully cited in Chap. 11 endnote 41).

[43] John Rowan, *Discover Your Subpersonalities: Our Inner World and the People in It* 79 (Routledge 1993) (emphasis in the original) [subsequently, Rowan, *Discover*].

[44] Schwartz, *IFS Therapy*, p. 232 (fully cited in Chap. 11 endnote 39).

[45] John Rowan provides the following list of common types: The Protector/Controller; the Critic; the Pusher; the Perfectionist; the Central Organizing Subpersonality; the Inner Child (which can include, inter alia, the "Good, Socialized Adapted Child"); the Little Professor; the Natural Child; the Nurturing Parent; the Power Brokers; and the Shadow ("what we would least like to be like"). Rowan, *People Inside Us*, pp. 6–10 (fully cited in Chap. 11 endnote 2). Rowan also lists some more specific Subpersonalities that his clients have identified: "the Hag, the Mystic, the Materialist, the Idealist, the Pillar of Strength, the Sneak, the Religious Fanatic, the Sensitive Listener, the Crusader, the Doubter, the Grabbie, the Frightened Child, The Poisoner, The Struggler, The Tester, The Shining Light, the Bitch Goddess, the Great High Gluck and the Dummy." Rowan, *Discover*, p. 6 (fully cited in Chap. 11 endnote 43).

[46] See Richard C. Schwartz, *Introduction to the Internal Family Systems Model* 111 (Trailheads Publications 2001) [subsequently Schwartz, *Intro to IFS Model*].

[47] Id at 127–28.

[48] Sometimes, however, Managers also induce extreme and dysfunctional behavior. For instance, a Manager might foster patterns of excessive work that could damage the person's health or might encourage a tendency to avoid seeking promotions or additional responsibilities.

[49] See *Seinfeld: The Invitations*, NBC television broadcast (Season 7, Episode 22, May 16, 1996).

[50] Richard C. Schwartz, *Dealing with Racism: Should We Exorcise or Embrace Our Inner Bigots?*, in *Innovations and Elaborations in Internal Family Systems Therapy* 124–132 (Martha Sweezy & Ellen L. Ziskind eds., Routledge 2016) [subsequently, Schwartz, *Dealing with Racism*].

[51] See American Psychiatric Association, *Diagnostic and Statistical Manual of Mental Disorders*, Dissociative Identity Disorder, 300.14 (F44.81) (5th ed. 2013). For an excerpted online description of the disorder, see American Psychiatric Association, Psychiatry Online, https://psychiatryonline.org/doi/10.1176/appi.books.9781585625048.gg24 (last visited Mar. 23, 2022).

[52] Schwartz, *Intro to IFS Model*, pp. 44–58 (fully cited in Chap. 11 endnote 46). Schwartz attributes other positive qualities to the Self: "joy, humor, forgiveness, and gratitude." Id. at 48. In contrast, when "the Self is buried beneath the noise and emotion," the person is "closed, confused, clouded" and the like. Id. For support for this idea, see Holmes et al., *Parts Work*, pp. 23–26 (fully cited in Chap. 11 endnote 20); Schwartz, *IFS Therapy*, p. 37 (fully cited in Chap. 11 endnote 39).

[53] Schwartz, *IFS Therapy*, p. 57 (fully cited in Chap. 11 endnote 39).

[54] It is very difficult to describe or define the IFS Self in concrete, understandable terms. Three leading authorities writing about IFS in their training manual say "The Self is the core of psychic balance, the seat of consciousness and inner source of love. Everyone has a Self . . . But the Self is perhaps most simply introduced to clients as 'the you who is not a part.' " Frank G. Anderson, Martha Sweezy & Richard C. Schwartz, *Internal Family Systems Skills Training*

Manual: Trauma-Informed Treatment for Anxiety, Depression, PTSD & Substance Abuse 9 (PSI Publishing & Media 2017) [subsequently, Anderson et al., *IFS Training Manual*].

55   Schwartz, *IFS Therapy*, pp. 57–58 (fully cited in Chap. 11 endnote 39).

56   The Self has some qualities of a continuum. To use the language of physics, it has "wave-like" and "particle-like" aspects. The wave-like qualities include pure awareness. The particle-like qualities include its ability to interact with Parts. See Schwartz, *IFS Therapy*, p. 38 (fully cited in Chap. 11, note 39); Schwartz & Sweezy, *IFS 2nd* (fully cited in Chap. 11, endnote 41).

57   See Schwartz, *IFS Therapy*, pp. 40–41 (fully cited in Chap. 11 endnote 39).

Chapter 12. Managing the Luxor Carriage Situation with IFS (pp. 139–151)

1   Confession: Good Time Charlie has rarely exercised much influence during my adult life.

2   According to IFS, the Self is always "present" to some degree. Richard C. Schwartz, Founding Developer, Center for Self-Leadership, Email to author (Aug. 6, 2011) (on file with author). So it might be more accurate to say that the Coalition of the Small-Minded put the Self under house arrest. In any event, for a period of time, it deprived the Self of the ability to lead.

3   The core-concerns approach is covered in Section A, Chapter 3.

4   This train of reasoning is an example of the "fundamental attribution error," which is described above in Chapter 4. Daniel Kahneman explains that fast thinking, also known as System 1, automatically makes causal attributions. See Kahneman, *Thinking*, pp. 74–77 (fully cited in Chap. 11 endnote 15).

5   See Douglas Stone, Bruce Patton & Sheila Heen, *Difficult Conversations: How to Discuss What Matters Most* 111–14 (Penguin Books 1999) [subsequently, Stone et al., *Difficult Conversations*].

6   Here is another way to understand what happened, with the benefit of the IFS perspective. When we interact with another person—directly or indirectly, consciously or subconsciously—we typically are dealing with one or more of that person's Parts. And we are doing so through one or more of our Parts. Usually, we are not aware that our interactions have this limited nature. Our Parts generally bring out, in the other person, similar Parts and similar (or complementary) emotions, thoughts and behaviors. When person A's active Parts and person B's active Parts are in conflict, based on their perceptions and goals, we think that A and B are in conflict. If person A's active Parts and Person B's active Parts are getting along, A and B think they are not in conflict, and they feel comfortable. So, in the interaction between Mr. Hassan and me, in this view, although "I" thought that "I" was in conflict with Mr. Hassan, it is more accurate to say that a Part or Parts of me thought that I was in conflict with Mr. Hassan. But what my Parts-in-Charge thought was "Mr. Hassan" was really just a Part or Parts of him. Mr. Hassan's behavior, like mine, was dictated by his Parts-in-Charge. And which of his Parts were in charge, and what they did, resulted from his entire life experience and his interpretation of my behavior, which was produced by my temporarily ruling Coalition of Parts.

When we connect on a Self-Self level, we feel something like joy. See Schwartz, *Intro to IFS Model*, pp. 46–47 (fully cited in Chap. 11 endnote 46).

7   At this point, if not before, some readers will wonder about my own mental health or, at least, about the extent to which I believe that (1) the Parts and the Self are "real"; and (2) that they "actually did" what I have ascribed to them. (Before even answering those questions, I must confess to what is already obvious: I have reconstructed and described these external and internal events many years after they occurred. There is no reason to think that my

recollections or reconstructions are accurate, but I hope they seem plausible.) As to the first question, I believe neither that the Self and Parts are real nor that they are not real. These entities are constructs that are components of the IFS model of the mind and of psychotherapy. We should judge this model, as well as other models—such as the rational actor in economics and reasonable person in law, as well as Freud's id, ego, and superego (from his *Complete Introductory Lectures*, fully cited in Chap. 11 endnote 8)—based on the extent to which they are useful for a particular purpose. I believe that the IFS model provides a distinctive and effective way to access, understand, and deal with internal conflict-related processes. As psychologist Jay Earley puts it, "You may treat the idea of subpersonalities as simply a useful metaphor for viewing the psyche, which it is, but it is much more than that. If you treat the components of your psyche as real entities that you can interact with, they will respond to you in that way, which gives you tremendous power for transformation." Jay Early, *Self-Therapy: A Step-by-Step Guide to Creating Wholeness and Healing Your Inner Child Using IFS, A New Cutting-Edge Psychotherapy* 17 (2nd ed., Mill City Press 2012) [subsequently, Early, *Self-Therapy*].

[8]   See van der Kolk, *The Body Keeps the Score, passim* (fully cited in Chap. 11 endnote 33).

[9]   For more technical explanations of the processes by which IFS can help a person understand and transcend such barriers and other sequalae of trauma, see id. at 279–97.

[10] See Anne Bockler, Lukas Herrmann, Fynn-Mathis Trautwein, Tom Holmes & Tania Singer, *Know Thy Selves: Learning to Understand Oneself Increases the Ability to Understand Others*, 1 J. Cognitive Enhancement 197 (2017); Flynn-Mathis Trautwein, Philipp Kanske, Anne Bockler & Tania Singer, *Differential Benefits of Mental Training Types for Attention, Compassion, and Theory of Mind*, Cognition 194 (Jan. 2020).

[11] Schwartz, *No Bad Parts*, p. 34 (fully cited in Chap. 11 endnote 41).

[12] I explained, similarly, how mindfulness can change from a state of mind to a trait of mind in Chapter 5.

[13] This could be understood as a conflict between the "experiencing self" and the "remembering self" described by Kahneman. See Kahneman, *Thinking*, p. 381 (fully cited in Chap. 11 endnote 15).

[14] For more about this, see Schwartz, *No Bad Parts*, p. 74 (fully cited in Chap. 11 endnote 41).

[15] Id. at 51.

[16] See generally Leonard L. Riskin, *Decision-Making in Mediation: The New Old Grid and the New New Grid System*, 79 Notre Dame Law Rev. 1 (2003) (describing various approaches to mediation); Leonard L. Riskin & Nancy A. Welsh, *Is That All There Is?: "The Problem" in Court-Oriented Mediation*, 15 George Mason Law Rev. 863–932 (2008). See generally Kenneth Kressel, Tiffany Henderson, Warren Reich & Claudia Cohen, *Multidimensional Analysis of Conflict Mediator Style*, 30 Conflict Resolution Q. 135 (2012) (discussing various mediation approaches).

[17] See generally John Forester, *Dealing with Differences: Dramas of Mediating Public Disputes* (Oxford Univ. Press 2009) (discussing mediation in public and private settings); Susan L. Podziba, *Civic Fusion: Mediating Polarized Public Disputes* (Paperback ed., American Bar Assoc. 2013) (describing how people with different values reach consensus in public policy matters).

[18] See Philip J. Harter, *A Cure for the Malaise*, 71 Georgetown Law J. 1, 28 (1982); Philip J. Harter, *Assessing the Assessors: The Actual Performance of Negotiated Rulemaking*, 9 N.Y.U. Environmental Law J. 1, 32 (2000).

[19] For more on IFS methods for working with Parts, see *The Power of Self to Heal Our Parts: An Empowering Approach to Transforming Inner and Outer Relations*, Interview of Richard Schwartz by Soren Gordhamer, Wisdom 2.0 2017 (Feb. 28, 2017), https://www.youtube.com/watch?v=LuJLv98ks-I.

For helping Protector Parts differentiate from the Self, some IFS practitioners use the "Six Fs": "Find, Focus, Flesh-out, Feel, beFriend, and Fears." See Susan McConnell, *Somatic Internal Family Systems Therapy: Awareness, Breath, and Touch in Practice*, 24–31, 56–60, 252–53 (North Atlantic Books 2020).

[20] For specifics about depolarization, see Jay Earley, *Resolving Inner Conflict: Working Through Polarization Using Internal Family Systems Therapy* (Pattern Systems Books 2012); Schwartz & Sweezy, *IFS 2d*, pp. 147–60 (fully cited in Chap. 11 endnote 40).

[21] See Schwartz, *IFS Therapy*, pp. 225–30 (fully cited in Chap. 11 endnote 39. Schwartz's Summary Outline for Working with Individuals suggests the following steps in group decision-making (which would come after a good deal of work on the preceding steps).

1. As decisions emerge in the person's life, Self assembles parts for internal board meetings in which the group discusses the decision.

2. The Self listens to this discussion and then makes the decision.

3. Self takes care of those parts that lost out in the decision and tries to maintain balance such that no part or group of parts always loses.

Id. at 230.

[22] I might have used some of these methods to add another voice to the internal processes. Some Exiles listed in Box D-2 might have had concerns about what was happening but did not try to exercise influence. The most promising candidate with whom I might have worked, however, is Gandhi. He was a Protector at the beginning of the incident who was quickly transformed into an Exile—by the ruling Coalition—after he urged me toward kindness and generosity. I might have tried to recruit Gandhi and treat him as a full-fledged member of the Protector group. At that point, it would have become obvious that he and some or all Coalition members were polarized or disagreeing, and that I wanted Gandhi's voice.

[23] See Schwartz, *IFS Therapy*, p. 230 (fully cited in Chap. 11 endnote 39).

[24] See id. at 108–10. Note that IFS includes detailed procedures for working with the Parts. In one of these, the Self seeks permission from a Protector to talk directly to an Exile in order to "unburden" the Exile of one or more of the obligations it believes it carries—such as protecting the person's financial assets. See id. at 109. For other explanations, designed primarily for non-professionals, see Early, *Self-Therapy* (fully cited at Chap. 12 endnote 7); Jay Earley & Bonnie Weiss, *Freedom from Your Inner Critic: A Self-Therapy Approach* (Sounds True 2013).

[25] See Leonard Riskin, Chris Guthrie, Richard C. Reuben, Jennifer K. Robbennolt, Nancy A. Welsh & Art Hinshaw, *Dispute Resolution and Lawyers: A Contemporary Approach* 127 (6th ed., West Academic Pub. 2019) [subsequently, Riskin, et al., *DRL 6th*].

[26] Schwartz, *No Bad Parts*, p. 163 (fully cited in Chap. 11 endnote 41).

[27] Id.

[28] Id.

[29] Schwartz, *Dealing with Racism*, pp. 129–31 (fully cited in Chap. 11 endnote 50). For an exercise on working with your racist Parts, see Schwartz, *No Bad Parts*, pp. 163–65 (fully cited in Chap. 11 endnote 41).

[30] Schwartz, *Dealing with Racism*, p. 125 (fully cited in Chap. 11 endnote 50).

[31] Id. at 129.

Chapter 13. Managing Your Own Conflicts with IFS (pp. 153–157)

[1] It is usually important to protect privacy when using this exercise in a group setting, which is why I distribute file folders that the participants can close. I never ask individuals to show their drawings to others in the room, but I invite them to do so, if they wish.

² In my experience, this kind of strong identification is not unusual at some U.S. colleges and universities.

Chapter 14. Synergies Between IFS and Negotiation (and Mediation) (pp. 159–161)

¹ Hoffman, *Mediation, Multiple Minds*, p. 318 (cited in Chap. 11 endnote 38). IFS also can provide language or concepts with which a negotiator or mediator (or an advisor or counselor) can communicate more helpfully with clients and other participants. In a letter to a mediation party, Hoffman illustrates how a mediator might influence a party's internal negotiation using IFS language that is easily understood, even without any familiarity with IFS:

> All of us, the social scientists would say, are hardwired to desire revenge when we feel wronged. But there are other parts of us that are equally powerful—for example, in the mediation, we heard you articulate some of the other concerns and interests you have. For example, there's a part of you that is a welfare-maximizing, rational person that's got goals like saving time, money and effort. There's an altruistic part of you that wants to use these vast family resources to help people most in need, as opposed to financially comfortable lawyers and, indeed, mediators. There's a part of you that has emotional goals, such as restoring some semblance of family feeling for the next generation, even if that's not possible for this generation. Those other parts may want a larger role at the negotiation table, and they may even argue that there's been enough retribution, in the form of a court judgment, depositions, trial testimony, articles in the newspaper—and that now's the time for both sides of the family to put down the swords, resolve the remaining disputes as cost-effectively as possible, and use the resources that remain for more useful and altruistic goals.

Id. at 318–19.

More recently, Hoffman has elaborated on how he uses IFS during mediation. See David A. Hoffman, *The Self-Led Mediator: Using IFS in Dispute Resolution* (video prepared for IFS Institute Conference (Oct. 2022)), https://drive.google.com/file/d/1WDryewWgVYKlg Vvz8n69WHcx7lfCdVeN/view.

² See Gary Friedman & Jack Himmelstein, *Challenging Conflict: Mediation Through Understanding* (ABA & Harvard PON, 2009).

³ Robert A. Baruch Bush & Joseph P. Folger, *The Promise of Mediation: The Transformative Approach to Conflict* (rev. ed., Jossey-Bass, A Wiley Imprint 2005).

⁴ Susan L. Podziba, *Civic Fusion: Mediating Polarized Public Disputes* (American Bar Assoc., 2013); see also Susan C. Podziba, *Civic Fusion and the Hidden Connective Energies of Conflict* (Jan. 20, 2022) (a workshop/presentation), https://www.pon.harvard.edu/events/cpodziba-civic-fusion-hidden-connective-energies-conflict/.

Chapter 15. Synergies Between IFS and Mindfulness (pp. 163–165)

¹ For explanations of how mindfulness can enable a person to transcend these obstacles, see Chapter 8. To see how IFS can achieve the same goals using similar methods, see Chapter 14.

² Jack Engler & Paul R. Fulton, *Self and No-Self in Psychotherapy*, in *Wisdom and Compassion in Psychotherapy: Deepening Mindfulness in Clinical Practice* 176, 182 n. 1 (Christopher K. Germer & Ronald D Siegel eds., Guilford Press 2012). They continue: ". . .[A]ny image or belief I have about myself. . .can only be a part of me, never who I truly am. When I do not refer my seeing or thinking or doing back to a 'me,' I am thinking and perceiving from no-self." Id.

³ Richard C. Schwartz, *Moving from Acceptance Toward Transformation with Internal Family Systems Therapy*, 69 J. Clinical Psychology: In Session 805, 807 (2013). Richard Schwartz and

Robert Falconer describe various ideas within Buddhism that resemble the IFS conception of Self. Richard C. Schwartz & Robert R. Falconer, *Many Minds, One Self: Evidence for a Radical Shift in Paradigm* 185–200 (Trailheads Publications 2017).

Here is another way to understand this shared goal of mindfulness and IFS. Both embrace the goal of transcendence. The original and best-known version of the hierarchy of human needs described by the psychologist Abraham Maslow is a list of motivations, beginning with the most basic physiological or survival needs at the bottom, and moving up through safety needs, belonginess and love needs, esteem needs, and at the top, self-actualization. But he had more to say. In 1969 he wrote that self-actualization was not the highest need or motivation level. "Transcendence" stands above it. Maslow presented twenty-four different meanings or examples of transcendence. They included the kinds of changes that both mindfulness and IFS are meant to promote, such as transcending the ego or the small self (the idea of self that is created by IFS Parts and by social roles and beliefs), which should include or foster a realization that all beings and all things are connected, which should lead to or accompany treating themselves and others with kindness and compassion. See Abraham H. Maslow, *The Farther Reaches of Human Nature*, 1 J. Transpersonal Psychology 1 (1969) (article); Abraham H. Maslow, *The Farther Reaches of Human Nature* 259–288 (Penguin 1976) (book of essays); Mark E. Koltko-Rivera, *Rediscovering the Later Version of Maslow's Hierarchy of Needs: Self-Transcendence and Opportunities for Theory, Research, and Unification*, 10 Rev. of General Psychology 302 (2006).

4   Thich Nhat Hanh, *Peace is Every Step: The Path of Mindfulness in Everyday Life* 52–54 (Bantam Books 1992) (emphasis added).

5   See, for example, Tara Brach, *Fear and Love* (Blog entry with You Tube video link) (Nov. 10, 2021) https://www.tarabrach.com/fear-and-love/.

6   A trailhead "is the point at which a trail begins." *Merriam-Webster.com Dictionary*, s.v. "trailhead," accessed September 16, 2022, https://www.merriam-webster.com/dictionary/trailhead. In many managed areas a sign at the trailhead shows the destination(s) and gives other information.

7   Flint Sparks, *The Buddha as IFS Therapist*, recording of a presentation by Flint Sparks at the 2011 Annual Conference of the Center for Self-Leadership Oct. 2011, Providence, Rhode Island. Downloaded from https://courses.ifs-institute.com/account/login?returnUrl=%2Fviewer%2Fclassroom%2F9907317.

8   The Four Noble Truths and the Noble Eightfold Path are covered in Section B, Chapter 5.

For additional insights on the relationships between IFS and mindfulness or Buddhism, see Paul Ginter, *IFS and Mindfulness Meditation,* available for download from https://ifsca.wpenginepowered.com/wp-content/uploads/IFS-and-Mindfulness-Meditation-by-Paul-Ginter-Ed.D..pdf; Monica Sanford, *Actualizing Buddhanature Using Internal Family Systems Therapy* (2014) (Journal Article Draft), https://www.academia.edu/7204782/Actualizing_Buddhanature_with_the_Internal_Family_Systems_Model.